Queer Migrations

Sexuality, U.S. Citizenship, and Border Crossings

Eithne Luibhéid and Lionel Cantú Jr., Editors

University of Minnesota Press
Minneapolis • London

All royalties generated by this collection will be donated to the Lionel Cantú Memorial Award Fund at the University of California, Santa Cruz.

Chapter 7, by Martin F. Manalanson IV, was previously published as chapter 4 of *Global Divas: Filipino Gay Men in the Diaspora* (Durham, NC: Duke University Press, 2003). All rights reserved. Used by permission of the publisher.

Published by the University of Minnesota Press
111 Third Avenue South, Suite 290
Minneapolis, MN 55401-2520
http://www.upress.umn.edu

Library of Congress Cataloging-in-Publication Data

Queer migrations : sexuality, U.S. citizenship, and border crossings / Eithne Luibhéid and Lionel Cantú Jr., editors.
    p.   cm.
    Includes bibliographical references and index.
    ISBN 0-8166-4465-9 (alk. paper) — ISBN 0-8166-4466-7 (pbk. : alk. paper)
    1. Gay men—Latin America—Social conditions—Congresses.
2. Lesbians—Latin America—Social conditions—Congresses.   3. Hispanic American gays—Migrations—Congresses.   4. Hispanic American lesbians—Migrations—Congresses.   5. Asylum, Right of—United States—Congresses.
6. Emigration and immigration—Latin America—Congresses.
7. Emigration and immigration—United States—Congresses.
I. Luibhéid, Eithne.   II. Cantú, Lionel, d. 2002
    HQ76.3.L29Q56 2005
    306.76'6—dc22   2004013509

Printed in the United States of America on acid-free paper

The University of Minnesota is an equal-opportunity educator and employer.

12 11 10 09 08 07 06 05   10 9 8 7 6 5 4 3 2 1

Contents

Acknowledgments

Many thanks to my coeditor, the late Lionel Cantú, for his dedication, hard work, and enthusiasm for the project. Heartfelt thanks also to the authors whose work is included in this volume, not only because of their significant contribution to the emerging debates about immigration, citizenship, racialization, and sexuality, but also because they were unfailingly supportive and practically helpful throughout this volume's production.

Two conferences provided forums in which many of these essays were critically discussed. These were "Sexuality, Migration, and the Contested Boundaries of U.S. Citizenship," held at Bowling Green State University on February 28 and March 1, 2002; and "On the Line: Gender, Sexuality, and Human Rights in the Americas," held at the University of California, Santa Cruz, on March 8 and 9, 2002.

At Bowling Green State University, the Dean's Office of College of the Arts and Sciences, the Department of Ethnic Studies, and the Institute for the Study of Culture and Society (ICS) generously provided financial support for the first conference. I also extend deepest thanks to Don Nieman, dean of the College of Arts and Sciences; Michael Martin, chair of the Department of Ethnic Studies; Vicki Patraka, director of ICS; Hai Ren, Department of Popular Culture; Kathy Rahrig, Department of Ethnic Studies; Taeyon Kim, American Culture Studies Department; Ellen Berry and Valerie Rohy, Department of English; and Rob Buffington, Department of History, whose tremendous intellectual and material labor made the conference both possible and productive.

Heartfelt thanks to Patricia Zavella and the Chicano/Latino Research Center at the University of California, Santa Cruz, for all their work, which ensured the success of the second conference, "On the Line."

Thanks to Xiaohong Wang for thorough, careful editorial assistance during the book's final stages. The University of Minnesota Press editorial and production staff, who were unfailingly enthusiastic and helpful at every stage, have my everlasting gratitude. Three anonymous reviewers substantially contributed to making this a stronger volume. Thanks to Nancy Naples for practical advice and encouragement.

Do Hai le grá.

INTRODUCTION

Queering Migration and Citizenship

Eithne Luibhéid

International migration and related globalization processes have profoundly altered every aspect of U.S. social, political, economic, and cultural life in the past quarter century. Despite rich scholarship about the causes and consequences of international migration, there has been little consideration of how sexual arrangements, ideologies, and modes of regulation shape migration to and incorporation into the United States. Thus, important questions about sexuality and migration have yet to be addressed. These include: How does sexuality shape migration processes? How do concerns about sexuality shape U.S. immigration control strategies and constructions of citizenship? How has mass migration in the past quarter century transformed U.S. queer communities, cultures, and politics? In what ways is sexuality a source of conflict within migrant communities, and between migrant and U.S. communities? This collection, which focuses on queer of color migrants and communities in the United States, theorizes these and other questions.

Queers migrate from every region, but here we particularly address migration from Mexico, Cuba, El Salvador, and the Philippines. We do not claim to provide representational justice to the geographic regions from which queers migrate.[1] Rather, the purpose of these essays—which utilize history, literary theory, cultural studies, queer and race theory, anthropology, women's studies, sociology, and the visual arts—is to bring immigration scholarship and sexuality scholarship into productive dialogue, in ways that challenge existing frameworks in both fields while indicating how the lives of queer migrants can be usefully studied. Drawing on the strengths of both immigration and sexuality scholarships, the essays also indicate new areas for research. For example, the essays participate in theorizing sexuality beyond the horizon of the nation-state by exploring how U.S.-based sexual politics and communities are imbricated in the dynamics of globalization and imperialism, and at the same time they analyze how nation-state and citizenship boundaries are continually redrawn, despite globalizing processes that challenge their salience, through practices of discipline and surveillance directed at migrants. By focusing on queer migrants, the essays conceive multiplicity and heterogeneity within queer communities and significantly open queerness to the transnational, the global, and the migrant, and to critical analyses of the impact of queer migrants on U.S. sexual, gender, racial, and ethnic communities, cultures, and politics. Moreover, the essays identify the U.S. immigration control apparatus as a crucial target for queer intervention because it significantly regulates sexuality and reproduces oppressive sexual norms that are gendered, racialized, and classed.

Until recently, exploration of these connections between sexuality and migration was greatly hindered by the fact that lesbians and gay men were legally barred from migrating to the United States. They came anyway, but most kept their lives and experiences hidden lest they face deportation. In 1990, the ban on lesbian and gay immigrants was finally lifted, and in 1994 Attorney General Janet Reno deemed that lesbians and gay men were eligible to apply for asylum if they had been persecuted for sexuality. Lesbian, gay, trans, and queer migrants to the United States continue to face substantial obstacles. But these changes, not to mention the significance of immigration and sexuality in contemporary U.S. politics, mean that a collection of essays about the experiences and impact of queer migration is both possible and timely.

Before proceeding further, a brief explanation of how I use the terms "queer" and "migrant" is necessary. "Queer," a particularly contested term, is used here as a category that is intended to register several key ideas. First, according to Michael Warner, "'queer' rejects a minoritizing logic of toleration or simple political-interest representation in favor of a more thorough resistance to regimes of the normal."[2] This definition is particularly useful because it echoes this collection's call to transform, rather than to seek accommodation within, existing social structures. The definition also underscores that transformation needs to occur across a wide range of regimes and institutions, not just the sexual—but not without addressing the sexual, either. Therefore, "queer" must be "calibrated to account for the social antagonisms of nation, race, gender, and class as well as sexuality."[3] Finally, "queer" is used to mark the fact that many standard sexuality categories were historically formed through specific epistemologies and social relations that upheld colonialist, xenophobic, racist, and sexist regimes. Consequently, although the collection addresses varied migrant sexual practices and identities, these cannot necessarily be accommodated within institutional and socially sanctioned categories. The use of the term "queer" is also intended to register this difficulty.

Another category that I use throughout the essay is "migrant." This category refers to anyone who has crossed an international border to reach the United States and makes no distinction among legal immigrants, refugees, asylum seekers, or undocumented immigrants. In my view, such distinctions do not reflect empirically verifiable differences among migrants, who often shift from one category to another. Rather, the distinctions are imposed by the state and general public on migrants in order to delimit the rights that they will have or be denied, and the forms of surveillance, discipline, and normalization to which they will be subjected.[4] My use of the term "migrant," then, rejects the claim that such distinctions refer to different "types" of migrants, and instead directs analytic attention to the ways that these distinctions function as technologies of normalization, discipline, and sanctioned dispossession.

This introduction has three major sections. First, I discuss how concerns about sexuality guided U.S. immigration control, which in turn connected to the production of exclusionary versions of nation and citizenship. Next, I describe how a small group of scholars have brought migration and sexuality scholarship into critical conversation and, in the process, created foundational research about queer migrants' lives. Finally, I describe how each essay in the volume builds on this foundation while opening up new questions for consideration.

Queer Immigration and Citizenship: A History of Exclusion

Immigration and citizenship controls function in a double sense: as the means to delimit the nation, citizenry, and citizenship and, conversely, as the loci for contesting and reworking these limits. Therefore, this section provides an overview of the history of how U.S. immigration control has provided a means to delimit the nation and citizenry, and how the resulting immigration exclusions have their counterparts not only in exclusionary citizenship laws but also in symbolic exclusions that mark certain U.S. citizens as Others, despite their formal legal membership in the community. Their experiences make clear how thoroughly and complexly immigration and citizenship practices, policies, discourses, and norms implicate one another, in a continuously spiraling process.

In terms of immigration control as the means to delimit the nation, citizenry, and citizenship, we must differentiate between "regular" immigration control and the refugee/asylum system. Regular immigration control, which came under the management of the federal government in the late nineteenth century, remains guided by the plenary power doctrine, which holds that sovereign nations have the right to control the entry of noncitizens into their territories. This doctrine can usefully be read in light of Benedict Anderson's argument that although nations appear to be timeless and eternal, in fact they are relatively recent historical forms that require continual labor to maintain and reproduce.[5] The state's ongoing efforts to control the entry of noncitizens into U.S. territory are among the key technologies through which the nation and its sovereignty get continually reconstructed in the present. Moreover, according to the plenary power doctrine, this process may be carried out in a discriminatory manner.[6] Thus, U.S. immigration control has historically discriminated among potential immigrants based on sexuality, gender, race, class, and other factors.

For example, as mentioned earlier, lesbians and gays were barred for decades from entering the United States as legal immigrants. Some scholars date lesbian and gay exclusion from 1917, when people labeled as "constitutional psychopathic inferiors" were first barred from entering the United States. This category included "persons with abnormal sexual instincts" as well as "the moral imbeciles, the pathological liars and swindlers, the defective delinquents, [and] many of the vagrants and cranks."[7] The 1952 McCarran-Walter Act recodified exclusion categories to include a ban on psychopathic personalities. There is no doubt that lesbians and gay men were targeted: a U.S. Senate report related that "the Public Health Service has advised that the provision for the exclusion of aliens afflicted with psychopathic personality or mental defect which appears in the instant bill is sufficiently broad to provide for the exclusion of homosexuals or sex perverts."[8] Court cases from the 1950s and 1960s show that the Immigration and Naturalization Service (INS) (which, on March 1, 2003, became divided into three agencies administered by the Department of Homeland Security) used the ban on psychopathic personalities as grounds for excluding men and women whom they thought were, or might become, homosexual. In 1965, when immigration law underwent another sweeping revision, lesbian and gay exclusion was again recodified, this time under the ban on "sexual deviates."

In 1990, exclusion based on sexual orientation was finally removed from immigration law. But lesbian/gay migrants still face substantial barriers, which reveal the enormous gap between removing explicit discrimination from the law and ensuring that equal access can be realized in practice. For example, the two most common ways to become a legal permanent resident (LPR) are through direct family ties or sponsorship by an employer. But lesbian/gay relationships—unlike heterosexual ones—are not recognized as a legitimate basis for acquiring LPR status. This disparity was reinforced in 1996 by the Defense of Marriage Act, which defined marriage as a relationship between a man and a woman for domestic and immigration purposes. Thus, binational lesbian/gay couples must "rely on a wide variety of visas and artifices to keep them together," including student, tourist, and work visas.[9] But these are often difficult to get—especially for those without financial resources—and they expire. As a result, binational lesbian/gay couples continually face the prospect of separation and are unable to plan for the future. Some break up; others move to a third country; still others engage in sham heterosexual marriages to get legalized. Thus, as South Asian lesbian Grace Poore describes, a lesbian may experience the hypocrisy of "having left her home country to avoid marriage, only to end up marrying [a man] in the U.S. for the right to stay."[10] As researchers have documented, these sham marriages subject the migrant to great risk of exploitation and abuse. Lesbians and gays who seek residency through employer sponsorship, rather than family ties, may not fare much better than binational couples; they are often "exposed to the indignities and exploitation of employers who use the power imbalance [associated with legal status] to their advantage."[11]

HIV/AIDS exclusions have also become an issue for all migrants. In 1987, U.S. immigration law added HIV to the list of dangerous, contagious diseases for which immigrants should be excluded and required that all applicants for legal permanent residence must test negative for HIV. Although President Clinton pledged that he would end HIV immigration exclusion, congressional legislation in 1993 actually consolidated HIV exclusion, mandating "the exclusion of HIV-positive aliens applying for immigrant visas, refugee visas, and adjustment to permanent resident status."[12] The legislation further stated that as a matter of law, and regardless of medical opinion, HIV constituted "a communicable disease of public health significance." As a result, the Immigration and Nationality Act was amended to exclude all HIV-positive noncitizens from the United States, except under very exceptional circumstances.[13]

Finally, although lesbians and gays may no longer be explicitly excluded on sexuality grounds, their sexuality still makes them liable to be constructed as lacking good moral character or otherwise ineligible for residency and citizenship.[14]

Lesbian and gay exclusion never functioned as an isolated system, but instead was part of a broader federal immigration control regime that sought to ensure a "proper" sexual and gender order, reproduction of white racial privilege, and exploitation of the poor. The 1875 Page Law, which mandated the exclusion of Asian women who were thought to be coming to the United States for "lewd and immoral" purposes, marked the beginning of this restrictive regime. Working-class Chinese women were particularly affected by the law, since after its passage immigration officials generally presumed that they were all entering the United States to work in the sex industry, and accordingly tried to exclude them.[15] The Page Law also provided the blueprint through which the U.S. immigration system became transformed into an apparatus for regulating sexuality more generally, in relation to shifting gender, racial, ethnic, and class anxieties.[16]

Following passage of the Page Law, restrictive immigration legislation multiplied. For instance, Chinese exclusion became law in 1882, and by 1924 had been extended to prevent the entry of all Asians.[17] Southern and Eastern European arrivals were also significantly reduced after 1924 because of racial and cultural concerns. Class restrictions multiplied, including bans on contract laborers and those deemed liable to become public charges.

At the same time, a preference for nuclear, heteropatriarchal families increasingly structured U.S. immigration law. As a result, in the early decades of the twentieth century, women who were not excluded on racial and class grounds faced growing difficulties entering the United States unless they came under the protection of a male who seemed "respectable" and could provide support.[18] Immigration law also expanded the provisions against women coming to the United States for prostitution, and added bans on polygamists and immoral women.[19] Immorality encompassed a wide range of sexual (and other) behaviors, including cohabiting and having sex outside of marriage.

The focus on heteropatriarchy also legitimated the exclusion of gender-transitive people. Edward Corsi, an Italian immigrant who became the commissioner of immigration and naturalization at Ellis Island in New York, described the experiences of immigrant Alejandra Velas when she reached Ellis Island in the 1910s: "She proved to be, upon examination, despite her earlier insistence to the contrary, a young woman. Vehemently she insisted that her identity had not been questioned before. When Dr. Senner asked her why she wore men's clothes, she answered that she would rather kill herself than wear women's clothes."[20] Velas was denied entry, apparently on the grounds of cross-dressing, and was sent to England.[21]

The immigration system's anxious production of heteropatriarchal families became explicitly linked to the reproduction of racial and class exclusions. Asian wives, in particular, were continually singled out for investigation of possible sexual immorality. When not barred for alleged immorality, they were often barred on racial or class grounds. Exemplifying these restrictions was the 1920 Ladies Agreement, which ended the migration of Japanese brides joining husbands in the United States because restrictionists claimed that these brides' childbearing rates threatened white supremacy.[22] Poor and working-class wives of all backgrounds were increasingly refused entry on the grounds that they were "liable to become public charges," such as through bearing children in publicly funded hospitals.

Revisions to immigration law in 1965 not only reaffirmed lesbian and gay exclusion but also further codified heterosexual, nuclear family relations as the primary basis for admission to the United States by reserving nearly three-quarters of all permanent immigration visas for people with those ties.[23] As David Reimers's research shows, these family preferences not only upheld patriarchal gender and sexual regimes but also were tacitly intended to perpetuate racial exclusion. Particularly since

Asians and Africans had been barred from immigrating for many decades, lawmakers calculated that they would lack the family ties necessary for legal immigration under the 1965 revisions.[24] In 1996, further revisions to immigration law codified the neoliberal drive to create "responsible" immigrant families through exclusionary measures.[25] Those whose incomes did not reach at least 125 percent of federal poverty guidelines became ineligible to sponsor family members for migration. Those who met income requirements had to sign a legally binding affidavit of support for each sponsored family member—even while the 1996 revisions also stripped legal immigrants of eligibility for many federal support programs. Representative Lamar Smith explained the rationale for the affidavits: "Just as we require deadbeat dads to provide for the children they bring into the world, we should require deadbeat sponsors to provide for the immigrants they bring into the country."[26] As Kathleen M. Moore described, Smith's rhetoric equates immigrant families with welfare users in a way that justified punitive policies toward both.[27]

In short, since its inception in the late nineteenth century, federal immigration control centrally focused on sexuality as a ground for controlling newcomers' entry. But sexuality always operated in tandem with gender, racial, class, and cultural considerations. As the immigration control apparatus evolved to address these interlocking concerns, it did not simply apply preexisting sexual, gender, racial, class, and cultural categories to individuals, but rather actively participated in producing these distinctions and linking them to broader processes of nation-making and citizenship.[28] As the essays in this volume show, contemporary examinations of queer immigration must take this history and its legacies into account.

The immigration system, however, was not the only channel through which noncitizens sought to enter and often settle in the United States. Noncitizens' entry has also been structured through the refugee/asylum system, which developed after World War II. Unlike the immigration system, which frames entry as a privilege that can be granted in a discriminatory manner by a sovereign nation-state, the refugee/asylum system is underpinned by a different logic. Here, admission is supposed to be granted based on the United States' commitment to upholding international human rights laws, which provide asylum to those fleeing persecution on the basis of race, religion, nationality, political opinion, or membership in a particular social group. This international standard, codified by the 1951 Convention on the Status of Refugees, was formally incorporated into U.S. law through the 1980 Refugee Act, which also systematized admission and resettlement procedures for refugees.[29]

Despite its grounding in international human rights regimes, refugee/ asylum law has historically been interpreted in ways that presumed a male subject seeking to assert his individuality against an oppressive state.[30] But in recent years, the refugee/asylum system has had to develop a more gender-sensitive process and interpretive framework.[31] Competing claims about how to interpret "membership in a particular social group," and about what counts as a legitimate "political opinion" for purposes of asylum, have also opened up the asylum process to new actors and issues. Moreover, since the 1990s courts have considered and issued contradictory rulings about the significance of gender and sexual identities and practices in establishing eligibility for asylum. In particular, courts have addressed persecution on account of sexual orientation, gender identity, and noncompliance with social gender norms. They have also addressed persecution that takes gendered or sexualized forms, including rape, FGM (female genital mutilation), forced sterilization or abortion, and domestic violence. Nonetheless, such cases remain difficult to win, and the asylum process is still most accessible to those who are male, heterosexual, economically privileged, and from particular "racial" and national origins (see Randazzo's essay in this volume)—and most inaccessible for those whose persecution involved several intersecting axes of subordination (see Randazzo's and Solomon's essays). Thus, the refugee/asylum system also perpetuates exclusions similar to those that structure immigration control.

Exclusions are also generated because the refugee/asylum system involves an inherent tension between, on the one hand, providing protection to people who are persecuted by national governments and, on the other hand, respecting the sovereignty of individual nation-states. As a result, refugee/asylum determinations are often driven as much by U.S. foreign policy considerations as by the merits of individual claims (the disparate treatment of Haitian versus Cuban asylum seekers, historically, is an example). Furthermore, asylum adjudications provide opportunities for the construction or reiteration of racist, imperialist imagery that has material consequences on a global scale (see the essay by Cantú, Luibhéid, and Stern).[32]

Finally, Jacqueline Bhabha suggests that the refugee/asylum system plays a crucial role in maintaining and legitimating exclusionary immigration regimes in so-called developed countries, including the United States. As is well documented, the United States in recent years has facilitated the ever-expanding flow of capital, goods, information, and technology across borders—while at the same time cracking down on immigration, especially by the poor. Bhabha suggests that because the refugee/asylum system is supposed to grant protection to persecuted people, "asylum . . . keeps migration exclusion morally defensible"—even when only a tiny fraction of the world's persecuted people actually has the means to lodge an asylum claim, much less muster the resources needed to possibly win such a claim.[33]

The production of national sovereignty and citizenship through controlling the entry of refugees, asylum seekers, and immigrants has resulted in the proliferation of border zones and detention centers, where various categories of suspect people—legal immigrants, asylum seekers, the undocumented—are detained pending adjudication of their status. Located within U.S. territory, these are nonetheless "zones of exception" where a semblance of rights and protections rarely applies.[34] Investigations of the U.S.–Mexico border have consistently documented a pattern of serious human rights abuses, including beatings, rapes, and deaths, which occur there.[35] Similarly, those incarcerated in immigrant detention centers are often subjected to abuse, threats, coercion, and violence that they rarely have the means to challenge (see Solomon's essay).[36] Border zones and detention centers not only disrupt the presumed homology between territory, nation, and citizenship, but also highlight the structured exclusions, limits, and ongoing violence through which normative constructions of nation, citizenry, and citizenship are actively produced and contested.

Detention centers and border areas provide a means to understand how immigration control practices implicate citizens who have historically been excluded from full belonging in the nation-state. Addressing this issue takes us to the second sense in which immigration control functions: as a process through which the meanings and limits of nation, citizenry, and citizenship become contested and reworked. Many citizens' bodies are, as Robert Chang expresses it, marked as racial, sexual, cultural, gender, and class outsiders, regardless of their formal citizenship

status.[37] In turn, these marked citizens are affected by immigration control in ways that reflect and reinforce, but sometimes provide an occa-
sion to challenge, their subordinated status. One example of the ways
that marked citizens become affected by immigration control is that
slightly over half of all civil and human rights violations identified by
the American Friends' Service Committee in a five-year study of immigration control practices at the U.S.–Mexico border region were perpetrated against Latinos who were U.S. citizens or legal residents.[38]

Citizens who are marked as outsiders are particularly affected by immigration control in two interrelated ways. First, the discriminatory
immigration laws described above had their counterpart in discriminatory citizenship laws, and each reinforced the other. Thus, although citizenship involves rights and obligations that are supposedly available to
all members of the national community, in practice, in the United States
and elsewhere, citizens who were not white, male, able-bodied, property-
owning, and sexually reproductive faced great struggle in becoming formally recognized as full, rights-bearing members of the national community. The 1790 naturalization law reserved U.S. citizenship for free
whites only, and it was only in 1952 that all formal racial barriers to citizenship were dismantled.[39] Citizenship was gendered, so that as men of
different racial groups gained citizenship, women from these groups
were also enfranchised, but as dependents of men rather than as equal
citizens.[40] Citizenship was bound up with class relations; "it was on the
basis of property and wealth that citizenship rights, voting in particular,
were first determined."[41] The intimate connections between citizenship
and a patriarchal sexual order that sought to maintain "white" racial
purity and related property relations have been well documented.[42] Shane
Phelan further characterizes U.S. citizenship as increasingly heterosexu-
alized during the twentieth century.[43] Lauren Berlant extends Phelan's
claim to examine how citizenship norms and practices became increasingly privatized after the late 1970s through the aggressive promotion of
an idealized heterosexual family sphere.[44] More generally, M. Jacqui
Alexander argues that "heterosexuality is at once necessary to the state's
ability to constitute and imagine itself, while simultaneously marking the
site of its own instability."[45] Clearly, the abstract ideal of universal citizenship, supposedly available to all, was in reality very unequally distributed.[46] And these inequalities were mirrored in and reinforced by discriminatory immigration laws, which admitted immigrants based on

sexual, gender, racial, and class criteria. Changes in one area of law had ramifications in the other area. Moreover, as immigrants who did gain admission sought to become citizens, their possibilities for doing so were mediated by these exclusionary logics (see Somerville's essay).

A second important way in which marked citizens are deeply affected by U.S. immigration control involves the symbolic realm. In addition to immigration control strategies and citizenship law, representational systems powerfully construct a sense of national belonging and identification. Stuart Hall elaborates, "people are not only legal citizens of a nation, they participate in the idea of the nation as represented in its symbolic culture."[47] Representations of immigration are one of the most important motifs through which the U.S. nation and citizenry get imagined; as Lauren Berlant suggests, "immigration discourse is a central technology for the reproduction of patriotic nationalism."[48] Yet, all representations of imagined national community also entail exclusions, and this is certainly true in regard to immigration. Mainstream representations of the United States as a nation of immigrants depend on expunging histories of genocide, slavery, racialized heteropatriarchy and economic exploitation, and these representations in turn contribute to a national culture that expels racialized queer migrants, metaphorically and often literally (see Rand's essay).

Renato Rosaldo describes how the exclusions that founded normative constructions of U.S. citizenship and nation concomitantly "defined the parameters of dissident traditions that have endured into the present."[49] These dissident traditions provided a basis from which the meanings and limits of nation, citizenry, and citizenship have been fiercely contested and partly remade. All the essays in this volume, but especially the three ethnographies by Peña, Roque Ramírez, and Manalansan, provide rich, detailed analyses of efforts to contest and rework the limits of nation and citizenship, from the perspective of racialized queer migrants and the heterogeneous peoples with whom they live, work, mobilize, and love. Building on Rosaldo's redefinition of citizenship as a category to be studied not from the top down, in terms of legal definitions of rights and obligations, but from the bottom up, in terms of everyday practices that inhabit, transform, and extend the meaning of citizenship, the essays make clear how complex citizenship actually is. They also underscore the necessity of moving beyond single-axis analyses that address only the citizen/alien dichotomy, or the experiences of citizens subordinated along one axis, to theorize how aliens' and citizens' statuses complexly implicate one another, and how people who are multiply marginalized negotiate nationhood and citizenship. The essays ground dissident traditions not only in the legacies of U.S. exclusions but also in the cultural forms of other countries to which migrants have ties.

By centering racialized queer migrants, these essays both build on and usefully extend scholarship on immigration, sexuality, citizenship, nation-making, and racialization.

Placing Migration and Sexuality Scholarship in Critical Conversation

A small group of dedicated scholars including Martin F. Manalansan IV, Olíva Espín, and M. Jacqui Alexander has published pioneering studies of queer migration.[50] Essays in a handful of special editions of journals, and some anthologies, have also broadened the scope of our knowledge. These include essays in "Thinking Sexuality Transnationally," a special issue of *GLQ;* "Queer Transexions of Race, Nation, and Gender," a special issue of *Social Text;* Cindy Patton and Benigno Sánchez-Eppler's collection *Queer Diasporas;* and anthologies such as David Eng and Alice Hom's *Q & A: Queer in Asian America.*[51] Personal accounts, too, contained in edited collections, have contributed to our knowledge.[52] In various ways, these works have brought immigration and sexuality scholarship into critical conversation in a manner that resonates within theories of citizenship, nation-making, and racialization. Without wanting to oversimplify the vast literatures involved, some basic ideas in each area must be grasped in order to appreciate the essays that bring them together. I want to review these basic ideas briefly, then describe how some of the scholars listed above have linked them to create an important body of work on which this collection builds.

To begin, immigration scholarship has undergone vast revision in recent decades, impelled in part by the enormous growth in migration worldwide. Traditionally, studies of immigration have been framed by a view of migrants as individual actors making rational choices based on cost-benefit analysis, the horizon of the nation-state, and models of assimilation. The contemporary reorganization of capitalism, growing globalization, and increased worldwide migration have forced a rethinking of these frameworks, however. Thus, scholars such as Saskia Sassen have posited that immigration to the United States is not only driven by

at the individual level. It is also driven by historic
_ges that have been crafted between the United States
_tries, which create "bridges for migration."[53] Substanti-
_ɒassen's argument that large structural relations significantly con-
tribute to migration is the fact that it is not usually people from the
poorest countries who migrate to the United States, but rather people
from countries with which the United States has had close historic ties.
This includes people from Mexico, the Philippines, and South Korea,
who have steadily migrated in the past quarter century, even during periods of economic growth in their own countries. Sassen's argument
challenges not only the reduction of migration to individual cost-benefit
decisions,[54] but also frameworks that treat the sovereign nation as an
unquestioned horizon of analysis without consideration of wider, unequal global relations.[55]

If scholarship like Sassen's has greatly complicated traditional models
of why people migrate, others have similarly challenged traditional
models of assimilation. Assimilation describes a process whereby migrants are expected gradually to alter their beliefs and cultural forms to
conform to the mainstream United States. Of course, many scholars
have convincingly argued that this model only works for "whites"; as
race theorists Michael Omi and Howard Winant describe, communities
of color historically found that adopting mainstream ways did not ap-
preciably alter the racial discrimination to which they were subjected.[56]
Challenges to assimilation models have emerged in contemporary immigration scholarship, too, including through the work of scholars
Nina Glick Schiller, Linda Basch, and Cristina Blanc-Szanton, who have
developed an influential model of transnationalism. Transnationalism
views migrants as individuals who "take actions, make decisions, and
develop identities within social networks that connect them to two or
more societies simultaneously."[57] Thus, growing familiarity with and
involvement in U.S. society and culture does not necessarily result in
withering ties to home countries, nor does it presuppose a unilinear
process of assimilation. Patricia Pessar has outlined structural factors
that often contribute to sustaining such home country ties. According
to Pessar, changes in the structure of capitalism on a global scale "contribute to deteriorating social and economic conditions in both home
and host societies with no locale being, necessarily, a secure site of permanent settlement." Moreover, institutional racial discrimination dis-

courages "immigrants of color" from "pursuing long-term or permanent settlement in the United States." Finally, nation-building projects in both host and home societies solicit migrants' loyalties. President Aristide's efforts to draw on the resources of overseas Haitian migrants, whom he characterized as Haiti's "Tenth Department" and integral to Haiti's future, is just one among many examples of how "sending" countries continue to solicit migrants' loyalties.[58] Such contemporary immigration scholarship on transnationalism—not to mention the vast literature on diaspora[59]—radically revises assimilationist understandings of how and why migrants form identities and communities or take action. Moreover, it relates these processes to social institutions, ideologies, and local/global arrangements of power in ways that have enormous implications for the theorization of race, sexuality, gender, class struggle, and citizenship at different scales.

Since the 1970s, immigration scholarship has variously addressed how race, class, and gender relations and ideologies structure migration processes. But it has not generally addressed sexuality, which tends to be deemed unimportant or equated with gender. However, as Eve Sedgwick cogently explains, "the question of gender and the question of sexuality, inextricable from one another though they are . . . are nonetheless not the same question." Furthermore, Sedgwick warns, "a damaging bias toward heterosocial or heterosexist assumptions inheres unavoidably in the very concept of gender."[60] Her argument suggests that migration scholarship's attention to gender cannot substitute for an analysis of sexuality as a crucial, related, but distinct axis that structures all migration processes.

An analysis of sexuality begins from the understanding that sexuality is not the last bastion of the "natural" or the biological in an increasingly technological world. Biology certainly plays a role, but biology is always experienced through cultural mediation.[61] Consequently, sexual norms, identities, experiences, and arrangements vary historically and culturally. Efforts to regulate sexuality have been important in all societies, perhaps because sexuality is situated at the juncture of two major axes of concern: the individual, who must be "properly" formed; and society, including "the future growth, well-being, health, and prosperity of the population as a whole."[62] In the United States in the nineteenth century, sexual regulation underwent a significant change as the locus of control shifted from families and churches to the medical profession and state, including its developing criminal, health care, education, and welfare systems. Shifts in sexual regulation were also evinced by the development of sexual typologies, with particular attention to "deviant" or "dangerous" sexualities. Deviant sexuality was no longer viewed as simply involving undesirable acts, but rather as a marker of individual identity. Foucault's most famous illustration of these changes concerns homosexuality. According to Foucault, although sodomy had long been prohibited as an immoral or criminal *act,* persons who engaged in sodomy were not necessarily considered distinct *types* of persons. That changed in the nineteenth century when "the homosexual became a personage, a past, a case history, and a childhood, in addition to being a type of life, a life form.... The homosexual was now a species."[63] Homosexuals and other "deviants" were the first groups to be delineated by sexologists, but heterosexuality as a normative and desirable identity became elaborated, promoted, and consolidated by the 1920s. These sexual typologies became incorporated into immigration law, as described earlier.

Efforts to regulate sexuality have been inextricable from racial, gender, and class controls. These interconnections have been richly documented by scholars in many disciplines, including ethnic studies, women's studies, queer theory, sociology, history, and literature. Scholars have also theorized how sexual regulation facilitated imperial projects. According to Ann Laura Stoler, "the regulation of sexual relations was central to the development of particular kinds of colonial settlements and to the allocation of economic activity within them." Indeed, "the very categories of 'colonizer' and 'colonized' were secured through forms of sexual control."[64] As discussed earlier, the regulation of sexuality, carried out in tandem with immigration control, has also been a central technology for continually reconstructing the nation-state and citizenry within particular limits, historically and at present.

Finally, scholarship by feminists of color and queers of color emphasizes that interconnections among sexuality, race, class, gender, nation, and imperialism transform each category, necessitating new modes of theoretical engagement. Thus, Eng and Hom's analysis of queer Asian Americans stresses:

> We are not delineating an additive model of social inequity.... Sexuality and race cannot be brought into symmetrical alignment with each other. They are not commensurate oppressions easily catalogued or equated.

> Instead, the two share a constitutive and dynamic relationship, one whose dialectical combination often yields unrecognized, unacknowledged and understudied configurations.[65]

These rich analyses of how sexuality is implicated in multiple relations of power, domination, and resistance provide valuable tools for the study of queer migration, on its own terms and in relation to nation-making and citizenship processes.

Liberationist Narratives and Revisions

Despite pioneering research about queer migrants' lives, which has brought sexuality and migration scholarship into productive dialogue, the majority of accounts of queer migration tend to remain organized around a narrative of movement from repression to freedom, or a heroic journey undertaken in search of liberation. Certainly, it is appropriate to describe and appreciate the struggles and fierce dreams that have impelled queer migration. Queer migrants—not only those seeking asylum from persecution, but also those whose stories are more quotidian—often describe their experiences using precisely these terms. Scholars and activists also often use the terms. The difficulty arises, though, when the search for "freedom" and new possibilities become the only elements of queer migration that are addressed. When that happens, complex migration processes become reduced to oversimplified dynamics that reinscribe dominant nationalist myths of the United States as a land of freedom and democracy and erase the struggle, suffering, and resistance experienced by subordinated groups. Furthermore, queer migrants' experiences risk becoming appropriated to serve foreign policy objectives, and their subjectivities and histories become represented within colonialist, racist understandings of culture and identity. I want to briefly address these points, drawing on the work of many of the scholars mentioned earlier, who provide ways to study queer migration without becoming enmeshed in these difficulties.

Martin F. Manalansan IV has built on transnational, diasporic, and other models that reject strictly nation- and state-centered analyses in favor of analyses that highlight the salience of historical and ongoing links among different regions. In a 1997 essay, he highlights these linkages in order to underscore that while queer Filipino migrants may be searching for freedom from oppression, their oppression has been significantly shaped by the legacies of U.S. colonization and by ongoing economic and political relationships between the United States and the Philippines.[66] Under these circumstances, queer Filipinos' migration emerges not simply as a search for freedom in the United States, but also as a search for alternatives to circumstances in the Philippines in which the United States is centrally (though not solely) implicated. Consequently, queer Filipino immigration cannot be read as a comfortable reiteration of dominant U.S. nationalist myths.

By stressing historical and ongoing connections between the United States and the Philippines, Manalansan makes clear that queers migrate not simply as sexual subjects, but also as racialized, classed, gendered subjects of particular regions and nations that exist in various historic relationships to U.S. hegemony.[67] In this way, he echoes a crucial thread of sexuality scholarship that insists on treating queers not solely as sexual subjects, but in relation to multiple identities that directly affect them. At the same time, he revises that scholarship by transporting it to a global field structured by historic legacies and contemporary forms of inequality and exploitation between and among nations and regions. He also revises migration scholarship by centering sexuality as a critical structuring factor.

Scholars such as Manalansan document that although queer migrants may be searching for multiple forms of freedom, that does not mean they will find it. For the narrative of the United States as a land of freedom and opportunity, which often implicitly guides writings about queer and other migrations, represses the long history of how freedom and opportunity for some has generally been purchased at the expense of the many. This includes subordinated racial and ethnic groups, women, poor and working people, and queers. When queers migrate to the United States, they become inserted into that history and inherit its many legacies. The fact that lesbians and gays were barred from even legally entering the United States as immigrants until 1990, and still face forms of subtle and not-so-subtle discrimination in the immigration system, clearly challenges any simple claim that migration to the United States involves the attainment of freedom.

Olíva Espín has provided a detailed examination of how homophobia, racism, sexism, language, and legal status affect Latina lesbian migrants in the United States. According to Espín, Latina migrants frequently find themselves caught "between the racism of the dominant society and the sexist expectations of [their] own communit[ies]" as they struggle to negotiate identity and community.[68] Since women are typically constructed as the repositories of cultural tradition, their sexual behavior tends to become viewed—by both migrant communities and dominant cultures—as "evidence" of the worth of the group, and policed accordingly. Of course, contestations about the worth of particular migrant groups cannot be separated from the global histories and linkages that Manalansan has described. For Latinas in the United States, these factors make claiming a lesbian identity particularly complicated. Moreover, they underscore the need to revise triumphal stories based on assimilationist models.[69]

Espín not only speaks to issues described in migration and sexuality scholarship, but also raises questions for each of them. For instance, while migration scholars have examined conflicts between migrants and various U.S. communities, they have paid little attention to sexuality as a particular area of conflict. Moreover, centering migrant homosexuality as a site of conflict suggests that accounts of migrants' settlement, community formation, and cultural transmission are organized around implicitly heterosexist norms that require significant revision. At the same time, the ways that heterosexuality itself becomes reconstructed through migration also requires critical attention.[70]

Anne Maguire's "The Accidental Immigrant" affirms the difficulty of creating a sense of "home" for lesbian migrants in the United States—even those who are white and English speaking—with the resulting turn by some toward political activism. The Irish Lesbian and Gay Organization (ILGO) was founded to address the specific concerns of immigrant Irish lesbians and gays. Yet, as Maguire describes, the question of whether ILGO should be allowed to participate in New York City's St. Patrick's Day parade soon overshadowed all other functions of the group. The U.S. Supreme Court eventually affirmed ILGO's exclusion from the parade. As Maguire sums up, the parade "is where our 'coming out' took place in Irish America and where we were told that we did not belong, nor were we welcome." These struggles also affected St. Patrick's Day parades in other U.S. cities, including Boston and San Francisco, and in Ireland. As Maguire describes, "the greeting, 'Hello New York' jumped out at us from a photograph of the thirty lesbians and two gay men who marched in the St. Patrick's Day parade in Cork [Ireland] in 1992. This brave act of solidarity and support caused much joy, pride, amusement, and a little sadness in ILGO."[71] ILGO's struggle also resonated with struggles over "out" lesbian, gay, bi, trans, and queer participation in other major ethnic and national parades, such as the India Day Parade.

Maguire's essay certainly suggests that sexuality scholars' accounts of queer activism need to be revised to understand and account for the forms of activism and specific political concerns of queer migrants. Echoing Maguire, Grace Poore describes how fear of the immigration control authorities leads some queer immigrants to restrict their associations and activities: "We understand why some of us never march on the outside of Gay Pride contingents in case of cameras. Why many of us fear going into bars in case of a raid. Why we only do radio interviews, never have our photographs taken." At the same time, Poore describes how she negotiated these restrictions: "If I couldn't sign petitions, I distributed them; if I couldn't lead meetings, I organized them; if I couldn't do civil disobedience, I wrote." But these forms of activism, which represent migrants' creative adaptation to their circumstances, remain liable to misinterpretation by individuals and activists who privilege only one form of "being out," and see other forms as betrayal, inauthenticity, or lack of developed political consciousness.[72] For these reasons, queer migrants' contributions to political activism have only recently begun to be appreciated and analyzed.[73]

Queer migrants' contributions to cultural work, like Guillermo Reyes's play *Deporting the Divas*, have also largely remained "undocumented and unexamined," according to David Román. Román's critical analyses felicitiously combine José Muñoz's framework of "queer acts" with Lisa Lowe's theorization of "immigrant acts" to suggest that queer migrants' cultural works constitute "queer immigrant acts" that both expand theatrical representation and demand critical interrogation of race, gender, and sexuality as these intersect with histories of displacement and migration.[74]

Other scholars have problematized how the U.S. state appropriates queer migrants' presence for foreign policy objectives.[75] Lourdes Arguelles and B. Ruby Rich have charted "the construction of an anti-Castro campaign [in the United States] predicated on Cuba's repression of homosexual-rights,"[76] which oversimplified and misrepresented gay Cuban migrants' experiences and the larger circumstances of their journeys. This campaign substantially reinforced and shored up the U.S. government's policies toward Cuba. As a result, many gay and lesbian Cuban migrants felt themselves to be torn between "total integration into the American gay (frequently racist and classist) mainstream or an all-Cuban émigré existence," neither of which seemed like adequate alternatives.[77] They struggled to craft other options, although some did not survive the process.

Arguelles and Rich call for further investigation into and critique of the "U.S. use of émigré communities in foreign policy and domestic control initiatives."[78] Such an investigation would need to address not only the points raised by Arguelles and Rich, but also how queer asylum seekers' testimonies are elicited in ways that reinforce dominant nationalism and imperialism without necessarily leading to sanctuary for the individuals concerned.

These scholarly writings make clear that migration rarely represents a clear-cut resolution to the difficulties that queers face. Rather, they must deal with racial, gender, class, cultural, sexual, and language barriers that are inextricable from global histories of imperialism and exploitation that link the United States to other countries and regions.[79] Queer migrants also experience jeopardy based on their status as noncitizens—a jeopardy that has significantly intensified since the events of September 11, 2001.[80] By highlighting these issues, a foundational body of queer migration scholarship has revised the liberationist narrative of queer migration as a heroic personal search for freedom—celebrating personal actions, but placing them in a larger critical context.

Several scholars, while not explicitly concerned with queer migration across international borders, have advanced arguments that are very useful. One important area of research concerns patterns of queer migration *within* national borders. Carl Stychin observes, "the significance of [internal] migration in the constitution of lesbian and gay subjectivities is increasingly documented, particularly from within the discipline of geography."[81] Historian John D'Emilio has drawn attention to the significance of internal migration, especially after World War II, when demobilization, new employment opportunities, and the increased sexualization of commerce drew tens of thousands of gay men and lesbians to major U.S. cities.[82] In subsequent decades, as Kath Weston describes, the "Great Gay Migrations" to cities continued. In the process, gays, lesbians, and others crafted identities structured around "a symbolics of urban/rural relations [that located] gay subjects in the city" while transforming cities into sites of community and political power.[83] Such scholarship, which attends to the ways that mobility *within* countries has been central to the constitution of lesbian, gay, and queer identities, interrupts monolithic nationalist narratives of the United States and fragments the United States into spaces of both freedom and oppression, possibility and constraint. It also invites us to consider possible linkages among U.S. and migrant queers, based on histories of mobility.[84]

Another valuable area of emerging scholarship examines how identities—such as queer, lesbian, gay, bi, and trans—circulate in local and global contexts, including through queer tourism, and are variously claimed, inhabited, and rearticulated. This scholarship builds on several sources, including analyses of globalization and theories that situate cultural changes within relations of power and inequality.[85] Lisa Rofel, writing on men in Beijing, China, who call themselves gay, offers an example of this scholarship and its use for the study of queer migrants. Rofel begins by noting that claims of gay identity by men who are not white, Western, and middle-class tend to be conceptualized as evidence that globalization has modernized, Westernized, and homogenized various cultures. The result, according to some scholars, is the emergence of global gay identity.[86] But Rofel challenges the equation of globalization with Westernization and homogenization. As she suggests, globalization is never simply a matter of Western standards entering China or other countries "as an unimpeded cultural flow" that results in homogenization.[87] Rather, gay men in China actively engage Western (and other) models of gayness, but in the process transform and rework them.[88]

Rofel not only challenges notions of globalization as homogenization and Westernization, but also refuses the colonialist models of culture on which such notions implicitly hinge. As she explains, the belief that claiming gay identity is a consequence of Westernization participates in colonialist models that view non-Western culture "as timeless, bounded, homogenous, and unchanging." Moreover, "there appears to be a 'stepladder' version of culture and modernity here such that the more one looks like the West, the more one sheds any markers of culture." According to Rofel, such models of culture have been roundly critiqued in anthropology. Nonetheless, they continue to implicitly and explicitly structure scholarship about gays in other countries and cultures, such that "gay men in Asia can be either universal or Asian but not both, even as their Asianness continues to leave them in the place of otherness to global gayness."[89]

Rofel's analysis of the ways that men engage and rework various models of gayness that circulate through Beijing leads her to conclude that "what gay identity ends up looking like in any one place in the world today is not a foregone conclusion; certainly, it is not a straightforward matter of joining the global gay human race."[90] Similarly, when migrants in the United States claim gay, queer, or other identities, these claims do not simply reflect assimilation to dominant Western sexuality norms. Rather, they reflect complex processes of cultural transformation that occur within relations of power. When migrants claim queer identity, they strategically invoke, inhabit, and transform the term in relation to these wider cultural and historical processes.[91]

These scholarly works have reformulated "migration as liberation" narratives along more complex lines and, in the process, offered valuable tools for the continued study of queer migrants. The essays in this volume build on that foundation, while extending the debates into new realms.

Disciplining Queer Migrants and Queering Racial/Ethnic Communities

The essays in this volume are divided into two thematic groups. "Part I: Disciplining Queer Migrants" provides historical, cultural, and structural analyses of norms, institutions, and discourses that affect queer (and other) migrants in the United States. "Part II: Queering Racial/Ethnic Communities" offers rich ethnographic and sociological studies of queer migrants' lives and communities in Miami, New York, and San Francisco, which are key settlement cities for contemporary U.S. migrants.

Scholars in the first group of essays historicize the multiple modes of regulation and discipline to which migrants are subjected, including practices that have made them into one of the fastest-growing incarcerated groups in America. Alisa Solomon's essay focuses on the experiences of Cristina Madraso, a Mexican transsexual woman who sought asylum in the United States but was instead locked up at the Krome Detention Center in Florida, where she was raped twice by a guard. Solomon's analysis examines how guards and other officials use gender and sexual violence to informally demarcate who, in their view, does and does not belong within the U.S. nation. She also urgently problematizes how multiply subordinated people like Madraso remain literally "illegible" within rights regimes that are supposed to offer protection. At the same time, Solomon details how Madraso has challenged these violent erasures, seeking to craft her own "American dream."

Carceral practices involve not only the institutions in which migrants become detained, but also the immigration control apparatus, the judicial system, Congress, and public discourses used to frame, explain, and legitimize migrants' treatment. Tim Randazzo's essay offers insight into this more expansive version of the carceral network by providing a history of how, in 1994, persecuted lesbians, gay men, and transgender people came to be designated as eligible to apply for asylum. Although the asylum system offers protection to some people, Randazzo shows it also significantly participates in multiplying distinctions and inequalities among queers based on gender, race, class, and national origin.

Cantú, Luibhéid, and Stern provide a case study of how the asylum system multiplies inequalities not only on a national but also an international scale. The case study was initially composed by Cantú. After his sudden death in 2002, Luibhéid and Stern revised his draft to clarify the theoretical questions he wanted to raise. Focusing on cases involving Mexican-origin queers, the essay shows how the discourses and practices for processing asylum claims perpetuate essentializing, colonialist, and binarized conceptions of sexual, racial, gender, and national identities—even while transnational processes weave U.S. and Mexican people, communities, and cultures into ever closer contact. Thus, there exists a contradiction between colonialist models of hermetically sealed identities and cultures, and the reality of increasing trade, contact, and cultural and population exchange between Mexico and the United States. As these authors suggest, the asylum system's role in perpetuating colonialist imagery has material consequences for U.S.–Latin American relations, U.S. Latinos, and Latin Americans seeking asylum in the United States.

The perpetuation of inequalities through the asylum system echoes the history of disparate citizenship possibilities for peoples within the United States, as Siobhan Somerville addresses. Focusing on the McCarran-Walter Act of 1952, which established the framework through which immigration and naturalization remain controlled today, Somerville inquires into the shifting links between racial and sexual controls in the production of U.S. citizens through naturalization. Somerville draws on congressional testimonies, letters from the public, court documents, and other materials to suggest that sexuality exclusions in the McCarran-Walter Act provided lawmakers with a means to reinvigorate a hegemonic national fantasy of "pure blood," with its associated property relations, in the absence of an explicit discourse of race. Somerville's "queer" analysis of the heterosexual and racial imaginaries that undergird the production of American citizenship valuably theorizes race, sexuality, and citizenship as thoroughly intertwined in one another.

Erica Rand concludes the first group of essays. Drawing on popular and commodity cultural materials, her playful veneration of the Statue of Liberty as an erotic icon both recuperates a hegemonic national symbol into queer history and resituates queerness at the center of mainstream immigration narratives. Her analysis of the ceremonies and celebrations staged around Lady Liberty's restoration in 1986 reveals the systemic occlusions of gender, sexual, racial, and class oppression that underpin dominant discourses of America as a melting pot and bastion of liberty, and render racialized queer migrant subjects literally unthinkable. Rand's expository style, as much as her analysis, insists on queering traditional scholarly studies of immigration.

Part II complements the first part by providing complex analyses of how queer migrant individuals and communities negotiate disciplinary and regulatory structures while simultaneously crafting identities, communities, cultural forms, and political activism. The essays establish central linkages among sexuality and other modes of regulation in migrants' lives. Not just economics, but gender, national origin, racialization, and class processes, as these intersect with sexuality, are addressed. While the essays remain grounded in specific communities, they make abundantly clear how transnational communities, relations, and processes continually reconfigure these locales. The essays also document histories that have been literally ignored and unexplored. These include the lives of queer migrants, to be sure, but more specifically histories such as queer Salvadorans negotiating identities in relation to Mexican and Chicano queer communities in the San Francisco Bay Area. In these ways, the essays document struggles not only within communities, but also across communities and locales that reveal points of alliance, collaboration, and transformation. They enormously complicate our understanding of citizenship as lived practice versus legal rights and obligations and the dynamic interplay between these forces. The focus on migrants' lives within cities is particularly apposite because significant numbers of contemporary migrants live in cities and because, as Holston and Appadurai argue, cities "are especially privileged sites for considering the current renegotiation of citizenship."[92]

Cuba and Miami, Florida, emerge as crucially linked locales in Susana Peña's essay. Peña analyzes the 1980 Mariel exodus from Cuba as a means for understanding both how queer migrant histories become silenced within official records and how queer migrant cultures develop. Prior to their migration, gay Marielitos had experienced repression for engaging in "ostentatious" public displays of homosexuality through transgressions of gender codes of dress, style, and conduct. Yet, the U.S. media extended Castro's logic of erasing homosexuality from the public sphere by rarely acknowledging the presence of these gay men among the Mariel arrivals. When serious discussion about gay Marielitos appeared in the media, it was quickly silenced and delegitimated through statements issued by a prominent U.S. immigration scholar, Cuban American Alejandro Portes, and others. Peña's essay traces how one of this century's significant queer migrations has been rendered invisible and unspeakable by media, scholars, local communities, and queers themselves.

Although the Cuban state and U.S. forces worked in tandem to render the men invisible, the Mariel migrants had a palpable impact on culture in Miami. According to Peña, Marielitos drew on their premigration experiences in Cuba and the possibilities offered by Miami to fashion a vibrant gay male Cuban American culture that was substantially organized around visible gender transgression. Cuban American men in Miami, then, negotiate their sexual and cultural identities within the competing logics of silence and visibility and in relation to a circuit of Cubanidad that implicates the island and Miami in continually changing ways.

Martin Manalansan uses ethnographic techniques to examine the private spaces and everyday lives of queer Filipino migrant men living in another major migrant city, New York. He shows that while engaged in mundane activities, such as dressing for work and using the telephone, his informants confront and negotiate transnational structures of imperialism, racism, and gender and class oppression that are lived with local, everyday immediacy. The everyday, then, provides a site for understanding how diasporic queers of color forge selves, intimacy, and home in the face of these multiple displacements and forms of violence. Manalansan convincingly argues that disaporic Filipino gay men live an alternative modernity that is neither dependent on Western mainstream queer culture nor reducible to an assimilative framework, but rather demands new methodologies and theories—which Manalansan's essay models—in order to be understood. For these men, Manalansan argues, citizenship is not a matter of birthright or of romantic dissidence, but about survival.

Despite very useful developments, citizenship scholarship still tends to presume either that all queers are legal citizens or that all immigrants are heterosexual. Horacio Roque Ramírez's essay bridges that gap and illuminates the experiences of queer Latino migrants who negotiate citizenship and social membership in the San Francisco Bay Area through cultural work. Roque Ramírez situates the production and reception of two cultural works—the Salvadoran-based play *El Corázon Nunca Me Ha Mentido* (1984) and the film *Del Otro Lado* (1998)—in relation to transformations wrought by migration, AIDS, and anti-immigrant organizing in San Francisco neighborhoods. As he beautifully shows, these cultural works constituted important sites through which community identities, histories, memories, and collective action became contested and reworked within those changing neighborhoods and in relation to larger transnational circuits.

As a collection, the essays establish queer migration as central in the making of migrant, racial, ethnic, and sexual communities, politics, cultural work, and struggles for social justice—historically and at present. Building on foundational work, as well as the best in contemporary sexuality and immigration scholarship, they open up multiple, pressing questions for further analysis. In particular, the authors urge that sexuality scholarship closely attend to the dynamics of past and contemporary immigration, and that immigration scholarship attend to the dynamics of sexuality—in all its forms—in structuring migration.

Notes

For assistance with conceptualizing this introduction, many thanks to Rob Buffington, Lionel Cantú, Hai Ren, Val Rohy, and Siobhan Somerville. For further revision suggestions, I am very grateful to Arlene Keizer, Susana Peña, Radhika Gajjala, Vicki Patraka, and John Warren.

1. Several essays that we solicited, which addressed lesbian migration, the reconstruction of heterosexuality through migration, and HIV and migration, were unavailable as this collection went to press. Future collections will have to address these important subjects. On the difficulties of generating scholarship about lesbians

and migration, see Eithne Luibhéid, *Entry Denied: Controlling Sexuality at the Border* (Minneapolis: University of Minnesota Press, 2002), chapter 4.

2. Michael Warner, ed., introduction to *Fear of a Queer Planet: Queer Politics and Social Theory* (Minneapolis: University of Minnesota Press, 1993), xxvi.

3. Philip Brian Harper, Anne McClintock, José Esteban Muñoz, and Trish Rosen, "Queer Transexions of Race, Nation, and Gender," *Social Text*, no. 52–53 (Fall/Winter 1997), 3.

4. Take the example of paid employment. Most migrants contribute to the U.S. economy through paid employment. Yet, legal distinctions have enormous consequences for migrants' employment possibilities. Legal immigrants may work without hindrance, except in certain federal jobs, and are technically eligible for the same protections (or lack thereof) as their citizen counterparts. Refugees may also work and are eligible for federally funded job training and placement assistance. Asylum seekers cannot legally work for at least six months (longer if the government has detained them) and must then apply to the government for permission. The undocumented are not supposed to hold paying jobs, but, given employers' demands for their labor, they often work anyway, under conditions of great exploitation and at continual risk of deportation. These contrasts make clear that legal status distinctions significantly shape conditions and possibilities for migrants.

5. Benedict Anderson, *Imagined Communities: Reflections on the Origins and Spread of Nationalism*, rev. ed. (London: Verso, 1991).

6. Thus, the production of U.S. nation, citizenry, and citizenship through immigration control operates through multi-axial differentiations that not only contrast citizens with noncitizens (or "aliens"), but also make differentiations *among* aliens. As we will see later, the differentiations among aliens both stem from and further reinforce actual differentiations that continue to shape life possibilities for U.S. citizens, too.

7. Sana Loue, "Homosexuality and Immigration Law: A Re-Examination," *Journal of Psychiatry and Law* (Spring/Summer 1990): 126n11.

8. *Revision of Immigration and Nationality Laws*, 82d Cong., 2d sess., 1952, S. Rep. 1137, 9.

9. Marta Donayre, "Binational Couples: Alliance of Fear," *Gay and Lesbian Review*, March–April 2002, 25.

10. Grace Poore, "Three Movements in A Minor: Lesbians and Immigration," *Off Our Backs*, August–September 1996, 12. On Valentine's Day 2000, Representative Jerrold Nadler introduced the *Permanent Partners Immigration Act* (HR 690), which was intended to enable migrants in binational lesbian/gay relationships to receive U.S. residency, but the bill has not yet received a hearing. Thus, binational couples remain a largely invisible constituency, who "keep their mouths shut" for fear of attracting INS attention and investigation (Donayre, "Binational Couples," 25). The Lesbian and Gay Immigration Rights Taskforce (LGIRTF), with fifteen chapters in the United States, has, however, provided a forum for binational couples. Additionally, according to Donayre, "the internet has [also] provided this community with a tremendous tool" (25).

11. Poore, "Three Movements in A Minor," 12.

12. Peter Barta, "Lambskin Borders: An Argument for the Abolition of the United States' Exclusion of HIV-Positive Immigrants," *Georgetown Immigration Law Review* 12 (Winter 1998): 336.

13. For a review of much recent scholarship, see Richard Parker, "Sexuality, Culture, and Power in HIV/AIDS Research," *Annual Review of Anthropology* 30 (2001): 163–79. On connections between HIV/AIDS and migration, see, for example, Mary Haour-Knipe and Richard Rector, eds., *Crossing Borders: Migration, Ethnicity, and AIDS* (London: Taylor and Francis, 1997). The editors state that "this, to our knowledge is the first book to have addressed" the intersections of migration and HIV/AIDS ("Introduction," 7). The collection focuses primarily, though not exclusively, on Europe, and the introduction usefully describes some of the reasons why the connections between migration and HIV/AIDS merit particular attention. See also Gilbert Herdt, ed., *Sexual Cultures and Migration in the Era of AIDS* (Oxford: Clarendon Press, 1997). On migrant laborers and HIV/AIDS in the United States, see, for example, Kurt Organista and Pamela Balls Organista, "Migrant Laborers and AIDS in the United States: A Review of the Literature," *AIDS Education and Prevention* 9, no. 1 (February 1997): 83–93; Shiraz I. Mishra, Ross F. Connor, and J. Raul Magaña, eds., *AIDS Crossing Borders: The Spread of HIV among Migrant Latinos* (Boulder, CO: Westview Press, 1996). On discourses about AIDS and their implication in neocolonialist imagery and practices, see Cindy Patton, *Inventing AIDS* (New York: Routledge, 1990); Patton, "From Nation to Family: Containing 'African AIDS,'" in *Nationalisms and Sexualities*, ed. Andrew Parker et al. (New York: Routledge, 1992), 218–34; and Patton, *Globalizing AIDS* (Minneapolis: University of Minnesota Press, 2002).

14. See Shannon Minter, "Sodomy and Public Morality Offenses under U.S. Immigration Law," *Cornell International Law Journal* 26 (1993): 771–818.

15. See George Peffer, "Forbidden Families: Emigration Experiences of Chinese Women under the Page Law, 1875–1882," *Journal of American Ethnic History* 6, no. 1 (Fall 1986): 28–46; Peffer, *If They Don't Bring Their Women Here* (Urbana: University of Illinois Press, 1999).

16. Luibhéid, *Entry Denied,* chapter 3.

17. Filipinos were the only group exempted from Asian exclusion since the United States had acquired the Philippines. Nonetheless, the Tydings McDuffie Act of 1934 reduced Filipino migration to fifty people a year. See Bill Ong Hing, *Making and Remaking Asian America through Immigration Policy* (Stanford, CA: Stanford University Press, 1993), 35.

18. See Donna Gabaccia, *From the Other Side: Women, Gender, and Immigrant Life in the United States, 1820–1990* (Bloomington: Indiana University Press, 1994); Doris Weatherford, *Foreign and Female* (New York: Schoken Books, 1984).

19. See Jane Perry Clark, *The Deportation of Aliens from the United States to Europe* (New York: Columbia University Press, 1931); E. P. Hutchinson, *Legislative History of American Immigration Policy, 1789–1965* (Philadelphia: University of Pennsylvania Press, 1981); Luibhéid, *Entry Denied.*

20. Edward Corsi, *In the Shadow of Liberty* (New York: Arno Press, 1969), 81.

21. On transgender immigrants, see also Erica Rand's discussion of Frank Woodhull (née Mary Johnson) in "Heritage Sex," paper presented at the "Sex, Race, and Globalization" conference, University of Arizona, April 5, 2002.

22. For example, see V. S. McClatchy, *Four Anti-Japanese Pamphlets* (New York: Arno Press, 1978). See also Roger Daniels, *The Politics of Prejudice: The Anti-Japanese Movement in California and the Struggle for Exclusion* (New York: Athenium, 1972).

23. The preference system describes family relationships that qualify for immigrant visas and sets limits for how many visas may be issued each year for each category. Moreover, certain relatives qualify as "immediate relatives," and are exempt from annual numerical limitations. The exempt categories are currently spouses, unmarried children under twenty-one, and parents of adult U.S. citizens. Other family relationships that qualify one for an immigrant visa, but within quota limits, are described at http://uscis.gov/graphics/services/imm_visas.htm.

24. David Reimers, *Still the Golden Door: The Third World Comes to America* (New York: Columbia University Press, 1992). The 1965 emphasis on family also had an economic dimension; families were expected to generate growth through consumption.

25. Nikolas Rose, *Powers of Freedom* (Cambridge: Cambridge University Press, 1999).

26. Quoted in Kathleen M. Moore, "U.S. Immigration Reform and the Meaning of Responsibility," *Studies in Law, Politics, and Society* 20 (2000): 138. The affidavit remains in effect until the sponsored immigrant becomes a U.S. citizen, works for ten years, permanently leaves the country, or dies. It is not voided by divorce.

27. Ibid., 139.

28. At the same time, migrants, migrant communities, sending-country officials, and various U.S. constituencies have contested and renegotiated these distinctions.

29. For an overview of the history of the refugee/asylum system in the United States, see Norman L. Zucker and Naomi Flint Zucker, *The Guarded Gate: The Reality of American Refugee Policy* (San Diego: Harcourt Brace Jovanovich, 1987); and Philip Shrag, *A Well-Founded Fear: The Congressional Battle to Save Political Asylum in America* (New York: Routledge, 2000). Technically, the distinction between a refugee and an asylum seeker is that refugees have been preapproved for admission, based on human rights criteria, before they ever arrive in the United States. Asylum seekers, by contrast, seek asylum from within the United States' borders, having entered in some other way.

30. Jacqueline Bhabha, "Embodied Rights: Gender Persecution, State Sovereignty, and Refugees," *Public Culture* 9, no. 1 (Fall 1996): 8.

31. See Luibhéid, *Entry Denied*, 105–18.

32. See Sherene Razack, "Policing the Borders of the Nation: The Imperial Gaze in Gender Persecution Cases," in her *Looking White People in the Eye* (Toronto: University of Toronto Press, 1998), 88–129; and Jacqueline Bhabha, "Boundaries in the Field of Human Rights: International Gatekeepers? The Tension between Asylum Advocacy and Human Rights," *Harvard Human Rights Law Review* 15 (Spring 2002): 155–81.

33. Bhabha, "Boundaries in the Field of Human Rights," 161.

34. See Giorgio Agamben, *Homo Sacer: Sovereign Power and Bare Life*, trans. Daniel Heller Roazen (Stanford, CA: Stanford University Press, 1998), including his discussion of World War II concentration camps as "states of exception" that remain outside of, but at the same time foundational for, national sovereignty. Moreover, according to Agamben, "the camp is the very paradigm of political space at the point at which politics becomes biopolitics" (171), and thus the camp represents "the political space of modernity itself" (174). His analysis questions how "human beings could be so completely deprived of their rights and prerogatives that no act

committed against them could appear any longer as a crime," a question that demands urgent consideration in terms of detained migrants, too (171).

35. Amnesty International, *Human Rights Concerns in the Border Region with Mexico* (New York: Amnesty International, 1998); Human Rights Watch, *Brutality Unchecked: Human Rights Abuses along the U.S. Border with Mexico* (New York and Washington, DC: Human Rights Watch, May 1992). Human Rights Watch issued four other reports about the U.S.–Mexico border: *Frontier Injustice: Human Rights Abuses along the U.S. Border with Mexico Persist amid Climate of Impunity* (May 1993); *Crossing the Line: Human Rights Abuses along the U.S. Border with Mexico Persist amid Climate of Impunity* (April 1995); *Human Rights Violations by INS Inspectors and Border Patrol Agents Continue: Attorney General Janet Reno Urged to Address Abuse Problem* (an open letter to Janet Reno, January 13, 1997); and *Slipping through the Cracks: Unaccompanied Children Detained by the U.S. Immigration and Naturalization Service* (April 1997). See also Peter Andreas, *Border Games: Policing the U.S.– Mexico Divide* (Ithaca, NY: Cornell University Press, 2000); Timothy Dunn, *Militarization of the U.S.–Mexico Border, 1978–1992: Low-Intensity Conflict Doctrine Comes Home* (Austin: Center for Mexican American Studies, University of Texas at Austin, 1996); Joseph Nevins, *Operation Gatekeeper: The Rise of the Illegal Alien and the Making of the U.S.–Mexico Boundary* (New York: Routledge, 2002); and "Gatekeepers State: Immigration and Boundary Policing in an Era of Globalization," ed. Jose Palafox, special issue, *Social Justice* 28, no. 2 (2001).

36. See, for example, the report by the Office of the Inspector General, *The September 11 Detainees: A Review of the Treatment of Aliens Held on Immigration Charges in Connection with the Investigation of the September 11 Attacks* (June 2003), at http://www.usdoj.gov/oig/special/03–06/. See also Michael Welch, *Detained: Immigration Laws and the Expanding INS Jail Complex* (Philadelphia: Temple University Press, 2002).

37. Robert S. Chang, *Disoriented: Asian Americans, Law, and the Nation-State* (New York: New York University Press, 1999). In regard to citizenship, as James Holston and Arjun Appadurai explain, "Since the eighteenth century, one of the defining marks of modernity has been the use of two linked concepts of association—citizenship and nationality—to establish the meaning of full membership in society. Citizenship rather than subjectship or kinship or cultship has defined the prerogatives and encumbrances of that membership, and the nation-state rather than the neighborhood or the city or the region established its scope. What it meant to be a member of society in many areas of the world came to be understood, to a significant degree, in terms of what it means to be a rights-bearing citizen of a territorial nation-state." See James Holston and Arjun Appadurai, "Cities and Citizenship," *Public Culture* 8, no. 2 (Winter 1996): 187.

38. Maria Jiminez, "War in the Borderlands," *NACLA Report on the Americas* 26, no. 1 (July 1992): 33.

39. Moreover, citizenship law has been a site where individuals contested, and the courts imposed, particular definitions of who was white. See Ian Haney Lopez, *White by Law: The Legal Construction of Race* (New York: New York University Press, 1996).

40. See, for example, Candice Bredbenner, *A Nationality of Her Own: Women, Marriage, and the Law of Citizenship* (Berkeley: University of California Press, 1998).

41. Engin F. Isin and Patricia Wood, *Citizenship and Identity* (Thousand Oaks, CA: Sage, 1999), 75.

42. E.g., Martha Hodes, ed., *Sex, Race, Love: Crossing Boundaries in North American History* (New York: New York University Press, 1999); Carole Pateman, *The Sexual Contract* (Stanford, CA: Stanford University Press, 1998); Dorothy E. Roberts, *Killing the Black Body: Race, Reproduction, and the Meaning of Liberty* (New York: Vintage Books, 1998). See also writings on nationalism and sexuality such as George Mosse, *Nationalism and Sexuality* (Madison: University of Wisconsin Press, 1985); and Parker et al., *Nationalisms and Sexualities*.

43. Phelan's argument carefully attends to the fact that heterosexuality as a normative category emerged in the first decades of the twentieth century in association with changes in capitalism. See Shane Phelan, *Sexual Strangers: Gays, Lesbians, and the Dilemmas of Citizenship* (Philadelphia: Temple University Press, 2001). On the emergence of heterosexuality, see Jonathan Ned Katz, *The Invention of Heterosexuality* (New York: Dutton, 1995).

44. See Lauren Berlant, *The Queen of America Goes to Washington City* (Durham, NC: Duke University Press, 1997). Other valuable books on sexuality and citizenship include: David Bell and Jon Binnie, *The Sexual Citizen: Queer Politics and Beyond* (Cambridge, England: Polity Press, 2000); David Evans, *Sexual Citizenship: The Material Construction of Sexualities* (London: Routledge, 1993); Diane Richardson, *Rethinking Sexuality* (Thousand Oaks, CA: Sage, 2000).

45. M. Jacqui Alexander, "Erotic Autonomy as a Politics of Decolonization," in *Feminist Genealogies, Colonial Legacies, Democratic Futures*, ed. Chandra Talpade Mohanty and M. Jacqui Alexander (New York: Routledge, 1997), 65.

46. T. H. Marshall's foundational work conceived citizenship as involving an evolutionary succession of rights: civil or legal, political, and social. See, for example, T. H. Marshall, *Citizenship and Social Class and Other Essays* (Cambridge: Cambridge University Press, 1950). Recent scholarship also addresses consumer rights and cultural rights as dimensions of citizenship.

47. Stuart Hall, "The Question of Cultural Identity," in *Modernity and Its Futures*, ed. Stuart Hall, David Held, and Tony McGrew (Cambridge, England: Polity Press, 1992), 292.

48. Berlant, *The Queen of America Goes to Washington City*, 195.

49. Renato Rosaldo, "Cultural Citizenship, Inequality, and Multiculturalism," in *Latino Cultural Citizenship*, ed. William V. Flores and Rina Benmayor (Boston: Beacon Press, 1997), 29.

50. E.g., Olíva Espín, *Latina Realities: Essays on Healing, Migration, and Sexuality* (Boulder, CO: Westview Press, 1997); Espín, *Women Crossing Boundaries: A Psychology of Immigration and Transformation* (New York: Routledge, 1999); M. Jacqui Alexander, "Not Just (Any) Body Can Be a Citizen: The Politics of Law, Sexuality, and Postcoloniality in Trinidad and Tobago and the Bahamas," *Feminist Review* 48 (Autumn 1994): 5–23; Alexander, "Erotic Autonomy as a Politics of Decolonization," in *Feminist Genealogies*, ed. M. Jacqui Alexander and Chandra Talpade Mohanty, 63–100; Martin F. Manalansan IV, "Searching for Community: Filipino Gay Men in New York City," *Amerasia Journal* 20, no. 1 (1994): 59–73; Manalansan, "Speaking of AIDS: Language and the Filipino Gay Experience in America," in *Discrepant Histories: Translocal Essays on Filipino Cultures*, ed. Vicente Rafael (Philadelphia: Temple

University Press, 1995), 193–220; Manalansan, "In the Shadows of Stonewall: Examining Gay Transnational Politics and the Diasporic Dilemma," in *The Politics of Culture in the Shadow of Capital,* ed. Lisa Lowe and David Lloyd (Durham, NC: Duke University Press, 1997), 485–505; Manalansan, "Diasporic Deviants/Divas: How Filipino Gay Transmigrants 'Play With the World,'" in *Queer Diasporas,* ed. Cindy Patton and Benigno Sánchez-Eppler (Durham, NC: Duke University Press, 2000), 183–203; Manalansan, *Global Divas: Filipino Gay Men in Diaspora* (Durham, NC: Duke University Press, 2003). See also Lourdes Arguelles and Anne M. Rivero, "Gender/Sexual Orientation Violence and Transnational Migration: Conversations with Some Latinas We Think We Know," *Urban Anthropology* 22, no. 3–4 (Fall–Winter 1993): 259–75.

51. *GLQ* 5, no. 4 (1999); *Social Text,* no. 52–53 (Fall–Winter 1997); Patton and Sánchez-Eppler, eds., *Queer Diasporas*; David Eng and Alice Hom, eds., *Q & A: Queer in Asian America* (Philadelphia: Temple University Press, 1998).

52. Some earlier anthologies that contain rich accounts of queer migrants' lives include Sharon Lim-Hing, ed., *The Very Inside* (Toronto: Sister Vision Press, 1994); Juanita Ramos, ed., *Compañeras: Latina Lesbians* (New York: Latina Lesbian History Project, 1987); Rakesh Ratti, ed., *Lotus of Another Color: An Unfolding of the South Asian Gay and Lesbian Experience* (Boston: Alyson Publications, 1993); Makeda Silvera, ed., *Piece of My Heart: A Lesbian of Colour Anthology* (Toronto: Sister Vision Press, 1991). Joseph Beam's pioneering *In the Life: A Black Gay Anthology* (Boston: Alyson Publications, 1986) includes an account by Panamanian-born Gilberto Gerald, "With My Head Held High," that describes his struggles to gain U.S. citizenship. More recent anthologies also include valuable discussions of queer migrant experiences.

53. Saskia Sassen, "Why Migration?" *NACLA Report on the Americas* 26, no. 1 (July 1992): 14–19; Sassen, *Losing Control? Sovereignty in an Age of Globalization* (New York: Columbia University Press, 1996).

54. This cost-benefit framework reaffirms dominant nationalist narratives that suggest that migrants come because the United States is simply "better" than wherever they are from. Lauren Berlant has described how such narratives construct the immigrant as "someone who desires America" in a manner that validates dominant North American nationalist identity. See Berlant, *The Queen of America Goes to Washington City,* 195. See also Bonnie Honig, *Democracy and the Foreigner* (Princeton, NJ: Princeton University Press, 2001).

55. Moreover, Sassen and a group of other scholars argue that the government's control of migration actually provides the means through which nation-states continue to constitute themselves *as* nation-states precisely at a moment when globalization is reworking the salience of the nation-state. For example, see Roxanne Lynn Doty, "The Double Writing of Statecraft: Exploring State Responses to Illegal Immigration," *Alternatives* 21 (1996): 171–89; Nevzat Soguk, *States and Strangers: Refugees and Displacements of Statecraft* (Minneapolis: University of Minnesota Press, 1999).

56. Michael Omi and Howard Winant, *Racial Formation in the United States: From the 1960s to the 1980s* (New York: Routledge, 1986), 22.

57. Nina Glick Schiller, Linda Basch, and Cristina Blanc-Szanton, "Transnationalism: A New Analytic Framework for Understanding Migration," in their *Towards a Transnational Perspective on Migration: Race, Class, Ethnicity, and Nationalism Reconsidered* (New York: New York Academy of Sciences, 1992), 1–2.

58. Patricia Pessar, introduction to *Caribbean Circuits: New Directions in the Study of Caribbean Migration*, ed. Pessar (New York: Center For Migration Studies, 1997), 4–5.

59. On diaspora in general, see James Clifford, "Diasporas," in *Cultural Anthropology* 9, no. 3 (1994): 302–38; Paul Gilroy, *The Black Atlantic: Modernity and Double Consciousness* (Cambridge, MA: Harvard University Press, 1993); Stuart Hall, "Cultural Identity and Diaspora," in *Identity: Community, Culture, Difference*, ed. Jonathan Rutherford (London: Lawrence and Wishart, 1990), 222–36. In addition, there exists an important body of scholarship that discusses the utility and limits of diaspora models for queer theory. For example, see Gayatri Gopinath, "Funny Boys and Girls: Notes on a Queer South Asian Planet," in *Asian American Sexualities: Dimensions of Gay and Lesbian Experience*, ed. Russell Leong (New York: Routledge, 1996), 119–27; JeeYeun Lee, "Toward a Queer Korean American Diasporic History," in *Q & A: Queer in Asian America*, ed. Eng and Hom, 185–209; Sonia Otalvaro Hormillosa, "The Homeless Diaspora of Queer Asian America," *Social Justice* 26, no. 3 (Fall 1999): 103–22; essays by Cindy Patton and Benigno Sánchez-Eppler in *Challenging Boundaries: Global Flows, Territorial Identities*, ed. Michael J. Shapiro and Hayward B. Alker (Minneapolis: University of Minnesota Press, 1996), 361–401; Patton and Sánchez-Eppler, eds., *Queer Diasporas*; Jasbir K. Puar, "Transnational Sexualities: South Asian (Trans)nation(alism)s and Queer Diasporas," in *Q & A: Queer in Asian America*, ed. Eng and Hom, 405–22; Alan Sinfield, "Ethnicity, Diaspora, and Hybridity," in his *Queer and After* (London: Serpent's Tail, 1998), 18–44; Simon Watney, "AIDS and the Politics of Queer Diaspora," in *Negotiating Lesbian and Gay Subjects*, ed. Monica Dorenkamp and Richard Henke (New York: Routledge, 1995), 53–70.

60. Eve Sedgwick, *Epistemology of the Closet* (Berkeley: University of California Press, 1990), 30, 31.

61. Ellen Ross and Rayna Rapp, "Sex and Society: A Research Note from Social History and Anthropology," in *Pleasure and Danger: Toward a Politics of Sexuality*, ed. Carole S. Vance (London: Pandora Press, 1983), 153–68; on the issue of how culture constructs "nature" (and nature constructs "culture"), see Bruce Braun and Noel Castree, eds., *Remaking Reality: Nature at the Millenium* (New York: Routledge, 1998).

62. Jeffrey Weeks, *Sexuality* (London: Travistock, 1986), 34. See also Michel Foucault, *The History of Sexuality* (New York: Vintage Edition, 1990), 1: 145–46.

63. Foucault, *The History of Sexuality*, 1: 43.

64. Ann Laura Stoler, "Making Empire Respectable: The Politics of Race and Sexual Morality in Twentieth-Century Colonial Cultures," in *Dangerous Liaisons: Gender, Nation, and Postcolonial Perspectives*, ed. Anne McClintock, Aamir Mufti, and Ella Shohat (Minneapolis: University of Minnesota Press, 1997), 347, 345.

65. David Eng and Alice Hom, "Introduction: Q & A; Notes on Queer Asian America," in *Q & A: Queer in Asian America*, ed. Eng and Hom, 12.

66. Manalansan, "In the Shadows of Stonewall." Moreover, when situated within Sassen's framework, Filipino migration is clearly connected to the imperial, economic, and military ties that exist between the United States and the Philippines.

67. Similarly, Nice Rodriguez describes how not just sexuality but also "Third World realities," including difficulty making a living, structured her migration from the Philippines. See Nice Rodriguez, "Straight People, Wild Ducks, and Salmon," in *Piece of My Heart: A Lesbian of Colour Anthology*, ed. Silvera, 204.

68. Espín, *Latina Realities: Essays on Healing, Migration, and Sexuality*, 175.

69. Chandan Reddy and Javid Syed valuably note that even gaining legal residence or citizenship need not be read within a linear narrative of assimilation to dominant national culture, for acquiring the documents that accompany these statuses may be migrants' primary goal. Such documents help "to ward off violences committed to immigrants here in the U.S." See Chandan Reddy and Javid Syed, "I Left My Country for This?" *Rice Combo* 20 (April–May 2001), at www.apiwellness.org/v2o/ricecombo/mycountry.html.

70. See Gloria González López, "Beyond the Bed Sheets, Beyond the Borders: Mexican Immigrant Women and Their Sex Lives" (Ph.D. diss., University of Southern California, 2000).

71. Anne Maguire, "The Accidental Immigrant," in *Lesbian and Gay Visions of Ireland: Towards the Twenty-First Century*, ed. Íde O'Carroll and Eoin Collins (London: Cassell, 1995), 205, 211.

72. Poore, "Three Movements in A Minor," 12.

73. E.g., Larry La Fountain-Stokes, in "1898 and the History of a Queer Puerto Rican Century," analyzes migrant Puerto Ricans' contributions to queer and mainstream politics on the island, the mainland, and between these two areas (in *Chicano/Latino Homoerotic Identities*, ed. David William Foster [New York: Garland, 1999], 197–215). Eric Wat's *The Making of a Gay Asian Community* (Lanham, MD: Rowman and Littlefield, 2002) shows the relationships among immigrant and U.S.-born men who develop a distinctly gay Asian American community in Los Angeles in the 1980s. See also Gina Masequesmay, "Negotiating Multiple Identities in a Queer Vietnamese Support Group," *Journal of Homosexuality* 45, no. 2–4 (2003): 193–215; and Trinity Ordoña, "Asian Lesbians in San Francisco: Struggles to Create a Safe Place," in *Asian/Pacific Islander Women: A Historical Anthology*, ed. Shirley Hune and Gail M. Nomura (New York: New York University Press, 2003), 319–34.

74. See David Román, "Visa Denied," in *Queer Frontiers*, ed. Joseph Boone et al. (Madison: University of Wisconsin Press, 2000), 351. Also, José Esteban Muñoz, *Disidentifications: Queers of Color and the Performance of Politics* (Minneapolis: University of Minnesota Press, 1999); and Lisa Lowe, *Immigrant Acts: On Asian American Cultural Politics* (Durham, NC: Duke University Press, 1996). Tim Miller's "Glory Box" (included in his *Body Blows: Six Performances* [Madison: University of Wisconsin Press, 2002]), a play about the struggles of a binational gay couple separated by immigration law, has received critical attention in recent years.

75. Carl Stychin has analyzed how the figure of the homosexual as a threat gets used in the service of nation-building, particularly in times of crisis: "homosexuality has been associated with Communism, fascism, bourgeois capitalism, colonialism, the West and north, the east and south, environmentalism, Europe, and North America. In the project of nation building, homosexuality is a ready discursive tool that can be conflated with any enemy of the state, in the process of becoming the enemy within." See Carl F. Stychin, *A Nation by Rights: National Cultures, Sexual Identity Politics, and the Discourse of Rights* (Philadelphia: Temple University Press, 1998), 194.

Conversely, other scholars have analyzed how the figure of the homosexual gets strategically deployed as a sign of a nation-state's claim to modernity and democracy. Such uses are intended to alter nation-states' position within the hegemonic "family of nations," but are not necessarily indicative of progressive agendas on gay/

lesbian/queer matters. For example, Gabriel Giorgi suggests that the Spanish government deployed images of Chueca, Madrid's new gay quarter, as "an example of the new openness that allegedly characterizes Spain today" (60). This deployment reveals the Spanish government's wish to be seen as aligned with "older, so-called advanced democracies" (61), and its repudiation of selective aspects of Spain's past.

Significantly, however, Giorgi also describes how the gays that populate Checua are discursively constructed and governed in ways that oppose them to Third World immigrants, who are associated with dangerous "tradition." Thus, the gay citizen or tourist and the Third World immigrant function as binary figures through which Spain's modernity gets constructed. Needless to say, the Third World queer immigrant becomes literally inconceivable. Moreover, it is evident that governments' utilization of gay figures to signal modernity and democracy replicates, remakes, and/ or complicates hierarchies among queers based on race, gender, class, and nationality and, in the Spanish case, positions queers and immigrants as hostile. See Gabriel Giorgi, "Madrid en Tránsito: Travelers, Visibility, and Gay Identity," in "Queer Tourism: Geographies of Globalization," special issue, GLQ 8, no. 1–2 (2002): 57–79. See also Cindy Patton, "Stealth Bombers of Desire: The Globalization of 'Alterity' in Emerging Democracies," in Queer Globalizations: Citizenship and the Afterlife of Colonialism, ed. Arnaldo Cruz-Malavé and Martin F. Manalansan IV (New York: New York University Press, 2002), 195–218.

76. Lourdes Arguelles and B. Ruby Rich, "Homosexuality, Homophobia, and Revolution: Notes toward an Understanding of the Cuban Lesbian and Gay Male Experience, Part II," Signs 11, no. 1 (Autumn 1985): 134. While the article's analytical framework has been strongly questioned by some scholars, the issue that the authors raise about how the U.S. state uses queer migrants' presence to advance foreign and domestic policy remains significant. Moreover, the article represents one of the earliest scholarly analyses of queer migrants, and merits attention for that reason, too. For a summary of controversies generated by this article, see Lawrence La Fountain-Stokes, "De un pájaro las dos alas: Travel Notes of a Queer Puerto Rican in Havana," GLQ 8, no. 1–2 (2002): 26–27n4.

77. Arguelles and Rich, "Homosexuality, Homophobia, and Revolution," 125.

78. Ibid., 135.

79. Moreover, scholarship has shown that, after a number of years, many migrants who are considered people of color within the U.S. racial order develop increasingly negative and pessimistic perceptions of their possibilities in the United States—even when their earnings improve. For example, see Alejandro Portes and Robert L. Bach, "America in the Eyes of the Immigrants," in their Latin Journey (Berkeley: University of California Press, 1985). In regard to gender, Tienda and Booth summarized the results of a wide range of studies of how immigration affected women's gendered positions, roles, and possibilities. Rather than finding that women experienced "liberation" from gender oppression through migration—which is the common assumption—they found that women generally confronted "restructured asymmetries." In other words, some aspects of gender oppression lessened, others worsened, and some new forms of oppression emerged. See Marta Tienda and Karen Booth, "Gender, Migration, and Social Change," in International Sociology 6, no. 1 (1991): 51–72.

80. As Muneer Ahmed describes, "Among the enormous violence done by the United States since the tragedies suffered on September 11 has been an unrelenting,

multivalent assault on the bodies, psyches, and rights of Arab, Muslim and South Asian immigrants. Restrictions on immigration of young men from Muslim countries, racial profiling and detention of 'Muslim looking' individuals, and an epidemic of hate violence against Arab, Muslim, and South Asian communities" have occurred (Muneer Ahmed, "Homeland Insecurities: Racial Violence the Day after September 11," *Social Text*, no. 72 [Fall 2002]: 101). There has also been an increased focus by police and immigration officials on noncitizens from Muslim and South Asian countries, "incommunicado detention, deporting citizens from those countries before citizens from elsewhere, and special admission and registration procedures for noncitizens from those countries" (Hiroshi Motomura, "Symposium on Confronting Realities: The Legal, Moral, and Constitutional Issues Involving Diversity, Panel II: Immigration Policy, Immigrants, and We the People after September 11," *Albany Law Review* 66 [2003]: 420).

Terrorists have also been portrayed as fanatics driven by their inappropriate masculinities and sexualities; "posters that appeared in midtown Manhattan only days after the attacks show a turbaned caricature of bin Laden being anally penetrated by the Empire State Building. The legend beneath reads, 'The Empire Strikes Back' or 'So you like skyscrapers, huh, bitch?'" (Jasbir K. Puar and Amit S. Rai, "Monster, Terrorist, Fag: The War on Terrorism and the Production of Docile Patriots," *Social Text*, no. 72 [Fall 2002]: 127). Conversely, most public expressions of grief relied on images of heterosexual families (usually white, not particularly poor, not evidently immigrant, and apparently models of approved gender and sexuality) as the primary victims of the attacks of September 11 and the means through which a response should be organized. The politics of sexuality, gender, race, ethnicity, and class, as these shape possibilities for migration and migrant life within the United States, have been radically restructured once more in the wake of September 11.

81. Carl F. Stychin, "'A Stranger to Its Laws': Sovereign Bodies, Global Sexualities, and Transnational Citizens," *Journal of Law and Society* 27, no. 4 (December 2000): 603.

82. John D'Emilio, *Sexual Politics, Sexual Communities: The Making of a Homosexual Minority in the United States, 1940–1970* (Chicago: University of Chicago Press, 1983); Allan Bérubé, *Coming Out under Fire: The History of Gay Men and Women in World War II* (New York: Free Press, 1990).

83. Kath Weston, "Get Thee to a Big City: Sexual Imaginary and the Great Gay Migration," in her *Long Slow Burn* (New York: Routledge, 1998), 41.

84. Of course, gender, racial, and class factors deeply shape opportunities for mobility, as many scholars have pointed out. The emerging scholarship on queer tourism valuably extends these analyses to show how differential access to mobility reconstructs neocolonial relationships and imaginaries. See "Queer Tourism: Geographies of Globalization," ed. Jasbir Kuar Puar, special issue, *GLQ* 8, no. 1–2 (2002).

85. For discussions of globalization and culture, see Arjun Appadurai, *Modernity at Large: Cultural Dimensions of Globalization* (Minneapolis: University of Minnesota Press, 1996); Fredric Jameson and Masao Miyoshi, eds., *The Cultures of Globalization* (Durham, NC: Duke University Press, 1998); Lowe and Lloyd, eds., *The Politics of Culture in the Shadow of Capital*. For models of culture that reject ideals of purity and evolutionary/assimilationist frameworks, see, for example, writings on *mestizaje* (Gloria Anzaldúa, *Borderlands/La Frontera: The New Mestiza* [San Francisco: Aunt Lute, 1987]; Jose Vasconcelos, *La Raza Cosmica* [Mexico: Espasa-Calpe,

1966]); transculturation (Fernando Ortiz, *Cuban Counterpoint, Tobacco and Sugar,* trans. Harriet de Onis [New York: Knopf, 1947]; Mary Louise Pratt, *Imperial Eyes: Travel Writing and Transculturation* [London: Routledge, 1992]); hybridity (Homi Bhabha, *The Location of Culture* [New York: Routledge, 1994]; Robert Young, *Colonial Desire: Hybridity in Theory, Culture, and Race* [London: Routledge, 1995]; Lisa Lowe, "Heterogeneity, Hybridity, Multiplicity: Asian American Differences," in *Immigrant Acts,* 60–83); and creolization (Edouard Glissant, *Caribbean Discourse: Selected Essays,* trans. and with an intro. by J. Edward Dash [Charlottesville: University Press of Virginia, 1989]). Especially useful for many contributors in this volume are works that use border theory, e.g., Anzaldúa, *Borderlands/La Frontera;* Renato Rosaldo, *Culture and Truth: The Remaking of Social Analysis* (Boston: Beacon Press, 1989); Hector Calderón and José David Saldívar, eds., *Criticism in the Borderlands* (Durham, NC: Duke University Press, 1993); D. Emily Hicks, *Border Writing: The Multidimensional Text* (Minneapolis: University of Minnesota Press, 1991); José David Saldívar, *Border Matters: Reconceptualizing American Cultural Studies* (Berkeley: University of California Press, 1997). For a useful discussion of some of the limits of border theory, see Scott Michaelson and David E. Johnson, eds., *Border Theory: The Limits of Cultural Politics* (Minneapolis: University of Minnesota Press, 1997).

86. E.g., Dennis Altman, "Global Gaze/Global Gays," *GLQ* 3, no. 4 (1997): 417–36.

87. Lisa Rofel, "Qualities of Desire: Imagining Gay Identity in China," *GLQ* 5, no. 4 (1999): 469.

88. Rofel describes her model as one of discrepant transcultural practices. She "emphasizes articulation, between Chinese gay men's desires for cultural belonging in China and transcultural gay identifications, in which these men nonetheless continuously discern and imagine differences compelled by China's colonial and socialist political histories with other nations. Transcultural practices resist interpretation in terms of either global impact or self-explanatory indigenous evolution. Instead, they open inquiry into contingent processes and performative evocations that do not presume equivalence but ask after confrontations charged with claims to power" (ibid., 457).

89. Ibid., 455.

90. Ibid., 470.

91. Manalansan's *Global Divas* most thoroughly addresses this issue in terms of gay Filipino migrant men in New York City, who craft identities through "complex engagements with temporalities and spaces" of diaspora (180). For a literary analysis of migrant queers that employs a transculturation model, see Kate McCollough's "'Marked by Genetics and Exile': Narrativizing Transcultural Sexualities in *Memory Mambo,*" *GLQ* 6, no. 4 (2000): 577–607. Her analysis examines how writer Achy Obejas negotiates Cuban and American histories in the life of her lesbian heroine, Juani Casas.

92. Holston and Appadurai, "Cities and Citizenship," 188–89.

PART I

Disciplining Queer Migrants

CHAPTER ONE

Trans/Migrant

Christina Madrazo's All-American Story

Alisa Solomon

[E]veryone can, should, will "have" a nationality, as he or she "has" a gender.
— Benedict Anderson, *Imagined Communities*

I need justice. That's all. I need to be respected as a woman.
— Christina Madrazo, asylum seeker

In April 2002, Christina Madrazo, a transsexual woman from Mexico seeking asylum in the United States, announced she was planning to sue the U.S. government for $15 million. She alleged that while she had been held in an immigration detention facility in Miami, Florida, in May 2000, a guard raped her. Twice.[1] The second assault occurred after she had already complained to authorities in the detention center about the first rape, yet the offending officer had been assigned to guard her again. Madrazo brought criminal charges first, and in August 2000 the guard, Lemar Smith, was indicted on two felony counts of rape and two misdemeanor counts of "sex with a ward," and he faced up to forty-two years in prison.[2] He copped a plea to the lesser charges and was sentenced to eight months in prison and a year's probation. Stunned and disappointed by the plea bargain, Madrazo pursued a civil suit under the Tort Claims Act as her only means of possible redress.[3]

These bare facts point to innumerable contradictions embedded within U.S. immigration policy, the American legal system, and the myths that underpin the dominant narrative of U.S. nationness. Why are asylum seekers—people fleeing persecution in their homelands for freedom in the United States—locked up in detention centers? Why is rape so easy to commit in such a place and, on the rare occasions when it is prosecuted, so easily reduced to misdemeanor charges? Why are the arcane systems of tort claims more accessible than criminal or civil rights laws? How can Madrazo's all-American dream of having the freedom "just to live my life and be myself" be so thwarted, indeed, so trampled, by a range of bureaucracies representing a state that claims to be founded on such ideals? How can it be that the very persecution from which she is seeking refuge was taken up as a cudgel by the state to which she appealed?

The answers—complex and troubling—are obviously connected to Madrazo's status as a transsexual transmigrant from Mexico. Certainly she is hardly the only migrant to be mercilessly detained and abused. But because she has refused to remain inside the official borders of gender and nation, Madrazo's case magnifies the various ways the regimes of gender and nation reinforce and mutually constitute each other. Her case reveals, too, how communities in the United States that one might expect to embrace her—gays and lesbians, settled Latino/a immigrants—draw their own boundaries as part of their assimilationist bargain as they strive for "naturalization."

In elaborating Madrazo's story, I hope to show how the liberal state labors to fortify its borders by designating who is, and who may become, "natural," and how gendered and sexualized discourses of American nationalism legitimate and render invisible extreme forms of gender and sexual violence. I begin with a material and ideological analysis of the "scene of the crime"—the United States' ever-expanding immigrant detention system—for Madrazo's experience, and the ideological machinations it reveals, cannot be understood outside the context of this self-contradictory and often abusive "civil" regime, which, in fact, emblematizes American policy more generally. I then look at "the unseen of the crime"—the various legal, juridical, and civic spheres that structurally cannot recognize Madrazo's claim, or even her personhood—thus revealing the limits of the liberal state even in arenas (such as asylum law) where it often appears to be most generous. For taking America at its word—seeking refuge in this country as well as an identificatory place as a subject in America's myth of self-making—Madrazo was brutally punished. Yet I hope, finally, to demonstrate that Madrazo's own brave and persistent pursuit of justice offers an important counterdiscourse in an era of narrowing national definition.

The Scene of the Crime

The alleged rapes took place at the notorious Krome detention center on the swampy outskirts of Miami. This is not the only site of ill-treatment in Madrazo's story. The first, arguably, is her home in Coatzacoalcos, a city in the Mexican state of Veracruz, where she was constantly bullied and beaten as a "maricón" (faggot); then various cities of Mexico where she endured more aggressive transphobic violence; then the punishing economic deprivations of Miami as she struggled to survive without the work authorization documented status provides; later, a psychiatric hospital where she was confined after alleging she'd been raped at Krome; and, finally, the courts that did not recognize the crimes she had suffered. But at Krome, all these injuries converged in an overdetermined and explosive manifestation of gender power as state power, and vice versa.

The Krome Service Processing Center of the Immigration and Naturalization Service (INS), about a forty-minute drive on the way to the Everglades from downtown Miami, is one of innumerable locations where the INS (as of March 2003, reorganized and renamed the Bureau of Immigration and Customs Enforcement) holds, on any given day, about twenty thousand individuals in deportation proceedings.[4] The INS has long been empowered to deport both those who are in the country illegally—either because they entered without documents or because they overstayed their visas—and those who, though here legally, have committed a crime classified as a deportable offense. The government explains that it must maintain custody of such individuals while their cases proceed to protect society from those it deems dangerous and to contain "flight risks," those it fears will slip out of the agency's radar and neglect to turn up for deportation hearings.

Unofficially—but perhaps more to the point when it comes to penning in traumatized asylum seekers—detention functions as a deterrent to other would-be immigrants. "If José's friends back home hear that José is sitting in Krome and not walking down streets paved with gold," a Miami district deportation officer once told me with a cocksure grin, "they might not be so quick to try sneaking over the border themselves."[5] (The invocation of "José"—as opposed to, say, Igor or Wang or even Mohammed—suggests just how centrally the southern border lurks in the anxious imagination of INS enforcers.)

Such thinking was reasserted as official policy at Krome early in 2002 when the government insisted on penning up some 165 asylum seekers from Haiti after the grounding of their ship the previous December. In response to a lawsuit filed the following March by immigrant advocates, charging racist treatment by the Bush administration in its effort to make an object lesson for others who might seek refuge from the impoverished and unstable nation, U.S. attorneys said in court filings that the blanket detention of Haitians was intended "to discourage further risk-taking and to avoid an immigration crisis of the magnitude which existed during the early 1980s and 1990s with the Haitian and Cuban mass migrations."[6] Even the UN high commissioner on refugees weighed in, asserting that using detention as a deterrent is "contrary to international standards" and amounts to "arbitrary detention."[7]

The logic of this policy first surfaced during the Reagan administration specifically in response to that influx of Cubans and Haitians arriving by boat in the 1980s. Indeed, according to Jonathan Simon, "immigration imprisonment was reinvented in 1981 in response to the massive immigration flow to south Florida in the spring of 1980 that came to be known as the Mariel boatlift" during which nearly 100,000 Cubans landed along the Florida coast. That event marked a major shift in U.S. attitudes toward immigrants, Simon argues, from a 1950s image of brave, entrepreneurial refugees seeking freedom from Communist oppression, to a Reaganite framing of refugees as deviant and driven to prey on American society as welfare recipients or criminals. "Mariel itself," Simon writes, "provided the most powerful visual imagery that Reagan could have wanted to illustrate his thesis that years of liberalism and social democracy had weakened the ability of the nation to assert itself against the predation of criminals and deviants."[8]

By 1989, the INS announced it would detain all applicants for political asylum entering the country through Texas—in other words, from Mexico—to deter others from joining them. The INS commissioner at the time said the policy would send a message to would-be Central American refugees: they would be held in conditions that "won't be like the Ritz Carlton."[9]

To be sure, detention conditions have improved considerably since then, thanks in large measure to a series of lawsuits brought by immigrant advocates and to public pressure over the last two decades; indeed, in early 2001 the INS announced detention guidelines that are supposed to be thoroughly implemented by 2003.[10] Nonetheless, the sometimes tacit, sometimes blatant, and always southern-directed aim of making detention scare would-be migrants from attempting to enter the United States combines with the cost-cutting efforts of private-prison companies, the entrenched corruption in some sectors of the INS, and the general lack of accountability throughout the agency. As a result, detention conditions remain minimal at best.

Absorbing the ideology of detention as deterrence, employees at detention centers come to understand that it is part of their job to make the lives of detainees as miserable as possible. As working-class government employees (many of whom are immigrants), INS guards and deportation officers may not be able to afford Ritz-Carlton conditions themselves (though that is often the hotel of choice for the conventions of the private-prison companies that run many of the INS facilities). Edward Stubbs, the officer in charge of Krome from 1998 to 2000, told me during his tenure, "Meaning no disrespect for my officers, they could change uniforms with the detainees and you couldn't tell one from the other."[11]

But through their labor, Krome's employees can assert their own American legitimacy—often precisely by emphasizing the differences between themselves and those they guard. Aggressive behavior is often the most available means of doing so, and it works most efficiently when deployed across a clear axis of power differential—such as gender or sexuality. Deportation officers and INS guards I've interviewed over the last eight years have often peppered their remarks about their charges with misogynist and homophobic language. Harassment and abuse of female detainees (who constitute less than a third of INS detainees nationwide) are rampant in INS jails.

INS detention functions ideologically in another way, too, as it fuels America's prison boom: the INS is building and expanding its own detention facilities around the country, signing ever more voluminous contracts with private-prison companies, and farming out detainees to dozens of county corrections departments. These facilities are harsh symbols of how America produces and protects its wealth. They stand at the crossroads of anti-immigrant anxiety and the roaring economy of incarceration, raking in profits and, at the same time, barring the supposed threat of teeming masses coming to snatch those profits away.[12] In emblematic terms, INS detention is a veritable fortress of American prosperity. In Miami, the iconography of what Jean Comaroff and John L. Comaroff call "millennial capitalism"—whose fastest-growing industries are prisons and gambling—is most stark. The Comaroffs show that the triumphalism of "*the* market" rests, among other things, on a cultural revaluation of gambling, both in the valorizing of the stock market and in the surge in the gambling industry.[13] The only other institutions in the isolated area where Krome is situated are just up the highway from the turnoff to Krome: casino hotels.

Since September 11, 2001, of course, the demand for security has poured more fuel into the economic engine of detention, adding a popular rationale for even further incarceration of immigrants—even for the racial profiling and blanket roundup of Muslim and Arab men. In a conference call with colleagues at the end of 2001, the CEO of the Houston-based private-prison company Cornell Companies noted with glee that INS detainees are excellent business for the company and gloated that "the events of September 11 are increasing that level of business."[14]

But even before September 2001, immigrant detainees were the fastest-growing segment of America's exploding jail population. Their daily numbers tripled between 1994 and 1999 to 16,400, and by 2001 had hit close to 24,000, at an annual cost to taxpayers of some $500 million.[15]

The detainee population began to swell in the early 1990s as Congress tightened immigration policy, and then skyrocketed after 1996 when the Newt Gingrich–led Congress passed a series of stringent immigration and "anti-terrorism" laws in 1996 as a direct response to Timothy McVeigh's bombing of the federal building in Oklahoma City. Although he was, of course, a home-grown terrorist, Congress promised that the new laws would help thwart violent attacks on America by getting tough on immigrants (as well as on drugs).[16] The 1996 laws made detention *mandatory* for almost everyone in deportation proceedings, taking away the agency's long-standing discretion to release immigrants on bond on a case-by-case basis. The legislation also broadened the definition of "aggravated felony"—the level of crime that leads to deportation—to include numerous nonviolent offenses. *And* it made the law retroactive. Thus, even permanent residents who had committed minor crimes years ago, had served out their sentences, and had gone on to lead productive, law-abiding lives, suddenly found the INS slapping them with deportation orders and hauling them off to detention.

Much to her shock—and illegally since she was never accused, much less convicted, of a felony—that happened to Christina Madrazo. Two old misdemeanor charges came back to haunt her when she appeared at an asylum hearing on May 4, 2000, anticipating—on the basis of an encouraging letter she'd received from the INS—that her request for asylum had been approved. In the early 1990s, Madrazo had been arrested twice for soliciting—one charge she calls routine harassment that trans women often face, the other a measure of "how desperate [for income] I was"—and these minor infractions were enough to thwart her aslyum claim and provoke an INS functionary to order her detention. After the judge gave her the heartbreaking news that her application had been denied, she left the courtroom to find two guards waiting for her. They put her in handcuffs and carried her right to Krome. "I'm ashamed of it," Madrazo says of the misdemeanor. "But do I deserve to be deported or raped because of it?"

Such cases have overwhelmed the INS, which has not been able to keep up with the surge in detainee population, even as it expands its own detention centers like Krome (where the number of beds increased from four hundred to eight hundred between 1998 and 2000, according to Edward Stubbs), while it also contracts out more detention services to private-prison companies and, when even these facilities overflow, rents more and more beds from county jails across the country, where the agency cannot exercise much oversight.[17] Detainees frequently languish for months, even years, in facilities meant to house people for no more than a week or two. And some four thousand of those who have been ordered deported are enduring de facto life sentences because the United States has no diplomatic relations with their home countries— Cuba, Laos, and Libya, among others—and thus can't secure travel documents for them. In June 2001 the Supreme Court ruled against such indefinite detention, yet thousands in this predicament have yet to be released.

People in deportation proceedings are administrative, not criminal, detainees—even those who are being deported because they committed crimes. In such cases, they have already served out criminal sentences before being turned over to the INS. Nonetheless, the regimented schedules of life in detention, the barbed wire and armed guards, the lack of freedom of movement, the regular use of handcuffs and ankle shackles when detainees are transported to immigration courts for hearings, the constant and sometimes arbitrary assertion of power by guards—all add up to a punitive atmosphere that does not differ from criminal prisons. "This is definitely a corrections environment," Edward Stubbs said of Krome.

In some ways, INS detention is even worse. Many times when I have interviewed "criminal aliens" turned over to the INS after completing a criminal sentence, they have told me they preferred state penitentiaries to INS detention. If nothing else, at least in prison inmates know when they can expect to get out: they have a sentence. But in INS detention, detainees have no idea how long they may remain, and depression, desperation, and even suicide attempts are not uncommon. Madrazo, for one, recalls that she was overcome by feelings of helplessness and acute anxiety throughout her detention ordeal—all exacerbated by Krome's notoriety. "I was afraid I could disappear in there," she says, "and anything could happen."

Krome has had a long-standing and well-earned reputation for abuse and corruption, and Edward Stubbs was brought there in 1998 expressly to clean it up. Authorities believed that the reform-minded officer with twinkling eyes and shiny shoes could help lift the facility out of the muck. Recruited by the INS from his position running the West Palm Beach office of the U.S. Marshall's Service, Stubbs brought a much-ballyhooed demand for more accountability and openness at Krome. He pushed through a $20 million renovation of the facility and, when he showed me around the grounds in March 2000, spoke enthusiastically about the "paradigm shift" he was trying to institute by creating a culture in which Krome's three hundred employees would "treat people with respect and human dignity." He admitted that "the place was in turmoil when I got here."

"Turmoil" is a perpetually good descriptor for the INS in general, of course. The beleaguered agency's many shortcomings were broadcast widely after the tragedy of September 11—the most egregious instance of INS incompetence, perhaps, being the revelation that a Florida flight school received notification that visas had been approved for hijackers Mohamed Atta and Marwan al-Shehhi, six months after they crashed jets into the World Trade Center. But the INS had long been—in the words of Congress member Zoe Lofgren, saying she was expressing bipartisan accord—"the worst-performing agency in government."[18] In addition to being, by the government's own report, a staggeringly inept bureaucracy that remains unaccountable to the public and even to the Congress that sets its agenda, the INS has a contradictory job: charged with facilitating immigration as well as containing it, the INS mirrors the schizophrenia of U.S. immigration policy. It's the paradigmatic American agency, embodying the nagging question of the liberal state: is government's role to provide services to people—or to police them?

The blundering, bunker-minded agency is under a constant barrage of accusations of misconduct. Between October 1, 2000, and March 31, 2001, the Justice Department fielded more than 3,200 allegations that INS personnel had committed, among other infractions, sexual assault, drug smuggling, theft, and even murder.[19] Many of those complaints involve INS detention centers. The charges, which range from denial of toiletries to threats, beatings, and sexual abuse—are not so different from the sort of grievances filed by inmates in prisons. But detainees, unlike people in criminal proceedings, are not guaranteed attorneys. Many don't understand English. It's easy, then, for INS personnel to abuse detainees—to coerce favors with promises of release, warnings of transfer to far-flung prisons, or threats of deportation (even when the officials don't really have the power to make such decisions). Madrazo recounts hearing of such intimidation from the moment she entered the facility.

From the day it opened, Krome has been at the center of allegations of abuse and misconduct. The site—an abandoned guided missile base—was first used by the INS to process refugees on the Mariel boat lift. Soon after, the INS began detaining all Haitians who arrived without documents, and Krome was in permanent business as an INS "Special Processing Center"—a bureaucratic euphemism for a detention camp surrounded by razor wire, just down the road from an INS pistol range. Gunshots reverberate across the compound throughout the day—an especially unsettling sound for asylum seekers fleeing violence. Over the last two decades, Krome has been built up. It now comprises six "pods"—dormitories—where detainees sleep and spend the better part of the day, especially in inclement weather. The older pods are cavernous rooms with sloping roofs, sheetrock walls, and green linoleum floors. They are crammed with bunk beds, and when there's an overflow problem, as is now permanently the case, cots are squeezed into the narrow spaces between the beds. A TV perched on a wall overhead blares throughout the day; a wall at one end has a line of pay phones—detainees can work in the cafeteria, laundry, the grounds, or other jobs for $1 per day to earn money for phone cards—and along another wall stand vending machines full of candy bars and soda. Toilet stalls line a third wall. They lack doors for "security reasons," so detainees must use them in public view. Newer pods, though outfitted in the same minimalist style, take advantage of developments in penal design, using metal caging along the hallways.

In 1985 detainees rioted to protest conditions, and twenty-four of them escaped. So did the chief administrator, who requested a hasty transfer. A year later, confrontation erupted again when officials tried to break up an extortion ring operating inside the facility, and 150 Mariel refugees pelted guards with rocks and set mattresses on fire.[20]

In 1990 the FBI was called in to Krome after detainees swore complaints that guards there routinely coerced sexual favors from them. Its findings were never disclosed, and, as far as advocates know, no disciplinary actions were taken. INS employees cited by detainees remained on the job—and their names came up again when scandal erupted a decade later. Meanwhile, detainees frequently protested their confinement by whatever means they could—45 Chinese detainees went on a hunger strike in 1990, saying that guards egged on Haitian detainees to beat them. Some 170 detainees started a hunger strike in 1991, claiming that officers were abusing them and that parole was not being granted fairly. Haitians went on hunger strike in 1993, objecting to increasingly punitive immigration policy, and Cubans refused to eat in 2000 to bring attention to the plight of indefinite detainees. A former officer pleaded guilty in 1996 to viciously beating a detainee a few years earlier, and later that year a Justice Department investigation found that some INS district managers had misled a congressional fact-finding mission about overcrowding by suddenly transferring detainees to other facilities; nine officials were demoted and transferred as a result. The health facility on the grounds—operated by the federal Public Health Service, not by the INS—was closed for renovation in 1999 after detainees complained of roach infestations, unwashed floors, lack of ventilation, and other substandard conditions.

When Christina Madrazo asserted that a guard raped her at Krome in 2000, her forthrightness emboldened about a dozen of the roughly one hundred women held there to come forward with further stories of sexual abuse as well as of drug trafficking by guards, prompting an investigation involving then U.S. attorney general Janet Reno, the Office of the Inspector General, and the FBI's civil rights division.[21]

In affidavits collected by attorneys and government officials, the women told myriad tales of sexual misconduct, ranging from adolescent-style flirtations to downright assault. Women told advocates that guards rubbed up against them or fondled them during searches. They said guards and deportation officers propositioned them, often promising gifts of cosmetics or other contraband in exchange for sexual favors. The women described barely concealed encounters between INS personnel and detainees, from a guard masturbating while a detainee danced for him to ongoing affairs. Many who weren't involved in such liaisons said they were threatened with deportation if they snitched. Two women got pregnant at Krome that year—one after sex with a guard, another after sex with a male detainee. All told, some fifteen officers were named. Nine were transferred from Krome to desk jobs after the allegations surfaced. Edward Stubbs abruptly resigned.[22]

Since George W. Bush's ascendancy to the White House—and the replacement of Janet Reno with John Ashcroft—the Justice Department has refused to comment on the ongoing investigation, and advocates for detainees fear that the government has turned down the heat and stopped far short of uncovering—and rooting out—widespread corruption and abuse.

In the meantime, Krome has stopped housing women altogether. As the investigation intensified, most of the women who gave testimony were released for their own safety, and in December 2000 all of Krome's remaining female detainees were transferred. Most were moved to a local high-security prison called the Turner Guildford Knight Correctional Center, where some were put into solitary confinement. Amnesty International summed up the move in the title of a statement on the scandal: "Women asylum seekers punished for state's failure to protect them."[23] Some witnesses to the alleged misconduct were deported. Many of the alleged abusers remained in their jobs.

Christina Madrazo was thrust into this environment without warning. That she chose to bring charges is a measure of the urgency of her own quest for justice as well as a radical intervention that breaks open the multiple enforcement apparatuses that govern her life in the United States—and that in more diffuse ways govern everyone's.

The Unseen of the Crime

It's hard to imagine a person less recognized by U.S. legal regimes than a transsexual undocumented migrant from Mexico. In myriad ways, her very humanness is disavowed by the limitations of civil rights and immigration laws and the policy principles that underlie them. Christina Madrazo's plight and plea were illegible, even invisible, to the guardians of these realms.

In recent years, a spate of new scholarship on transgender experience (much of it taking place within the field of legal studies) has examined ways in which, as Darren Rosenblum puts it, transgender people, who occupy "society's bottom rung," encounter "an array of intermingled and overwhelming legal dilemmas" that are crystallized especially when they are behind bars.[24]

Though two states and forty-three cities and counties have passed legislation that explicitly includes transgender people in human rights laws (and another seven jurisdictions prohibit discrimination against transgender people in public employment), to date transgender people are not included in the panoply of federal civil rights protections.[25] Indeed, proponents of legislation to extend federal workplace protections to prohibit discrimination on the basis of sexual orientation have worked hard to reassure legislators that the bill would expressly not apply to transphobic discrimination.[26] Case law is, predictably, erratic: In July 2001, for instance, a New Jersey appeals court found that a transgender physician may pursue sex and disability claims against a former employer that terminated her when she began to undergo the process of sex reassignment. Less than a year later, the supreme court of Kansas declared the marriage of a transsexual invalid.[27]

Within the criminal justice system—and particularly when it comes to incarceration—the rights of transgender people are frequently abused even, or especially, by those responsible for their protection. As Rosenblum points out, "Acts by the guards cross the line from deliberate indifference to acts of hostility and aggression. Not only do authorities turn a blind eye to abuse . . . of transgendered inmates [by other prisoners], but they permit and occasionally encourage the mistreatment of transgendered inmates by prison employees."[28]

Katrina Rose analyzes an especially hair-raising case in "When Is an Attempted Rape Not an Attempted Rape? When the Victim Is a Transsexual."[29] The case, *Schwenk v. Hartford,* was a civil rights action brought by a transsexual prisoner, Crystal Schwenk, alleging that her Eighth Amendment rights—not to be subjected to cruel and unusual punishment—had been violated by a guard who sexually assaulted her repeatedly. Rose argues that the judicial approach in the case—most of all the judge's assertion that Title VII barred discrimination not just on the basis of sex, but also on the basis of gender—has far-reaching significance for transgender rights in general. But she expresses alarm at the guard's defense put forward by the state: that his alleged actions—among them, pulling out his penis, demanding oral sex, grabbing Schwenk and turning her around forcibly, pushing her against the bars and grinding his exposed penis into her buttocks—constituted at worst " 'same-sex sexual harassment' and not sexual assault." Rose suggests that the state's claim that such actions do not constitute violent assault derive directly from the victim's status as transsexual. Though absurd, the state's conclusion follows a certain legalistic logic: Schwenk filed charges under the Gender-Motivated Violence Act (GMVA), part of the (soon revoked, and thus no longer applicable) Violence Against Women Act; the state of Washington (where Schwenk was doing time) insisted that the GMVA does not apply to transsexuals or men, even though it declares that "All persons within the United States shall have the right to be free from crimes of violence motivated by gender."[30] Thus, the state assumed that an assault that occurs because of a victim's transsexuality is not an assault because of gender and thus, under this law, not an assault at all. Under such a routine interpretation, in other words, violence against transsexuals does not register. The law simply does not recognize it.

Neither Rosenblum nor Rose discusses the differences between criminal prisons and INS detention for transgender inmates, but in some respects, INS detention is arguably worse insofar as it exaggerates many of the problems that plague penal institutions. Though prisons are increasingly built in backwaters, sensationalistic crime reporting and a constant barrage of TV cop shows keep the fact of prisons in the public eye (albeit in exactly the wrong way). Despite the spotlight shined briefly on the practice after the post–September 11 roundups, INS detention remains largely invisible. Detention facilities are typically unmarked, nondescript buildings on the outskirts of cities—for instance, two New York City–area detention centers are cinderblock former warehouses, one near JFK airport, another near Newark; a third occupies the fourth floor of a Manhattan federal office building from which detainees have no access to outdoor recreation or fresh air. Only family members or attorneys of detainees ever have reason to find these places. As for Krome, David Reiff calls it "an ulcer in Miami; apart from a few civil liberties activists and Haitian community leaders . . . it is never mentioned—as taboo a subject for dinner as one's recent colostomy or a new recipe for broiled dachsund."[31] Detainees are literally unseen by the American public. The government's insistence on holding secret hearings for post–September 11 detainees, barring their families and the press, hides them even more deeply.

Meanwhile, guards in prisons express their power by threatening violence or writing inmates up for infractions; guards in INS facilities, for example, can threaten detainees with immediate deportation, transfer to faraway places, or other reprisals if they report guards' advances or fail to comply with sexual demands. Though guards don't really hold such power, there's often no way for the detainees to know that, and affidavits from women harassed at Krome repeatedly refer to precisely such threats.

Detainees without attorneys are particularly vulnerable. What is more, because immigrant detainees don't have any idea how long they might be held, when they are harassed they live with the dread—again, attested to over and over in the Krome affidavits—that the persecution might go on indefinitely. Fearing exactly that, at one point during her confinement Madrazo actually "signed out"—agreed to be deported to Mexico—rather than remain at Krome for one more moment.

Worst of all, immigration law and policy erase the humanity of undocumented migrants, even in the very nomenclature these regimes use to describe such individuals: "illegal alien." There's a long-standing debate among legal scholars—and, worse, among policy makers and judges—over whether constitutional protections even apply to immigrants. Though the Supreme Court has ruled in a range of cases that immigrants are covered by the Bill of Rights, which expressly apply to "persons" not to "citizens," the history of U.S. immigration policy has always been a tense struggle between the principle of constitutional protections for immigrants and the broad discretion granted the executive and legislative branches of government to defend borders and sustain national security under the plenary power doctrine.[32] In the name of preventing sedition, Communist revolution, or terrorism, the government has often restricted the rights of immigrants. And again and again, their rights have been reestablished as challenges to restrictive laws have percolated through the courts—but not always. Sometimes, especially in times of fear, the courts wobble. The Supreme Court, after all, upheld actions against those speaking out against American involvement in World War I and also permitted the internment of Japanese immigrants during World War II. Advocates today caution that the government can use immigration civil proceedings, where standards of proof are lower and technicalities broader, to accomplish what cannot be accomplished through the criminal justice system. Immigration laws can be manipulated to circumvent the Constitution.

As the post–September 11 sweeps of Muslim, Arab, and South Asian men have demonstrated, it is not difficult to lose detainees in the system. They can effectively be denied phone calls, attorneys, family visits. Even before 9/11, attorneys had long complained that their clients in INS detention have been moved abruptly to different jails, often hundreds of miles away, often without their attorneys being notified.

Immigration law distinguishes among three types of immigrant prisoners, each governed by a distinct set of harsh and byzantine laws: "deportable aliens," who entered the country legally and then violated the terms of their entry by, say, overstaying a visa, or got in and stayed illegally; "criminal aliens," who lost their status when convicted of a crime; and "excludable aliens," those who were intercepted at a port of entry. The INS defines this last category as never having entered the country, and this legal fiction means they are not entitled even to the most basic rights that apply to anyone who touches down in America. (This is why it is in the government's interest to wade into the ocean to round up immigrants on ships like the *Golden Venture* before they can make it ashore.) An asylum seeker caught with a false passport at a U.S. airport and taken to an INS detention center is not, technically, in the United States—even if she has languished at Krome for months and months. Rights to due process do not apply.

When Madrazo was taken into INS custody on May 4, 2000, she was "deportable," having lived in the United States without documents on and off for six years before her arrest. But on top of her transgender and undocumented status, there was one more attribute calling into play another entrenched U.S. bias that made her humanity—her individuality—difficult to see: her country of origin is Mexico. The overwhelming majority of undocumented migrants entering the United States come in from Mexico; the numbers are so high that when the INS collects statistics, its charts distinguish between two categories: Mexicans and OTMs (Other Than Mexicans). For anti-immigration alarmists, Mexico is nothing more—or less—than a launching pad for the unwashed masses who want to invade America, take away our jobs, supplant our language, and corrupt our culture. (Who, precisely, is encompassed by that "our" is precisely the issue for these nativists.)[33] Mexico stands so centrally in the official American imagination as the source of its immigration "problem" that when the Bush administration supported extending a provision under which undocumented residents of the United States can apply to regularize their status, media coverage—and critics—presented it as a special plan for Mexicans, though the policy never named Mexicans and would have applied equally to people from dozens of nations.[34]

In 1993, an aggressive U.S. campaign to shore up the border with Mexico—Operation Hold the Line—invoked the specter of the "vestidas," the transgender sex workers who labor in the liminal space between Ciudad Juárez and El Paso, crossing the border each night to work. As Jessica Chapin has powerfully shown, the state mobilized the vestidas as an emblem of menacing excess and indeterminacy. "Homophobic and xenophobic sentiments converged in statements that cast the presence of transvestite prostitutes as an index of social disorder," she writes, and U.S. officials repeatedly cited the prostitutes' absence after the blockade as a sign of its success. Popular attitudes toward the vestidas fused the powerful discursive constructions of "illegal alien" and "homosexual." Chapin argues:

> During a period of heightened anxiety about the phantasmic integrity of the nation-state, the body of the Mexican transvestite border crosser emerged as a switch point, securing a link between civil law and natural law and endowing the former with the authority of the latter. The transvestite prostitutes became a potent cultural symbol because the visibility

of this small group allowed them to stand in for the much larger and less easily apprehended populations of immigrants and lesbians and gays, whose existence threatens naturalized hierarchies of gender and nation by undermining the illusion of self-evidence that sustains them.[35]

Madrazo walked into Krome, then, preceded by a potent rhetorical and juridical mindset that made her impossible to recognize outside these easily triggered tropes. They are so forceful, so automatic, that in reporting on the rape allegations the *Miami Herald* repeated a rumor that Madrazo had tried to hustle male detainees almost immediately after her arrival at Krome.[36] In the article, this accusation is attributed to an unnamed source—an appallingly low journalistic standard, especially for such a potentially libelous remark—and Madrazo is given no opportunity to reply. (I asked her about it later and she denied the accusation, expressing indignation at its being printed.) With alacrity and unexamined conviction, the reporter and, as a result, his readers put into play a syllogism that says: Mexican tranny equals perpetually sex-crazed prostitute, bringing perversion and pecuniary lust to America; therefore, she solicited sex. And therefore (though this is only tacitly implied) she could not have been raped.

The crooked reasoning seemed to work in the criminal case Madrazo brought against the guard Lemar Smith as well. Though she had reported the first alleged rape to Krome officials and others, and was so distraught after the second that the INS gave her the choice of either going to a psychiatric hospital or being deported to Mexico, Smith was able to plead to the misdemeanor charge of "sex with a ward"—in other words, his defense attorney argued that the sex was consensual. The prosecutor supposedly pressing the case on Madrazo's behalf explained to me that he wouldn't have been able to win a rape conviction "beyond a reasonable doubt" because in addition to the guard's semen (determined by DNA tests on underwear Madrazo had the presence of mind to keep as evidence) some of Madrazo's semen had also been found on a towel in her cell.[37] The possibility of a wet dream or involuntary ejaculation seems to have escaped the prosecutor, or at least to have seemed not at all compelling compared to the readily available assumption that a Mexican transsexual would have wanted it.

There is one domain, however, where Madrazo might have been legible as a trans/migrant body: American asylum law. Because it is constructed within a human rights framework as opposed to within an imperative to border fortification, political asylum can sometimes be a refreshingly progressive area of immigration law. And it is also, arguably, one of the most potentially progressive areas of any segment of the law on matters relating to sexuality and gender, particularly in case law—though of course there are grave limitations, embedded in the terms by which an asylum claim must be made as well as in the luck of the draw of a judge. Once the frenzy to erect impenetrable borders is taken out of the discourse, the frantic need to fortify sex/gender boundaries can either evaporate or harden within new contexts. The contradictions erupt because, on the one hand, as a sphere of immigration policy that focuses on taking in the vulnerable, not only can asylum law cope with dissident expressions—be they political, sexual, or gender-related—it requires them. On the other hand, to win a claim, the asylum seeker must conform to a new set of regulatory ideals—be they political, sexual, or gender-related—in order to be embraced by America. Often queer immigrants requesting asylum on the basis of sexual orientation find that they must completely renounce their homelands and backgrounds and exchange them for a mythic American beneficence. The legal scholar—and gay Pakistani immigrant—Saeed Rahman has explained how he found that winning his asylum claim in 1997 meant demonizing Pakistan in ways that were painful to him, as though showing how impossible it is for a gay man to live openly there required a thorough, even colonialist, indictment of the entire culture. At the same time, Rahman found he was expected to "buy into a simple discourse of how wonderful America is." Dreaming of coming here, he had "felt that in America I could live freely. Even if one is harassed or attacked for being gay, there's recourse to the law. But that narrative didn't factor in that I was non-white and going to be an immigrant."[38]

Madrazo had first come to the United States in 1991, crossing the border from Ciudad Juárez to El Paso and immediately boarding a bus for Miami, deliberately seeking refuge with a gay community where se habla español. She says she was fleeing lifelong violence and persecution, which began in her own family as her brothers tried to beat some machismo into her, and persisted as she sought to make a living in the big cities of Mexico. In Miami, it was tough just to scrape by; without documents she couldn't get a decent job, and in 1995 she returned to Mexico, hoping the atmosphere for transsexuals might have improved at least slightly. It hadn't. Madrazo endured more violence and penury, and after recuperating from an especially vicious queer-bashing, she crossed the border again in 1998. This time, though, she would try to become legal.

Immigration law had changed since she had first fled north. On June 19, 1994, Attorney General Janet Reno issued an order that directed immigration officials to recognize gay men and lesbians as a "social group"— a designation required for eligibility in political asylum cases. The order responded to a 1989 case of a gay Cuban man, the first to be granted asylum by an immigration judge on the basis of sexual-orientation discrimination. The Board of Immigration Appeals upheld the decision in 1990, and Reno's order made it a legal precedent (see Randazzo's essay in this volume).[39]

Though transgender people were not explicitly named as part of that "social group"—nor as a "social group" of their own—in immigration courts around the country, transgender applicants were beginning to win asylum on the basis of sexual orientation or gender persecution. In 1997, for instance, a male-to-female transsexual from Peru was granted asylum because she was "taunted, humiliated, and physically attacked by her family, classmates, teachers, and strangers on the street," and "arrested and detained [by the Peruvian police] for being a gay man."[40] And in a groundbreaking decision in 2000—albeit one that technically applies only locally—California's Ninth Circuit Court granted asylum to a Mexican named Geovanni Hernandez-Montiel, asserting that "gay men with female sexual identities in Mexico constitute a protected 'particular social group' under the asylum statute." (The Ninth Circuit thus overturned a Board of Immigration Appeals decision that had suggested that Hernandez-Montiel merely needed to alter his appearance—essentially, butch up—if he didn't want to be persecuted.)[41]

After her first hearing, Madrazo received a letter from the INS informing her that she had conditionally been granted asylum. She merely had to be fingerprinted and go through some other checks. At a second hearing, she was told that the agency was now having some doubts. Authorities were concerned that she had left the United States and come back and had also dug up the old soliciting misdemeanors. The INS told her she would have to attend a third hearing before a final decision would be made. Madrazo arrived at the hearing on May 4, 2000, carrying just a small purse. From there, she went directly to Krome.

As soon as she was removed from the discourse of asylum law, Madrazo shifted back into the category of "undocumented criminal alien." So her transgender status no longer cast her as a victim of a "primitive" land, requiring rescue by America; quite the contrary, it became a marker of her multivalent deviance from which America itself required rescue through her deportation. Madrazo's illegibility became quite literal: Krome authorities couldn't figure out whether to house her in the men's or women's dorm. So they put her in one of the punitive segregation cells.

Narrow and dank, about seven feet wide by eight feet long, Krome's solitary cells are furnished with a stainless steel toilet and a steel ledge sticking out of the wall with a thin plastic mattress on it. The fluorescent lights give off a faint buzz. The ceiling is scrawled with graffiti. When I had a look in 2000, a macho little poem graced the ceiling: "Deportame, no me importa / No llores como mujer / Lo que no supiste / Defender como hombre / Deportame no me importa" [Deport me, I don't care / Don't cry like a woman (over) / That which you didn't know how / to defend like a man / Deport me, I don't care]. I don't know whether Madrazo had to stare up at those dispiriting and gender-stereotypical words from that thin plastic mattress. What she did say about being in segregation was that it depressed and terrified her. And that it created the opportunity for Lemar Smith to assault her.

That Madrazo came forward with charges and has continued to pursue justice has enabled her, at last, to begin to claim a place within a discourse that does not disavow her reality. The narrative she provides of her own history and aspiration streams easily into the currents of the time-honored American immigrant story, though she appeared not to be representable within that mythic frame. She has insisted on entering it, asserting her own all-American progress narrative in which hard work, persistence, and deliberate self-invention carry her from oppression to freedom and, eventually, maybe even prosperity. What, after all, is more American than *becoming* an American by changing the nationality one "can, should, will have"? and, presumably, by extension, by changing the gender one "has"—that is, by fully engaging the task of self-making? That's not how it has worked out for Madrazo—not yet, anyway, as she still awaits a final decision on her asylum request as well as her lawsuit— but most likely it cannot work out that way. Precisely the failure of that logical extension exposes the limitations of the liberal state, where those hoary old hierarchies of naturalized gender and nation permit only so much flexibility within a rigid frame. Straight and "legal" immigrants, properly abject queer ones, and norm-abiding U.S.-born homosexuals can fit within it and be recognized as citizens. If, that is, no unruly spoilers tug too hard on the edges.

In Miami, Madrazo found that the Latino, mostly Cuban, and right-tilting community would not embrace her, nor would the largely affluent and conservative gay community claim her as one of their own. As surely as German Jews rushing to assimilate into New York's upper classes distanced themselves from the unacculturated proletarian Eastern European Jews who followed them across the ocean a century ago, the assimilationist white gay men of South Beach want nothing to do with a Mexican tranny. Quite the reverse, they expressly want not to be bound up with her lest their own advances be delayed, or even reversed, by the association.

In another self-Americanizing move, Madrazo has, however, become active with the LGBT Latino/a activist organization LLEGÓ, whose progressive principles of inclusion made it easy for them to welcome her into their fold. Madrazo delivered the keynote address at LLEGÓ's annual national dinner in 2002 to great acclaim. Back in Mexico, Madrazo had eked out a living lip-synching her way across the country, performing in drag shows with other trans women. The experience did not live up to the campy pleasure and gender-fuck euphoria that some U.S. academics like to ascribe to drag. On the contrary, it was a miserable existence: "It was a place for us to hide and cry together, a place for us to have some kind of community," she says. Still, Madrazo earned her diva chops in those shows, acquiring the aplomb, the snap, the comfort on stage that are feeding her activist work now.

Indeed, Madrazo has made a spectacular entrance in an act of what Lauren Berlant calls "Diva Citizenship":

Diva Citizenship occurs when a person stages a dramatic coup in a public sphere in which she does not have privilege. Flashing up and startling the public, she puts the dominant story into suspended animation; as though recording an estranging voice-over to a film we have all already seen, she re-narrates the dominant history as one that the abjected people have once lived sotto voce, but no more; and she challenges her audience to identify with the enormity of the suffering

she has narrated and the courage she has had to produce, calling on
people to change the social and institutional practices of citizenship
to which they currently consent.[42]

Madrazo asked America to protect her from persecution as a transsexual in Mexico. Instead, a guard working for the Immigration Service—acting on behalf of the state—tried to "protect" the state by persecuting her further for being a trans/migrant woman. By bringing the charges and not letting the case drop when Smith was granted his plea bargain, Madrazo is, indeed, renarrating the dominant history and challenging people in the United States to recognize her suffering and courage. To change the practices of citizenship to which we consent in these increasingly bellicose and nationalistic times may be the most difficult challenge for those of us who enjoy the comforts and privileges of that citizenship. Those who have not been recognized within those institutional practices—and who, like Madrazo, are seldom legible within them—may be the best ones to show us the fault lines we must learn to exploit.

Notes

My investigation of Christina Madrazo's case began as a journalistic report for the *Village Voice* ("Nightmare in Miami," March 26, 2002, 28–33, cover story). I want to thank Karen Cook, my editor at the *Voice*, for all the fruitful ways in which she helped shape my thinking and my writing. Though this essay is considerably different, much of the material used here is drawn from that report (and from nearly ten years of covering INS detention and immigration policy for the *Voice*.) I'm also grateful to Eithne Luibhéid, whose insightful comments and suggestions have helped transform my profile of Christina Madrazo into a more extended and analytical essay here.

1. All quotations from Christina Madrazo are based on author interviews conducted with her in Miami on January 23, 2002, and by telephone on several occasions between February 1 and March 15, 2002. Details of her case are based on these interviews as well as on complaint papers prepared by her attorney, Robert Sheldon, and on several interviews with Sheldon, conducted in Miami on January 23, 2002, and by telephone on several occasions between February 1 and March 15, 2002.

2. The two-count indictment of Lemar Smith is filed as *United States of America v. Lemar Smith*, 00–0704, CR-Graham, U.S. District Court, Southern District of Florida (filed on August 31, 2000).

3. In a letter dated March 2, 2002, Madrazo's attorney, Robert Sheldon, notified the government that Madrazo intended to file a $15 million federal lawsuit on April 1, 2002, against the Justice Department, but indicated that she'd prefer to settle the

case than to pursue the claim. A few months later, the government offered $15,000 as a settlement—an amount Madrazo and Sheldon regarded as insulting, given that they interpreted the offer of any amount as an admission of wrongdoing. On July 3, they filed suit seeking $1 million in damages.

4. Though the number of INS detainees is public information, it is not among the statistics available on the INS's Web site. The current numbers were provided by the INS press office in response to my request. In a statement before the House Committee on the Judiciary Subcommittee on Immigration and Claims on December 19, 2001, Edward McElroy, INS district director for New York, said that at that time the INS had access to 21,304 detention beds. Though the functions of the INS were divided into several divisions of the new Department of Homeland Security in March 2003, and the INS as a single entity was officially dissolved, Madrazo's experience took place under the old designation. In addition, the on-the-ground personnel of the Bureau of Immigration and Customs Enforcement is the same as that of the INS. Therefore, for the sake of clarity, I have chosen to refer to the immigration agency as the INS throughout.

5. The deportation officer, who spoke to me on the condition of anonymity, made these remarks in Miami in May 2000.

6. See "INS 'using racist policy against Haitians'—immigration advocates," Associated Press (AP), March 16, 2002; and "US Changes Detention Policy to Discourage Haitian Refugees," AP, March 19, 2002. Further details were provided in a March 16 telephone interview with Cheryl Little, an attorney representing the detainees through the Florida Immigrant Advocacy Center in Miami.

7. The UNHCR expressed these remarks in a written response dated April 15, 2002, to a "Request for Advisory Opinion on Detention of Asylum Seekers" from the Florida Immigrant Advocacy Center. On similar grounds, Amnesty International issued a public statement on April 29, 2002, urging the United States to "Stop Discriminating against Haitian Asylum-Seekers."

8. Jonathan Simon, "Refugees in a Carceral Age: The Rebirth of Immigration Prisons in the United States," *Public Culture* 10, no. 3 (1998): 577–607; quotations from pp. 579 and 583.

9. INS commissioner Gene McNary made this remark as he toured six newly erected tents at a detention center for Central Americans in Bayview, Texas. See Roberto Suro, "US Is Renewing Border Detentions," *New York Times*, February 8, 1990, A22, col. 1.

10. The INS issued national standards for treatment of its detainees on January 1, 2001, after scores of complaints and lawsuits alleging physical and mental abuse of immigrants detained in detention centers and county jails. The standards, covering such matters as visiting policies and grievance procedures, began immediately to be phased in at the INS's own facilities; state and local jails that house INS detainees had two years to comply. Continued complaints from detainees and advocates—and some lawsuits—suggest that the standards have not been strictly enforced. They do not have the weight of law, as ACLU Immigrants' Rights Project attorney Judy Rabinovitz said at the time, and could prove to be impossible to enforce.

11. Edward Stubbs presided over an extended tour of the grounds at Krome and spoke to me (and a delegation from the Women's Commission for Refugee Women and Children) on March 30, 2000.

12. The rise in immigrant detainees responds to a growing pressure to fill up empty cells. As the state prison population begins to decline, reversing a decadelong trend that produced a prison-building boom in the 1990s, those with an interest in keeping multitudes behind bars—public employees working in the prisons that expanded in the 1990s, for-profit prison companies—are coming to regard immigrants as their redeemers. Like agriculture, restaurants, hotels, and other realms of American business, the prison-industrial complex now looks to illegal immigrants as the most promising means of keeping them afloat. See Alisa Solomon, "Detainees Equal Dollars: The Rise in Immigrant Incarcerations Drives a Prison Boom," *Village Voice,* August 20, 2002, 46–48; and Judith Greene, "Bailing Out Private Jails," *American Prospect* 12, no. 16 (September 10, 2001).

13. In "Millennial Capitalism: First Thoughts on a Second Coming" (*Public Culture* 12, no. 2 [2000]: 291–343), Jean Comaroff and John L. Comaroff argue that "many of the enigmatic features of economy and society circa 2000—be they the allegorical transfiguration of the nation-state, the assertive stridency of racinated adolescence, the crisis of masculinity, and apotheosis of consumption, the fetishism of civil society, the enchantments of everyday life—are concrete, historically specific outworkings of millennial capitalism and the culture of neoliberalism" (334). See also Simon, "Refugees in a Carceral Age."

14. CEO Steve Logan reported on how good INS detainees are for the private-prison business and how that business is booming, especially after September 11, 2001, in Cornell Companies' third-quarter public conference call between executives and investment analysts in December 2001. Similar sentiments have been expressed by Logan's counterparts in other private-prison companies. Wackenhut Corrections Corporation's CEO George Zoley enthused in a quarterly conference call in August 2002 over the U.S. government's plans "to build up the capacity for detaining illegal immigration at a number of locations throughout the country."

15. Statistics provided by the INS press office; they are also echoed in Edward McElroy's presentation before Congress on December 19, 2001 (see note 4).

16. The Anti-Terrorism and Effective Death Penalty Act (ADEPA), a direct response to the 1995 bombing of the federal office building in Oklahoma City, was passed and signed into law in April 1996. Among many other provisions, it imposed mandatory detention and deportation even on long-term U.S. residents convicted of any drug offense (including possession of small amounts of marijuana), and it eliminated the long-standing right of those facing deportation under these terms to judicial review. The Illegal Immigration Reform and Immigrant Responsibility Act (IIRAIRA)—embedded in a budget bill and signed into law on September 30, 1996, with little debate—reiterated the authority to deport immigrants for minor crimes and further restricted humanitarian relief and access to asylum. Like ADEPA, IIRAIRA also further limited the power of the federal courts to review deportation decisions. It's easy to see now how both functioned as precursors to the USA PATRIOT Act, which restricts judicial review even further to encompass executive action, passed in a rush after the attacks of September 11, 2001.

17. According to the INS press office, in 2001 the INS housed detainees in nine hundred county jails and state correctional facilities around the country. Advocates have long charged that the INS keeps inadequate controls on the treatment of detainees in these far-flung facilities.

18. Senator Zoe Lofgren offered her assessment of the INS during the "Immigration and Naturalization Service Performance Issues Hearing before the Subcommittee on Immigration and Claims of the Committee on the Judiciary, House of Representatives, 107th Congress," on October 17, 2001 (www.house.gov/judiciary/75762.pdf).

19. These allegations are detailed in the U.S. Department of Justice, Office of the Inspector General, Semiannual Report to Congress, March 31, 2001 (www.usdoj .gov/oig/sa2001/invest.htm). For details on mismanagement at the INS—including the loss of weapons, automobiles, and other material provided to INS employees—see the statement of Glenn A. Fine, inspector general, U.S. Department of Justice, before the House Judiciary Committee, Subcommittee on Immigration and Claims, concerning "Immigration and Naturalization Service Enforcement and Service Performance Issues," October 17, 2001.

20. See Debbie Sontag, "Behind Krome's Doors: Ex-Inmates Tell of Abuse, Brutality by Guards," *Miami Herald,* April 11, 1990; Lizette Alvarez and Debbie Sontag, "Krome Haunted by Claims of Abuse," *Miami Herald,* April 28, 1991; Lizette Alvarez, "Guard, Chinese Detainee Fight at Krome," *Miami Herald,* May 2, 1991; Jody A. Benjamin and Vanessa Bauza, "Lack of Oversight Blamed for Krome Center Woes," *Florida Sun-Sentinel,* September 3, 2000 (especially the sidebar, "History of the Krome Service Processing Center").

21. In telephone interviews in March 2002, spokespeople from the U.S. Attorney General's Office, the Office of the Inspector General, and the civil rights division of the FBI all confirmed their agencies' involvement in investigations.

22. The affidavits, which were provided to me on condition that the complainants remain anonymous, are voluminous and repetitive: different women describe the same threats, promises, attempts at coercion, and sexual scenarios playing out around them, often in obsessive detail. See also *Behind Closed Doors: Abuse of Refugee Women at the Krome Detention Center,* a report issued by the Women's Commission for Refugee Women and Children, October 5, 2000.

23. Amnesty International issued the press release on October 12, 2001.

24. Darren Rosenblum, "'Trapped' in Sing Sing: Transgendered Prisoners Caught in the Gender Binarism," *Michigan Journal of Gender and Law* 6 (2000): 499–570, 502.

25. A first-rate source of up-to-date information on nondiscrimination legislation that includes transgender people is the Web site of the Transgender Law and Policy Institute (www.transgenderlaw.org).

26. For an excellent analysis of efforts to keep transgender (and other "deviance") out of the Employment Non-Discrimination Act, which would protect gay men and lesbians from workplace discrimination, see Patrick McCreery, "Beyond Gay: 'Deviant' Sex and the Politics of the ENDA Workplace," in *Out at Work: Building a Gay–Labor Alliance,* ed. Kitty Krupat and Patrick McCreery (Minneapolis: University of Minnesota Press, 2000), 31–51.

27. The New Jersey case is *Enriquez, M.D. v. West Jersey Health Systems,* Superior Court of New Jersey, Appellate Division, A2017–99T5 and A-5581–99T5 (May 31, 2001). The Kansas case is *In Re: Matter of Estate of Marshall Gardiner,* 85,030, Supreme Court of the State of Kansas (July 3, 2001).

28. Rosenblum, "'Trapped' in Sing Sing," 525.

29. Katrina Rose, "When Is an Attempted Rape Not an Attempted Rape? When

the Victim Is a Transsexual," *American University Journal of Gender, Social Policy, and the Law* 9 (2001): 505–40.

30. The Violent Crime Control and Law Enforcement (Gender-Motivated Violence) Act of 1994 (40302(c), 42 *U.S. Code* 13981 [1994 and Supp.]) permits the victim of a violent crime, committed because of the victim's gender, to sue the perpetrator in federal or state court.

31. David Reiff, *Going to Miami: Exiles, Tourists, and Refugees in the New America* (Boston: Little, Brown, 1987), 82.

32. A useful overview of the history—and a powerful critique—of the plenary power doctrine can be found in Anne E. Pettit's "'One Manner of Law': The Supreme Court, Stare Decisis and the Immigration Law Plenary Power Doctrine," *Fordham Urban Law Journal* 24 (Fall 1996): 165–215.

33. Among the groups pushing for immigration restriction, the most vocal is the Federation for American Immigration Reform (FAIR), whose rhetoric is quite bald. Couching similar ideology in more academic form, the Center for Immigration Studies (CIS) produces measured-sounding think-tank reports. One, written for CIS by James R. Edwards Jr. in 1999 ("Homosexuals and Immigration: Developments in the United States and Abroad"), goes beyond the usual warnings about the threat of Latin American or Muslim immigrants to detail how "For at least a decade, homosexual advocacy groups have made immigration one of the fronts on which they fight for their agenda."

34. The provision—known as 245(i)—was due to expire and was extended by Congress, with restrictions, in March 2002. It allows certain illegal immigrants to remain in the United States while they apply for legal residency rather than return to their country of origin to apply there, as long as they have a family member or employer willing to sponsor them and pay a $1,000 fine. They must have been present in the United States since December 2000. The White House estimated that two hundred thousand immigrants could be eligible. While most are from Mexico, the law itself does not single out Mexicans, and tens of thousands of others would benefit equally from the law. Nonetheless, egged on by FAIR and other restrictionists, the bill became known as a "Mexican amnesty"—in part because President Bush pushed for the legislation shortly before his departure for a UN summit in Mexico. The provision is not limited to Mexicans, nor is it an amnesty as it applies only to those who otherwise qualify for permanent residence. The *New York Times* report on passage of 245(i), by Robert Pear, had the misleading headline "House Passes Immigrant Bill to Aid Mexico" (March 13, 2002). In fact, the measure fell far short of bolder proposals that had been considered in negotiations between the United States and Mexico for greater extension of legal rights to millions of undocumented Mexicans here and for guest worker programs.

35. Jessica Chapin, "'Closing America's 'Back Door,'" *GLQ* 4, no. 3 (1998): 403–22, 403, 405.

36. See Andres Viglucci, "Detainee Alleges 2nd Sex Attack," *Miami Herald,* May 27, 2000. Viglucci writes, "Krome sources say Sheldon's client was initially placed in a small men's dorm adjacent to the camp clinic. She was removed to an isolation cell after officers received reports she was having sex with residents, the sources said."

37. Author interview with the prosecutor, Scott Ray, March 16, 2002.

38. Rahman elaborated this analysis in an interview with the author in June 1999; he earlier offered this argument on a panel, "Shifting Grounds for Asylum: Female

Genital Surgery and Sexual Orientation," held on October 16, 1997, at New York University School of Law. The transcript is published in *Columbia Human Rights Law Review* 29 (Spring 1998): 467–532.

39. See Fatima Mohyuddin, "United States Asylum Law in the Context of Sexual Orientation and Gender Identity: Justice for the Transgendered?" *Hastings Women's Law Journal* 12 (Summer 2001): 387–410.

40. See law office of Robert Jobe, press release, "Six More Gays Receive Asylum as Window of Opportunity Closes in April 1997," February 25, 1997, San Francisco, California.

41. *Hernandez-Montiel v. INS* (2000 U.S. App. LEXIS 21403), 98–70582, August 24, 2000, Ninth Circuit Court of California.

42. Lauren Berlant, *The Queen of America Goes to Washington City*, (Durham, NC: Duke University Press, 1997), 223.

CHAPTER TWO

Social and Legal Barriers

Sexual Orientation and Asylum in the United States

Timothy J. Randazzo

Under its asylum laws, the United States provides refuge to those fleeing persecution in their home countries. Once recognized as a bona fide asylum seeker, a person can remain legally in the United States, eventually applying for permanent residency and citizenship. Typically, an asylum applicant must argue his or her case before an asylum officer, who may grant the case or refer it to an immigration judge who makes the final decision. In some cases, asylum applicants or the Bureau of Citizenship and Immigration Services[1] may appeal these decisions to the Board of Immigration Appeals and, sometimes, eventually to a federal circuit court. Until relatively recently, discriminatory legislation barring the immigration of gays and lesbians had prevented the option of asylum for gays and lesbians fleeing persecution. In 1990, however, this legislation was repealed, paving the way for the possibility of seeking legal protection under the refugee laws of the United States. A recent Ninth Circuit Court of Appeals decision suggests that transgender individuals who face persecution may also be eligible for asylum.

The first part of this essay reviews the history and precedent-setting cases involving asylum based on sexual orientation. In the nine years since the first cases were granted in 1994, approximately six hundred people have received asylum based on their sexual orientation.[2] Still, this is a small proportion of the over one hundred thousand people granted asylum during the same period.[3] In the next part I examine the continuing social and legal barriers faced by lesbian, gay, and transgender asylum seekers, despite their recent victories. I then offer an overview of recent changes in immigration policy that have had a particularly harsh impact on lesbian, gay, and transgender asylum seekers. Finally, in the conclusion I argue that immigrant rights and GLBT rights are inherently overlapping and that activists from both groups must recognize this if we are to successfully expand the rights of gay, lesbian, and transgender immigrants.

Historical Development

It was not until the mid-1990s that the Immigration and Naturalization Service (INS) began to grant refugee protection to a limited number of individuals fleeing anti-gay persecution. The INS did award a very small number of cases prior to that date, but these cases were decided by appellate legal bodies whose decisions were limited in scope and made against the wishes of the INS. Complicating matters further, gays and lesbians were explicitly barred from immigration before 1990, since U.S. immigration law specified "psychopathic personality or sexual deviation, or a moral defect" as a ground for exclusion, which the Supreme Court affirmed as including gays and lesbians.[4] After Congress finally removed this prohibition from U.S. immigration law in 1990, gays and lesbians began to test the courts in greater numbers to see if their new eligibility to immigrate could be extended to refugee policy—would those who faced persecution because of their sexual orientation now have the option of seeking asylum?

When it passed the Refugee Act of 1980, Congress adopted the international refugee definition developed by the United Nations in its 1951 Convention and 1967 Protocol Relating to the Status of Refugees.[5] The Refugee Act defined a refugee as any person unable or unwilling to return to his or her country of origin because of "persecution or a well-founded fear of persecution on account of race, religion, nationality, membership in a particular social group, or political opinion."[6] Persecution may be carried out by the government or by individuals whom the government is unable or unwilling to control.[7] Interpreting the precise meaning of each element of the refugee definition has generated decades of legal debate and judicial precedent. The phrase "membership in a particular social group" has produced a considerable amount of deliberation. As the Third Circuit Court of Appeals has pointed out, "Read in its broadest literal sense, the phrase is almost completely open-ended. Virtually any set including more than one person could be described as a 'particular social group.' Thus, the statutory language standing alone is not very instructive."[8] In 1985, the Board of Immigration Appeals examined the category at length, and the board's decision in that case has subsequently been cited as authoritative in nearly every asylum claim involving membership in a particular social group. In *Matter of Acosta*, the board ruled that persecution on account of "membership in a particular social group" consists of

> [p]ersecution that is directed toward an individual who is a member of a group of persons all of whom share a common, immutable characteristic. The shared characteristic might be an innate one such as sex, color, or kinship ties, or in some circumstances it might be a shared past experience such as former military leadership or land ownership. The particular kind of group characteristic that will qualify under this construction remains to be determined on a case-by-case basis. However, whatever the common characteristic that defines the group, it must be one that the members of the group either cannot change, or should not be required to change because it is fundamental to their individual identities or consciences.[9]

In sum, the board ruled that only characteristics that, like the other four asylum grounds, form part of a person's fundamental identity or conscience should be understood as constituting a "particular social group."

In 1985, a gay man from Cuba named Armando Toboso-Alfonso petitioned for asylum and a second form of relief called withholding of deportation. Toboso-Alfonso's attorney argued before an immigration judge that his client was harassed and assaulted by government officials because of his membership in a particular social group—in this case homosexual men in Cuba. The Cuban government, according to Toboso-Alfonso, kept a register of homosexuals and required him to submit to detention and interrogation every few months. During these periods of detention, which would last for several days, police authorities would harass and assault him. During the 1980 Mariel boatlift, Cuban authorities ordered Toboso-Alfonso to leave the country or spend four years in prison for being gay.

Citing *Matter of Acosta*, the immigration judge ruled in Toboso-Alfonso's favor and, in an interesting twist, cited the exclusion of gays and lesbians from regular immigration channels as evidence that the U.S. government already considered homosexuals to be a "particularly identifiable group." He went on to state, "Though Congress may have intended to exclude homosexuals from entering the United States, there is no indication that Congress ever sought to condemn homosexuals to a life of suffering and persecution solely as a result of their sexual orientation."[10] The judge ruled that because he had committed certain minor crimes while in the United States, Toboso-Alfonso was not eligible for asylum, a discretionary form of protection under the Refugee Act. However, he was eligible for withholding of deportation, a mandatory provision similar to asylum but requiring the applicant to demonstrate the stricter standard of a "clear probability" of persecution rather than a "well-founded fear of persecution."

The Immigration and Naturalization Service appealed the judge's decision to the Board of Immigration Appeals (BIA), arguing, among other things, that to consider "homosexual activity" as the basis for membership in a particular social group under U.S. refugee law "would be tantamount to awarding discretionary relief to those involved in behavior that is not only socially deviant in nature, but in violation of the laws or regulations of the country as well."[11] In 1990, the BIA dismissed the INS's appeal and granted Toboso-Alfonso's petition for withholding of deportation. Though unprecedented, the case was not a total victory for gay and lesbian asylum seekers. Addressing the INS's concern that "socially deviant behavior" should not be made the basis for refugee protection, the board distinguished between homosexual *behavior* and *being* a homosexual. The board ruled,

> The government's actions against him were not in response to specific
> conduct on his part (e.g., for engaging in homosexual acts); rather, they
> resulted simply from his status as a homosexual. . . . The record indicates
> that rather than a penalty for misconduct, this action resulted from
> the government's desire that all homosexuals be forced to leave their
> homeland. This is not simply a case involving the enforcement of laws
> against particular homosexual acts, nor is this simply a case of assertion
> of "gay rights."[12]

Detaching identity from behavior, the board was careful to distinguish the Cuban government's abusive treatment of Toboso-Alfonso because of "his status as a homosexual" from other, presumably more benign, actions such as prosecuting homosexual acts or suppressing demands for gay rights. Despite the limited scope of the wording of its decision, the ruling is significant in that the board permitted sexual orientation to form the basis for membership in a particular social group. The board's decision was initially unpublished, however, meaning that other courts could not cite it as legal precedent in future asylum cases involving gays or lesbians.[13]

Gays and lesbians seeking asylum would have to continue to prove on a case-by-case basis that "membership in a particular social group" includes groups defined by sexual orientation. In 1993, for the first time, an immigration judge granted asylum based on sexual orientation.[14] The case involved Marcelo Tenorio, a gay man fleeing anti-gay violence in Brazil. After he was beaten and stabbed outside a gay disco by a group of men shouting anti-gay epithets, Tenorio fled to the United States and sought asylum. The immigration judge cited *Matter of Acosta* in his decision, and he also referred to a 1992 asylum decision issued by the Immigration and Refugee Board of Canada that reasoned that a person fleeing anti-gay persecution could fall within the UN Convention definition of a refugee. The judge ruled that Tenorio "is openly homosexual, a characteristic the court considers immutable, and one which an asylum applicant should not be compelled to change," and granted him asylum on the basis of his membership in a particular social group.[15] The INS appealed the judge's decision to the BIA, arguing that gays are not persecuted in Brazil and that sexual orientation is not a basis for membership in a particular social group under asylum law.[16] In 1999, the BIA dismissed the appeal, allowing Tenorio to remain in the United States.[17]

On March 18, 1994, the INS itself, not an immigration judge, granted asylum for the first time based on an applicant's sexual orientation. The grant was unusual in that it occurred while the INS was in the process of appealing *Matter of Tenorio* to the BIA, in part because it did not believe that homosexuality should be the basis for membership in a particular social group. The case involved Ariel Da Silva, a gay man from Mexico who had been harassed, beaten, and raped by police in his home country.[18] An INS spokesman commenting on the case warned against interpreting it as a precedent that might influence future asylum claims:

This doesn't mean that homosexuals in Mexico are persecuted. This means that this individual, due to the facts and circumstances, convinced an asylum officer that he has a well-founded fear of persecution that would justify asylum. It only relates to him. It doesn't relate to a class of people.[19]

Several months later, however, Attorney General Janet Reno would take an important step toward liberalizing INS policy in cases involving individuals fleeing anti-gay persecution.

By 1994, nine countries had recognized sexual orientation as a basis for asylum—Australia, Austria, Canada, Denmark, Finland, Germany, the Netherlands, New Zealand, and Sweden. At least forty cases were pending in INS offices and immigration courts in the United States. In order to provide direction to adjudicators on how to handle this new area of asylum law, Attorney General Janet Reno issued a memorandum on June 16, 1994, designating *Matter of Toboso-Alfonoso* as a legal precedent, making it no longer necessary for asylum applicants to prove on a case-by-case basis that being gay or lesbian constitutes a social group under the Refugee Act. In the memorandum, Reno stated,

> I have examined the case and conclude that it represents an appropriate application of the law to the facts as described in the opinion. I understand that there are now several cases involving similar issues before immigration judges, and believe that the publication of this decision will provide useful guidance to immigration judges and to the Immigration and Naturalization Service in evaluating such claims.[20]

Reno's decision was key in opening the door to other asylum claims involving gays and lesbians in the following months. In August and November, the INS granted asylum to gay men from Pakistan and Turkey, respectively. Both were granted asylum without appeals to an immigration judge.[21] By the end of 1996, over sixty people had been granted asylum on the basis of sexual orientation.[22]

While gay and lesbian applicants no longer need to argue that homosexuality should be considered a "particular social group," under U.S. refugee law they are not automatically granted asylum just for being gay or lesbian. They must still prove that they meet the other requirements for asylum as defined by the Refugee Act of 1980. First, applicants must prove that they have a "well-founded fear of persecution" if they return to their country of origin. While courts have interpreted the meaning of "persecution" in a variety of ways, it is generally understood to mean frequent or severe acts of abuse rather than isolated incidents of harassment or discrimination. In addition, acts of persecution must be perpetrated either by the government or by individuals whom the government is unable or unwilling to control.[23] These acts must be shown to have occurred *on account of* the applicants' race, religion, nationality, political opinion, and/or membership in a particular social group. Acts of persecution against lesbians and gays around the world have included rape, beating, attacks by paramilitary "death-squads," honor killings (killing an individual who has shamed the family), blacklisting to preclude employment, incarceration, forced "medical treatment," and numerous other forms of torture and violence.

Courts have been slow to recognize the meaning of "persecution" in a way consistent with the various forms of abuse experienced by gays and lesbians around the world. In 1997, the Ninth Circuit Court of Appeals decided a case that proved a major victory for lesbian and gay asylum seekers fleeing forced medical procedures. The case involved Alla Pitcherskaia, who sought asylum in the United States because she feared returning to Russia, where she would face psychiatric institutionalization and "medical treatments," including electric shock therapy, designed to "cure" her sexual orientation. After an immigration judge denied her petition for asylum, Pitcherskaia appealed her case to the BIA, which upheld the decision. The BIA's 1995 decision argued that the psychiatric treatment Pitcherskaia was forced to undergo did not constitute persecution because it represented an attempt to "cure" rather than "punish" her for her sexual orientation. In 1997, the Ninth Circuit Court of Appeals overturned the BIA's decision, finding that a supposed benevolent intent does not preclude an act from falling under the statutory definition of "persecution" under U.S. refugee law. The court found that "The BIA majority's requirement that an alien prove that her persecutor's subjective intent was punitive is unwarranted. Human rights laws cannot be sidestepped by simply couching actions that torture mentally or physically in benevolent terms such as 'curing' or 'treating' the victims."[24] The Ninth Circuit Court remanded the decision to the BIA for further consideration in light of a revised understanding of the meaning of "persecution." The BIA again refused to grant Pitcherskaia's asylum claim, however, this time minimizing the potential risk she would face if forced to return to Russia.[25] The board has ordered an immigration judge to review her claim, this time to address the question of whether or not Pitcherskaia's fear of persecution is "well-founded." Lambda Legal Defense and Education Fund, a national organization working to advance the rights of people based on sexual orientation, gender identity, and HIV/AIDS status, has worked with Pitcherskaia throughout the duration of her case and continues to assist her as she struggles to remain in the country.[26]

Despite Pitcherskaia's continued legal battle with the INS, the Ninth Circuit Court's finding that "persecution" need not have a punitive intent was an important victory for asylum seekers fleeing similar forms of abuse. Other countries, including China and Singapore, also engage in forced medical treatment of gays and lesbians.[27] The high-level ruling provides a substantial precedent for future cases involving coercive medical procedures and other "non-punitive" forms of persecution, particularly those falling within the jurisdiction of the Ninth Circuit Court.

The Ninth Circuit Court of Appeals decided another groundbreaking asylum case in August 2000. This time, the key issue centered on whether or not "sexual identity," in addition to "sexual orientation," constitutes a protected "particular social group" under U.S. asylum law. This distinction in formulating the definition of "social group" has the potential to make it easier for transgender applicants to win asylum. Geovanni Hernandez-Montiel sought asylum to escape beatings and rape that he suffered at the hands of Mexican police for adopting female dress and mannerisms. The BIA upheld an immigration judge's decision denying Hernandez-Montiel's asylum claim, arguing that he failed to prove his membership in a particular social group because "he was mistreated because of the way he dressed."[28] According to the board, Hernandez-Montiel himself was to blame for the persecution he endured, and he should merely dress differently in order to avoid being persecuted again in the future.

The Ninth Circuit Court found the board's decision to be "fatally flawed as a matter of law and not supported by substantial evidence." The court found that Hernandez-Montiel was, indeed, a member of a "particular social group" under asylum law, that of "gay men with female sexual identities in Mexico." Citing the "immutable characteristic" logic of *Matter of Acosta*, the Ninth Circuit Court quoted *Matter of Tenorio:* "Sexual orientation is arguably an immutable characteristic, and one which an asylum applicant should not be compelled to change." Arguing that the Hernandez-Montiel case "is about sexual identity, not fashion," the court concluded that "Geovanni manifests his sexual orientation by adopting gendered traits characteristically associated with women."[29] By including cross-gender dress and mannerisms within the category of sexual orientation, the Ninth Circuit Court's decision should make it easier for other transgender asylum seekers to win their claims along the same line of reasoning.

Through the efforts of gay, lesbian, and transgender asylum seekers and their advocates, at least six hundred people have won asylum based on their sexual orientation in the past decade.[30] A number of social and legal obstacles remain, however, and many potential refugees never win asylum. The following sections will explore some of the continued barriers facing gay, lesbian, and transgender people who leave their countries because of persecution on account of their sexual orientation.

Social and Legal Barriers

Even though asylum from persecution based on sexual orientation is now technically available for some, barriers involving gender, class, race, and ethnicity further constrain who is able to apply for and obtain asylum. These barriers can affect all asylum seekers, not just lesbian, gay, and transgender individuals. However, their marginality in relationship to immigrant communities and to white lesbian, gay, and transgender communities often exacerbates the impact of these obstacles on lesbian, gay, and transgender immigrants. After discussing these barriers, I return to the idea of double marginality, which Kimberlé Crenshaw describes in terms of structural and political intersectionality.[31] In her essay on violence against women of color, Crenshaw uses this concept to describe the ways that political and discursive structures of race and gender intersect to produce qualitatively unique experiences that cannot be understood as the simple quantitative addition of two separate identities. Similarly, the experience of being lesbian, gay, or transgender and an immigrant is not just a matter of membership in both groups. On the contrary, the intersection of these identities—not to mention their imbrication with gender, class, race, and ethnicity—can result in profound isolation and marginalization from supports and resources.

Departure

Many lesbian, gay, and transgender people who suffer persecution and wish to leave their countries never overcome the first obstacle to seeking asylum—making it to the United States. Leaving one's country, even without documents, requires at least some resources in order to secure transportation out of the country. Obtaining the proper travel documents for admission to the United States can require even more resources. Marcelo Tenorio, for example, an asylum seeker discussed earlier in this essay, remained in Brazil for six months after he experienced the anti-gay assault described in his asylum claim. On four occasions after his assault, Tenorio requested a visitor's visa from the U.S. Consulate so that he could come to the United States, but officials denied his request each time, saying that his income was inadequate. (The United States requires an applicant for a tourist visa to supply evidence that he possesses enough wealth in his home country that he is not likely to overstay the visa.) Tenorio eventually entered the United States without documents through Mexico.[32]

In many cases, it is poor gays and lesbians who suffer the most from anti-gay persecution, making economic barriers to departure particularly troubling. For example, according to Luiz Mott, an expert witness who testified at Tenorio's asylum hearing, high social status can often serve to buffer anti-gay harassment and violence in Brazil. It is black and poor gays, Mott testified, who are more likely to be targeted for harassment.[33] Economic barriers to departure disproportionately affect women as well, since women in many countries do not have the resources to leave their countries to come to the United States to request asylum.[34] As Shannon Minter has pointed out,

> In every country in the world, women earn less and have fewer economic resources than men. This economic stratification is even more severe for poor women, minority group women, and women living in third world countries devastated by structural adjustment programs.... For many lesbians, fleeing persecution is an economic impossibility.[35]

Furthermore, Minter points out, women may face social barriers that prevent them from leaving. In some countries, for example, a woman is not permitted to travel abroad without the permission of her husband or a male family member.[36]

Some gays, lesbians, and transgender people who are persecuted may still choose to remain in their countries in order to participate in ongoing struggles for equality; for others, however, the decision to leave or stay may be a decision between life and death.

Community Isolation

Those who do manage to escape persecution in their home countries do not necessarily find liberation after arrival in the United States. Because of language and cultural barriers, many immigrants join ethnic communities composed of people from their own country of origin. According to Dusty Aráujo, Asylum Program coordinator at the International Gay and Lesbian Human Rights Commission, such migrants may "find themselves in homophobic communities that are culturally similar to the ones they left behind." Living in such communities, many gay and lesbian immigrants "have learned to protect themselves by hiding and denying their sexual orientation. In many cases potential asylum seekers have never told anyone about their sexual orientation, they do not know of others in the same situation, and their sense of isolation is tremendous." Furthermore, immigration attorneys to whom a potential asylum seeker might turn often have close ties to the immigrant community, and interpreters may even be members of the community itself. "In such a situation," Aráujo explains, "a gay immigrant is unlikely to reveal his/her sexual orientation."[37]

At times, however, an immigrant might seek out lesbian and gay communities in the United States. These communities, while sometimes romanticized as sites of liberation and equality, typically reproduce the same racial and gender inequalities characteristic of the U.S. social order. Gay and lesbian immigrants, most of whom arrive from Asia, Latin America, and the Caribbean, must deal with U.S. gay and lesbian communities that often exclude or marginalize people of color. Gay and lesbian writers of color discuss this racism in many of their works. David Frechette, for example, describes the unwelcome reception many gays and lesbians of color face. "Most gay social groups have few black members and can't imagine why. Blacks often feel unwelcome or barely tolerated in many of these groups and fail to return after a few visits." He continues, "Gay literature—books, newspapers, and magazines—as well as film and theatrical efforts either studiously ignore blacks or gratuitously insult them."[38] Filmmaker Richard Fung describes the way people of color, particularly Asian American men, are often fetishized and marginalized by white gays in North America. "[T]he mainstream gay movement," he concludes, "can be a place of freedom and sexual identity. But it is also a site of racial, cultural, *and* sexual alienation sometimes more pronounced than that in straight society."[39]

Recently arrived immigrants, particularly immigrants of color, may not necessarily find advocacy and support networks in the gay and lesbian community that might lead them to find out about the asylum process as a means of seeking refuge from persecution. Homophobia in immigrant communities has the same effect; many newly arrived immigrants who depend on their immigrant communities for support are understandably hesitant to reveal their sexual orientation. In fact, many gay and lesbian immigrants mistakenly believe that revealing their sexual orientation would make them deportable from the United States.[40] The isolation resulting from their dual marginalization prevents many potential asylum applicants from even learning about the possibility of seeking asylum based on their sexual orientation. Aráujo explains,

> Because of the coming out process which significantly affects their ability to seek out immigration advice, many gay and lesbian asylum seekers take many years before they are comfortable enough with their sexual orientation to speak to an attorney about asylum. Of the asylum seekers who did seek out legal advice over the years many never divulged their sexual orientation and their adviser never asked. Not until by chance, either through a friend, through a flyer or some other haphazard way did they learn about asylum and called the Asylum Program.[41]

Furthermore, even when lesbian or gay immigrants are able to establish networks with mainstream gay and lesbian groups, they may still be unaware of the possibility of asylum based on sexual orientation. According to Aráujo, "Usually members of the gay community are United States citizens who do not know anything about immigration laws," and they can rarely offer any information on the asylum process to potential applicants.[42]

The consequences of applying for asylum on other grounds without revealing one's sexual orientation can be devastating to one's asylum case. For example, in 1998, an asylum officer in Houston denied the case of a gay Honduran asylum seeker because he failed to disclose his sexual orientation at an earlier hearing. Ashamed to reveal his abuse at the hands of Honduran police and others for being gay, the Honduran man had initially applied for asylum solely because of a land dispute. Explaining his denial of the man's claim, the asylum officer wrote,

> During your [earlier] hearing, you did not mention your homosexuality. You were embarrassed. You were not represented. You based your claim on problems that resulted from a land dispute. Your current testimony presented no new evidence regarding the land dispute. Your current testimony related to harm you suffered in the 1980s because of your homosexual orientation. This testimony could have been presented at your original hearing on November 20, 1996.[43]

After his initial hearing, the man was able to acquire the services of an attorney. She explained to the asylum office that with limited English and little knowledge of the asylum process, the gay Honduran man was forced to rely on other immigration detainees while in deportation proceedings to assist him with his asylum application. In her rebuttal of the officer's decision, the man's attorney described his isolation as a gay Honduran asylum seeker:

> In November, 1996, Respondent did not know that his homosexuality could be a basis for a claim of persecution. He tried to hide important aspects of his life which might have assisted the judge in understanding his fear of return to Honduras. Not wishing to present his homosexuality in a public forum seemed a reasonable and safe choice for the Respondent. He had, after all, almost been killed for his sexual orientation, even while trying to hide it. . . . He feared being ostracized by the only people whom he believed were capable of helping him with his claim: other detainees. Respondent had no one to confide in, no one to protect him physically nor to protect his legal interests. He thus chose what he thought would be his best protection, continuing to hide his homosexuality.[44]

Only after the tireless efforts of the man's attorney was he able to win withholding of removal, permitting him to remain in the United States.

Legal Barriers

Immigrants who do manage to apply for asylum face a number of legal barriers, including a bureaucracy that is difficult to navigate without an attorney, gender-related legal obstacles, and cultural and legal barriers to proving one's sexual orientation. Whether or not a person has the services of an attorney is a decisive factor in whether or not a person is successful during immigration proceedings. A study conducted in 2001 by the *Los Angeles Times* found that while 23 percent of individuals with attorneys were successful in immigration court, only 1 percent of those without attorneys received rulings in their favor.[45] One reason that lacking an attorney has such a negative impact on an applicant's success is the complicated nature of the legal bureaucracy involved in filing an immigration case. Lack of English fluency can add to this barrier for many immigrants. As Nicholas van Aelstyn, an attorney who often works with asylum seekers explains, "You can imagine that if a fairly sophisticated attorney who can speak English has a hard time dealing with INS documents, those without counsel fall through the cracks."[46] Attorneys also help asylum applicants to gather human rights documentation and contact expert witnesses. Such aid can be particularly crucial for lesbian asylum seekers, whose persecution is often hidden from the public sphere and rarely documented.[47]

Although some attorneys provide free legal representation to low-income immigrants, acquiring the services of an attorney is an expense that many poor immigrants cannot afford. Simona Todea, a lesbian asylum seeker from Romania, relates her difficulty obtaining an attorney:

> I lived there [Cleveland] for one year before I even began looking for advice. I was just trying to survive. But when I went to the lesbian and gay community center there, they referred me to an immigration attorney who wanted to charge me $12,000 to help me apply for asylum. That was impossible for me, obviously.[48]

Fortunately, Todea eventually came across the Web site of the National Center for Lesbian Rights (NCLR), whose Immigration Project put Todea in touch with an attorney who was willing to take her case for just a small fee.[49] With the support of NCLR and the help of her attorney, Todea eventually won asylum. Todea's case underscores the importance of legal aid during the asylum process.

The barriers faced by lesbian and gay asylum seekers are often intersecting in nature. As noted earlier in this essay, lesbian immigrants are typically poorer than their male counterparts. Being unable to afford an attorney is further compounded by the fact that documentation on lesbian human rights abuses, which an attorney could help locate, are difficult to assemble. It is not surprising that significantly fewer lesbians than gay men are granted asylum. Though official figures are not available, the Asylum Program of the International Gay and Lesbian Human Rights Commission (IGLHRC) has been able to track many of the cases it has come into contact with through its outreach and advocacy efforts on behalf of asylum seekers. The Asylum Program has recorded 686 asylum grants to men and just 87 to women, illustrating a severe gender disparity in the asylum process.[50]

Many lesbians also face legal barriers related to the way courts have typically interpreted gender-related forms of persecution under asylum law. The courts have typically considered human rights abuses more commonly associated with men, such as arrest and torture for government activism, as legitimate "political" persecution deserving asylum protection. On the other hand, acts of violence more often experienced by women, such as rape, forced marriage, or honor killings as punishment for refusing to conform to societal norms, have typically been labeled as "private" matters outside the scope of asylum law.[51]

For example, in 1996 an immigration judge denied asylum to a lesbian from Honduras who had been assaulted and raped for being a lesbian. The judge did not doubt the woman's credibility that she had been raped, and he also believed the fact that her attacker raped her in order to punish her for being a lesbian. However, the judge did not believe that the woman was raped *because* she was a lesbian, a critical connection that needs to be made for asylum purposes. Since the woman was raped by the brother of a woman she was having a relationship with, the judge framed her rape as in part punishment for having a relationship with the man's sister, not just because she was a lesbian. The judge ruled, "It is . . . not clear whether this act of rape, which would be considered persecution, was on account of her being a homosexual in the sense that not all homosexuals are being raped in Honduras." The judge believed the rape took place "because of a personal reason."[52] A more appropriate approach could have been to consider whether or not the rape would have taken place if the man's sister were having a relationship with a man instead of a lesbian. Furthermore, because of the often localized nature of violence against women, some immigration judges have difficulty framing such violence as part of a broader pattern of subordination against women in general and, in this case, lesbians in particular.

U.S. asylum policies regarding gender-related persecution affect gay men as well as lesbians. Gay men are often persecuted for transgressing societal norms, and the immigration courts frequently deny the asylum claims of gay men using the same rationale used to deny women's gender-related claims. In 1998, for example, an immigration judge denied asylum to Suhardy, an Indonesian man fleeing *sirik*, or honor killing. Both the family of his fiancée through an arranged marriage and the family of his boyfriend had vowed to kill Suhardy to preserve their honor. Despite the fact that the police habitually refuse to intervene in honor killings in Indonesia, a U.S. immigration judge ruled that the families were carrying out a "personal vendetta" and that Suhardy was, therefore, ineligible for asylum. Both the BIA and Fifth Circuit Court of Appeals have affirmed the decision of the immigration judge.[53] Like judges who rule that honor killings and sexual violence against women are "private matters" inappropriately remedied by asylum, Suhardy's judge found the kind of persecution he faced to be "personal" in nature.

In order to win asylum, applicants must convince an asylum officer or an immigration judge of the truthfulness and legal soundness of their claims. The emotional toll of hearing several cases daily, listening to multiple stories of abuse on a regular basis, and being responsible for determining their veracity can have profound consequences for the way adjudicators arrive at their decisions.[54] Asylum applicants can often be reduced to mere numbers on a court docket, and asylum officers and immigration judges, who are sometimes lied to by people desperate to remain in the United States, take out their frustration with one asylum seeker on subsequent applicants. A recent *New York Times* article discussing the documentary *Well-Founded Fear* observes the cynicism some asylum officers bring to their asylum interviews:

> Many [asylum officers] admit freely that the resentment they feel at being lied to by some applicants may carry over to subsequent cases. "Oh, another Chinese," mutters an officer named Jim, who later rolls his eyes during an interview with a man who cannot seem to get his story straight. Others joke about the similarity of people's tales of persecution. "You get lots of, 'I helped pull down the statue of the former dictator,'" says one officer.[55]

Having been deceived by some individuals with false asylum claims, many asylum officers and immigration judges carry their suspicions on to future applicants.

Indeed, the determination of an asylum claim is so subjective that one officer has referred to the process of winning asylum as "Russian roulette."[56] The level of scrutiny an adjudicator brings to an asylum case can vary widely. For example, a national study of asylum conducted by the *San Jose Mercury News* found that some immigration judges granted asylum in over half of the cases they heard, while others granted asylum in less than 2 percent of cases. The different grant rates include judges who hear similar kinds of cases.[57]

One aspect of gay and lesbian asylum claims that can fall under scrutiny is whether or not the applicant is, in fact, gay or lesbian. In order to win asylum based on sexual orientation, an applicant must demonstrate that he or she is a member of "a particular social group." In other words, it is necessary to "prove" one's sexual orientation.[58] This can be

problematic for applicants who are not "out," are single, or do not belong to any gay or lesbian organizations. McClure, Nugent, and Soloway
provide one such example from their experience working with gay and
lesbian asylum seekers:

> In a hearing on the merits of a gay asylum-seeker's claim, an Immigration
> Judge began to doubt whether the asylum-seeker was gay when the Trial
> Attorney pointed out that the asylum-seeker did not belong to any gay
> or lesbian organizations, was previously involved in a heterosexual rela-
> tionship, and had not "come out" to his doctor, family, or friends. The
> asylum-seeker's attorney had difficulty proving that the asylum-seeker
> was gay, in part because the asylum-seeker's sexual orientation had not
> been sufficiently established.[59]

In another instance, John Mburu, a gay asylum seeker from Kenya,
describes how an asylum officer questioned his sexual orientation during his asylum interview:

> I naively faced the process of seeking asylum, believing I would present
> my case and that I would be questioned in a non-adversarial manner.
> However, when the Immigration Officer interviewed me, I was surprised
> and offended by the battery of queries, particularly those designed to
> determine whether or not I was truly a gay man as I had asserted. From
> the start the interview felt more like an inquisition.
>
> "Do you have a lover?" The asylum case officer probed tactlessly. If
> by that he meant whether I had a live-in boyfriend with whom I slept
> every night, then I didn't. On the other hand, how could I explain more
> casual relationships to the stiff, unsympathetic interrogator sitting in
> front of me? Could I possibly explain the nuances of my life as a gay
> man in his twenties in San Francisco: Monday night rap sessions, mid-
> week romances, all-night dancing on Friday and Saturday? From his
> tone, I surmised that he would negatively judge my lifestyle. Was I less
> of a gay man, by implication, if I did not have a long-term relationship?
> If I could be a single (read closeted) gay man in the United States,
> couldn't I be the same in Kenya? If I didn't have a long-term boyfriend
> was I really out?[60]

The American gay concept of "being out" does not necessarily corre-
spond to the way many gay and lesbian immigrants construct their sexual identity. For example, Martin Manalansan has shown that, for some
Filipino gay men in the United States, concerns with being undocumented can be more immediate than matters related to being gay. For
others, sexual orientation is not something that must be openly announced. As one of Manalansan's informants explained, "I know who I

am, and most people, including my family, know about me—without any declaration."[61] Furthermore, demonstrating membership in gay or lesbian organizations or participation in any form of "public" gay life may not be possible for immigrants who are marginalized by mainstream gay communities or who fear jeopardizing their legal status through membership.

In some cases, an adjudicator might believe that the applicant is, in fact, gay or lesbian but deny the asylum claim because the person doesn't "look" gay or lesbian. In January 2003, an immigration judge in California denied asylum to Jorge Soto Vega, who fled anti-gay violence at the hands of the police in Mexico.[62] The judge believed Soto Vega's story of persecution but believed he could easily avoid persecution since he didn't "appear gay." The judge ruled, "It seems to me that if he returned to Mexico in some other community, that it would not be obvious that he would be homosexual unless he made that...obvious himself."[63] Lambda Legal and the Lesbian and Gay Immigration Rights Task Force are urging the Board of Immigration Appeals to review the case, pointing out that the judge's decision was based on stereotypes of what a gay man should look like rather than on Soto Vega's fear of persecution.

In sum, though asylum for gays and lesbians has become a possibility in recent years, social and legal barriers still restrict many gay and lesbian migrants from winning refugee status. Class and gender issues often affect who is able to flee to the United States and who is able to successfully navigate the complicated legal bureaucracy of the asylum system. Furthermore, isolation from immigrant communities as well as from mainstream gay and lesbian communities prevent many gays and lesbians from learning of the option to seek asylum. Gender-related legal barriers, racism, as well as problems proving one's sexual orientation, also limit asylum for many migrants.

New Restrictions: The Illegal Immigration Reform and Immigrant Responsibility Act of 1996

Despite the gradual opening of the asylum door for lesbian, gay, and transgender asylum seekers in *Matter of Toboso-Alfonso, Pitcherskaia v. INS,* and *Hernandez-Montiel v. INS,* recent anti-immigrant legislation threatens to offset these gains by exacerbating existing social and legal barriers. Three aspects of the euphemistically titled Illegal Immigration Reform and Immigrant Responsibility Act (IIRIRA) of 1996 have had a particularly harsh impact on lesbian, gay, and transgender asylum seekers: a one-year filing deadline, expedited removal, and mandatory detention.

The One-Year Filing Deadline

The IIRIRA established a policy that bars immigrants from seeking asylum if they have been in the United States for over one year, regardless of the strength of their claims.[64] Establishing a deadline for seeking asylum fails to take into account the difficulties most asylum seekers face after arriving in the United States. Often fleeing their home countries without belongings of any kind, they must think about immediate survival before beginning the task of applying for asylum. In addition, many people fleeing persecution suffer from severe trauma, fear government authorities, lack the skills and resources necessary to file an asylum claim, and often do not even know that petitioning for asylum is an option for them.[65] These factors make filing for asylum within one year of their arrival in the United States an unrealistic expectation for most asylum seekers.

Many gay and lesbian migrants are particularly at risk of losing the asylum option as a result of the new deadline. As discussed earlier in this essay, marginalization from mainstream gay and lesbian communities as well as isolation within immigrant communities prevents many gay and lesbian migrants from becoming aware of the possibility of seeking asylum based on sexual orientation. Peruvian asylum seeker Mario Cavero explains the ramifications of the new law, "because of our isolation and disenfranchisement, it can take years for us to learn of the asylum option, and by then it is too late."[66]

Asylum officers and immigration judges may waive the one-year filing deadline if the asylum applicant can show either "changed circumstances" related to eligibility for asylum or "extraordinary circumstances relating to the delay in filing the application."[67] Asylum applicants who miss the one-year deadline are at the mercy of asylum officers and immigration judges to determine whether or not their situation warrants an exception. Some adjudicators have been willing to take the isolation faced by many gay and lesbian immigrants into account when deciding their asylum claims. In 1998 an immigration judge in New Jersey did rule that a gay Honduran man's lack of knowledge that he could apply for asylum based on his sexual orientation constituted an "extraordinary circumstance" under the asylum statute.[68] Asylum officers and immigration judges have the discretion to make such determinations on a case-by-case basis; however, while at least one immigration judge has been sympathetic to the problems gays and lesbians face due to the new one-year filing deadline, it remains unclear whether or not other judges will follow suit. Many judges and asylum officers, particularly those holding anti-gay sentiments or who approach cases with suspicion, may be unconvinced that the barriers faced by lesbians and gays constitute "extraordinary circumstances." In addition, requesting an exception to the new deadline makes legal representation even more crucial for asylum applicants, leaving those unable to obtain an attorney and filing after the deadline more vulnerable than before.

Expedited Removal

Under the IIRIRA's expedited removal laws, immigration officers at ports of entry to the United States have been granted unprecedented authority to deport individuals who arrive with false or no travel documents. The officers' decisions are subject to virtually no review—there are no administrative and judicial appeals of their decisions. Asylum seekers, however, are one of a few classes of immigrants who are granted additional steps before being deported. If an immigrant expresses a fear of returning to his or her country of origin, the law requires that they be referred by the immigration officer to a "credible fear interview" with an asylum officer, who will then determine if the individual may apply for asylum.[69]

Because people fleeing persecution rarely have the time, luxury, or resources to obtain valid travel documents, asylum seekers are among those most harshly impacted by the expedited removal process. If an individual is unable to convince the asylum officer during the credible fear interview that he or she has a legitimate fear of returning to his or her country of origin, the expedited removal process allows the asylum officer to have the person immediately deported. The only recourse for the asylum seeker is to request that an immigration judge review the officer's decision.[70] However, it is unlikely that an individual would make such a request unless he or she possessed detailed knowledge of U.S. asylum policy. Moreover, most asylum seekers, who have often fled some of the most heinous abuse and human rights violations imaginable, are not always capable of recounting their appalling experiences to the first people they encounter after stepping off the plane. Gay and lesbian asylum seekers are even less likely to be willing to reveal their sexual orientation and abuse to immigration officers immediately on arrival in the United States. According to the Lesbian and Gay Immigration Rights Task Force, "Lesbian, gay and HIV+ aliens fleeing persecution are unlikely to know they may be eligible for asylum and are unlikely to establish the trust necessary to reveal their sexual orientation to a U.S. immigration officer at the port-of-entry, often thinking that being homosexual might be grounds for deportation itself."[71]

Furthermore, because of the unprecedented power given to immigration officers at ports of entry, even gay and lesbian asylum seekers who are able to express their fear of persecution are not guaranteed that their claims will be recognized. Despite attempts by the INS to restrict access to information on how the expedited removal process has impacted asylum seekers and others, nongovernmental organizations and researchers have documented numerous abuses of the unchecked power of immigration officers at ports of entry, including harassment of asylum seekers.[72] Even the INS itself has acknowledged that it is not uncommon for immigration officers at ports of entry to abuse their power. In its 1998 "Expedited Removal Training" memorandum, the INS stated, "There have been allegations of mistreatment of aliens and unprofessional behavior by officers during the expedited removal process." The memo went on to inform officers that they should refrain from using "derogatory language, racial slurs, verbal abuse, humiliation tactics, or accusations of lying when questioning aliens."[73] The fact that the INS needs to *instruct* its officers not to use "racial slurs" or "humiliation tactics" when questioning migrants and asylum seekers suggests that such abuses are not uncommon. In light of such abuses, what is to stop an anti-gay immigration officer from turning away lesbian, gay, and transgender asylum seekers? It seems likely that officers who would use racial slurs and humiliation tactics against asylum seekers also would not hesitate to harass and degrade individuals based on their sexual orientation or transgender status.

Mandatory Detention

Another controversial provision of the IIRIRA is the detention of asylum seekers while they await the final outcome of their asylum claim, involving a period of time that can last from weeks to years. Detention is mandatory for those in expedited removal proceedings,[74] and most individuals in deportation proceedings, including those who choose to seek asylum during the proceedings, are subject to detention as well.[75] Because the INS has insufficient space to house the new influx of detainees in its own facilities, it contracts out to local prisons, a highly profitable industry for many towns across the United States. INS detainees are generally not distinguished from the general prison population in terms of their treatment. The new policy of expedited removal has been widely criticized because it treats asylum applicants—people who are *fleeing* persecution—as criminals by incarcerating them for the duration of their asylum cases.

Human rights organizations have documented numerous abuses suffered by asylum seekers being held by the INS in prisons and detention centers, including harassment by prison staff; inadequate food, hygiene, and health care; and insufficient access to legal support and information about the asylum process.[76] Gays and lesbians held in prisons and detention centers must not only endure the same inhumane conditions as all asylum seekers (and criminal inmates), but they must also endure additional abuse when prison officials and inmates find out about their sexual orientation. According to the Lesbian and Gay Immigration Rights Task Force, "Gay, lesbian, bisexual, transgendered and HIV+ aliens are among the most vulnerable of detained individuals. Once their sexual orientation or HIV status is known, they not only face the degrading treatment by detention center employees but also continuous harassment from other detained individuals."[77] The task force also reports that gay men in detention have told of "serious physical and emotional abuse by other detainees and guards."[78]

Gay and lesbian asylum seekers are among the most vulnerable groups affected by the one-year filing deadline, expedited removal, and mandatory detention. Unless these provisions are repealed, gay and lesbian asylum seekers will continue to suffer abuses here in the United States even as they flee persecution in their home countries. More recent developments in immigration policy, however, suggest that more restrictions, rather than fewer, are on the horizon.

Growing Restrictions since September 11, 2001

Just prior to September 11, 2001, Congress had been considering relieving some of the harsh restrictions it had implemented in the 1996 Illegal

Immigration Reform and Immigrant Responsibility Act.[79] After the terrorist attacks, however, Congress began to pass legislation to further
restrict the rights of immigrants. Bush has already signed into law the
euphemistically titled U.S.A. PATRIOT Act, short for the Uniting and
Strengthening America by Providing Appropriate Tools Required to Inter-
cept and Obstruct Terrorism Act of 2001. This act includes a number of
anti-immigrant components, most notably a provision granting the attorney general unprecedented authority to imprison any immigrant he
has "reasonable grounds to believe" is a threat to the United States.[80]

Several changes in asylum policy since September 11, 2001, have made
it more difficult for applicants to win their claims. One change is that
adjudicators have put asylum claims under greater scrutiny, a harsh
change for many gay and lesbian asylum seekers who lack ample human
rights documentation or "evidence" of their sexual orientation. Another
change has been longer detention periods while applicants await extensive background checks.[81] As discussed earlier, lesbian, gay, and transgender asylum seekers frequently face harassment and other forms of
mistreatment while in detention, and the longer detention periods only
prolong the abuse they must endure before being granted asylum. Since
September 11, 2001, the Asylum Program of the International Gay and
Lesbian Human Rights Commission has seen an increase in requests for
aid from gay and lesbian immigrants in detention. Many requests have
come from gay Muslim immigrants held in detention after registering
with the Bureau of Citizenship and Immigration Services, as required
by law.[82]

A recent case in San Francisco illustrates the impact of post–September
11 policies, particularly on gay men from Muslim countries. In 1986, at
the age of seventeen, Keshav Jiwnani fled anti-gay and anti-Hindu persecution in Pakistan and arrived in the United States. Now thirty-four
years old, Jiwnani has lived as an undocumented immigrant in the United
States. On September 11, 2002, the Bureau of Citizenship and Immigration Services announced a program requiring males over the age of sixteen from a list of twenty-five predominantly Arab or Muslim countries
to register with the bureau. Because of his undocumented status, Jiwnani
found himself in deportation proceedings after registration. Terrified of
returning to Pakistan, he has applied for asylum, but Jiwnani's application is uncertain because he has applied after the one-year filing deadline.
His attorney is requesting an exception for "extraordinary circumstances"

because of the severe trauma Jiwnani experienced in Pakistan, and he is also helping Jiwnani to apply for withholding of deportation, a form of relief similar to asylum.[83] Jiwnani's case has been well publicized, and the gay and lesbian community in the Bay Area has rallied in support of his case, making his prospects for success rather promising. It is unknown, however, how many gays and lesbians seeking refuge from persecution have been silently deported in the wake of post–September 11 immigration policies.

Prospects for Human Rights Advocacy in an Anti-Immigrant Climate

In recent years, several gay and lesbian human rights organizations have begun offering services to their immigrant constituents, including assistance to those fleeing persecution. One notable organization is the International Gay and Lesbian Human Rights Commission (IGLHRC), which, through its Asylum Program, provides documentation of the human rights conditions of gays and lesbians around the world.[84] The materials provided by the Asylum Program have been a vital resource for gay, lesbian, and transgender asylum seekers, whose claims are strengthened when they can provide detailed documentation on country conditions to support their cases. In fact, documentation provided by the Asylum Program has been the deciding factor in a number of successful asylum cases in recent years.

Other organizations include the National Center for Lesbian Rights (NCLR) and the Lambda Legal Defense and Education Fund, which provide important legal support to gay, lesbian, and transgender immigrants and asylum seekers.[85] NCLR works closely with the Lesbian and Gay Immigration Rights Task Force (LGIRTF), an organization with chapters across the United States that serve binational couples, immigrants with HIV/AIDS, and people seeking asylum based on sexual orientation. LGIRTF offers a variety of programs, including legal service, educational outreach, and legislative advocacy.[86]

Despite their efforts, the resources of these organizations are limited, and they can reach only a small percentage of lesbian, gay, and transgender asylum seekers, many of whom are desperate for legal and emotional support. In fact, a survey of a number of prominent gay and lesbian rights organizations shows that few have implemented programs to assist their immigrant and refugee constituents. While it is still difficult for many gay, lesbian, and transgender immigrants to find support and advocacy from gay and lesbian rights organizations, neither can they always rely on immigration organizations and attorneys. The attitude of many immigrant rights advocates toward gay, lesbian, and transgender asylum seekers can range from uninformed to hostile. Pedro Luís Abosolo, a gay asylum seeker who fled to Houston from Mexico, sought legal advice for his asylum hearing; the first two lawyers he consulted with told him that sexual orientation was not considered a legitimate basis for asylum.[87] In another instance, a gay asylum seeker being held in El Paso, Texas, "could not find an attorney to represent him in the INS removal proceedings to return him to Indonesia. The local immigration organizations and attorneys lost interest when they learned he was gay."[88]

Kimberlé Crenshaw's concepts of structural and political intersectionality are useful for understanding the needs of gay and lesbian immigrants and asylum seekers and the roles that individuals and organizations can play in response. Crenshaw has written about the structural and political intersectionality that characterizes the lives of women of color.[89] By "structural intersectionality," Crenshaw refers to the qualitative distinctiveness of the experiences of women of color that cannot be accounted for by merely considering their race or gender in isolation. In addition, the political interests of women of color are not adequately addressed by organizations and movements that are primarily antiracist or feminist. Gay, lesbian, and transgender immigrants occupy a similar position of intersectionality, both in their experiences in the asylum system and in relationship to mainstream gay and lesbian organizations and immigrant rights advocates. As discussed in this essay, gays, lesbians, and transgender people fleeing persecution often face qualitatively unique social and legal barriers to winning asylum in the United States. Furthermore, their political needs often go unmet: gay and lesbian human rights organizations too often neglect immigration issues, and immigrant rights organizations do not always adequately assist gay and lesbian immigrants.

In the wake of renewed restrictive currents in immigration policy, it is more important than ever that gay and lesbian rights organizations as well as immigrant rights advocates recognize the connectedness of the issues they have too often viewed as unrelated. The reader might point out that to argue for coalition building is neither controversial nor new. Indeed, many progressive scholars and activists have advocated political cooperation across differences.[90] The case of gay, lesbian, and transgender immigrants and asylum seekers, however, illustrates the potential for coalition building around issues that, while often seen as separate, are actually interconnected in quite concrete ways.

First, advocates working with gay, lesbian, and transgender immigrants have a vested interest in broader immigration issues. As shown in this essay, seemingly neutral policies, such as mandatory detention and a one-year filing deadline, have a disproportionately harsh impact on gay, lesbian, and transgender asylum seekers. Furthermore, those working on broadly defined human rights for gays and lesbians should also be concerned with the treatment of these groups within immigration policy. Gay, lesbian, and transgender immigrants are part of this constituency, and their issues deserve to be recognized. Their struggles for equality in the immigration system expand the rights of all gays, lesbians, and transgender people by bringing issues of sexual orientation and gender identity to the forefront of legal and public discourse. For example, when the Ninth Circuit Court of Appeals rules that the persecution faced by a transgender individual in Mexico is "about sexual identity, not fashion," and that such individuals should not be expected to change their behavior, it is a victory for all transgender people, not just immigrants.

In addition, immigrant rights advocates should invest in supporting gay, lesbian, and transgender immigrants and asylum seekers not just because they represent a part of their constituency, but because doing so is crucial in efforts to increase the fairness of immigration policy generally. In their struggles for recognition in the asylum system, gay, lesbian, and transgender asylum seekers have changed asylum policy in a way that expands the rights of all immigrants. For example, when Alla Pitcherskaia convinced the Ninth Circuit Court of Appeals to rule that forced medical "treatment," even with a supposed benevolent intent, must be considered persecution under asylum law, she helped create a precedent for later asylum seekers, regardless of their sexual orientation.

With renewed anti-immigrant sentiment in the United States, it is more important than ever for marginalized groups to work together to protect the rights of everyone. Immigrant rights advocates alone cannot hope to shift the anti-immigrant sentiment that has intensified since September 11. Similarly, gay and lesbian rights advocates stand a better chance of advancing the rights of people based on sexual orientation and gender identity if they continue to ally themselves with other groups.

By pooling their knowledge and resources, gay, lesbian, and immigrant rights advocates not only can ensure the rights of gay, lesbian, and transgender asylum seekers who lie at the intersection of these groups' agendas, but can also simultaneously strengthen their own bases of support through mutual cooperation and coalition building.

Notes

I would like to thank Dusty Aráujo, Dominic Buyi, Sara Moore, and others at the International Gay and Lesbian Human Rights Commission who provided me with invaluable assistance during my internship with the Asylum Program.

1. On March 1, 2003, the Immigration and Naturalization Service (INS) was renamed the Bureau of Citizenship and Immigration Services and moved from the Department of Justice to the recently created Department of Homeland Security. See http://www.immigration.gov/graphics/aboutus/thisisimm/index.htm.

2. Monica Rhor, "US Grants Asylum to Gay Man: Rules Dominican Faced Threat at Home," *Boston Globe,* September 5, 2003. The data was provided by the International Gay and Lesbian Human Rights Commission, which tracks asylum cases related to sexual orientation. The Bureau of Citizenship and Immigration Services does not provide information regarding the number of asylum cases won on the basis of sexual orientation.

3. Bureau of Citizenship and Immigration Services, *2002 Yearbook of Immigration Statistics,* 65, http://www.immigration.gov/graphics/shared/aboutus/statistics/Asylees.htm.

4. Tracy J. Davis, "Opening the Doors of Immigration: Sexual Orientation and Asylum in the United States," *Human Rights Brief* 6 (1999): 19; Lucy H. Halatyn, "Political Asylum and Equal Protection: Hypocrisy of United States Protection of Gay Men and Lesbians," *Suffolk Transnational Law Review* 22 (Winter 1998): 142; Denise C. Hammond, "Immigration and Sexual Orientation: Developing Standards, Options, and Obstacles," *Interpreter Releases* 77, no. 4 (January 24, 2000): 114.

5. Karen Musalo, Jennifer Moore, and Richard A. Boswell, *Refugee Law and Policy: A Comparative International Approach,* 2d ed. (Durham, NC: Carolina Academic Press, 2002), 32, 35, 66.

6. INA § 101(a)(42); 8 *U.S. Code* § 1101(a)(42), quoted in ibid., 66.

7. Musalo, Moore, and Boswell, *Refugee Law and Policy,* 270.

8. *Fatin v. INS,* 12 F.3d 1233 (3rd Cir., December 20, 1993), 1238.

9. *Matter of Acosta,* 19 I&N Dec. 211 (BIA 1985), quoted in Musalo et al., *Refugee Law and Policy,* 557–58.

10. *Matter of Toboso-Alfonso,* A23–220–644 (IJ, February 3, 1986) (Houston, TX), 5, 6.

11. Quoted in *Matter of Toboso-Alfonso,* 20 I&N Dec. 819 (BIA, March 12, 1990), 822.

12. Ibid., 822–23.

13. Keith Donoghue, "Safe Harbor: U.S. Immigration Authorities Are Increasingly Willing to Grant Asylum on the Basis of Sexual Orientation," *Recorder,* October 25, 1995.

14. "IJ Grants Asylum to Brazilian Homosexual," *Interpreter Releases* 70, no. 32 (August 23, 1993).

15. *Matter of Tenorio*, A72–093–558 (IJ, July 26, 1993), 17.

16. "IJ Grants Asylum to Brazilian Homosexual."

17. Lambda Legal Defense and Education Fund, "Matter of Tenorio," 2000, http://www.lambdalegal.org/cgi-bin/iowa/cases/record?record=29.

18. In the original press reports regarding his case, Da Silva used the pseudonym Jose Garcia. Since his death shortly after his asylum victory, his name has been released. Jennifer Warren, "Asylum OKd on Basis of Homosexuality Immigration: Gay Man Said He Would Be Persecuted If Returned to Mexico," *Los Angeles Times*, March 25, 1994; "First Man Given Asylum as Gay Dies of AIDS," *San Francisco Chronicle*, August 30, 1994.

19. Quoted in Jim Doyle, "Political Asylum Granted to Gay from Mexico," *San Francisco Chronicle*, March 25, 1994.

20. "Reno Designates Gay Case as Precedent," *Interpreter Releases* 71, no. 25 (July 1, 1994).

21. "INS Grants Asylum to Turkish Gay Man," *Interpreter Releases* 71, no. 44 (November 14, 1994).

22. William Branigin, "Gays' Cases Help to Expand Immigration Rights: More Than 60 Homosexuals Claiming Persecution Have Been Granted Asylum in U.S.," *Washington Post*, December 17, 1996.

23. Jin S. Park, "Pink Asylum: Political Asylum Eligibility of Gay Men and Lesbians under U.S. Immigration Policy," *UCLA Law Review* 42 (April 1995): 8–12; Musalo et al., *Refugee Law and Policy*, 219–74.

24. *Alla Konstantinova Pitcherskaia v. Immigration and Naturalization Service*, 118 F.3d 641 (9th Cir., 1997), 648.

25. Lambda Legal Defense and Education Fund, "Disappointment for Russian Lesbian Seeking Asylum" (1998), http://www.lambdalegal.org/cgi-bin/iowa/documents/record?record=250.

26. Lambda Legal Defense and Education Fund, "In re Pitcherskaia" (2002), http://www.lambdalegal.org/cgi-bin/iowa/cases/record?record=28.

27. Ryan Goodman, "The Incorporation of International Human Rights Standards into Sexual Orientation Asylum Claims: Cases of Involuntary 'Medical' Intervention," *Yale Law Journal* 105 (October 1995): 288.

28. *Geovanni Hernandez-Montiel v. Immigration and Naturalization Service*, 225 F.3d 1084 (9th Cir., 2000), 3.

29. Ibid., 15, 9, 10, 30.

30. Rhor, "US Grants Asylum to Gay Man: Rules Dominican Faced Threat at Home."

31. Kimberlé Williams Crenshaw, "Mapping the Margins: Intersectionality, Identity Politics, and Violence against Women of Color," in *Critical Race Theory: The Key Writings That Formed the Movement*, ed. Kimberlé Crenshaw, Neil Gotanda, Gary Peller, and Kendall Thomas (New York: New Press, 1995), 357–83.

32. *Matter of Tenorio*, A72–093–558 (IJ, July 26, 1993).

33. Ibid., 10–11.

34. Shannon Minter, "Lesbians and Asylum: Overcoming Barriers to Access," in *Asylum Based on Sexual Orientation: A Resource Guide*, ed. Sydney Levy (San Francisco: International Gay and Lesbian Human Rights Commission and Lambda Legal Defense and Education Fund, 1996).

35. Ibid., 7.

36. Ibid.

37. Dusty Aráujo, "Declaration of Dusty Aráujo," Asylum Program coordinator, International Gay and Lesbian Human Rights Commission, August 9, 1999, on file with author.

38. David Frechette, "Why I'm Not Marching," in *Fighting Words: Personal Essays by Black Gay Men,* ed. Charles Michael Smith (New York: Avon Books, 1999), 132.

39. Richard Fung, "Looking for My Penis: The Eroticized Asian in Gay Video Porn," in *Asian American Sexualities: Dimensions of the Gay and Lesbian Experience,* ed. Russell Leong (New York: Routledge, 1996), 190. For other examples of racism by white gays against people of color, see Essex Hemphill, ed., *Brother to Brother: New Writings by Black Gay Men* (Boston: Alyson Publications, 1991); Alice Y. Hom, "In the Mind of An/Other," in *The Very Inside: An Anthology of Writing by Asian and Pacific Islander Lesbian and Bisexual Women,* ed. Sharon Lim-Hing (Toronto: Sister Vision Press, 1994), 272–75; Eric C. Wat, *The Making of a Gay Asian Community: An Oral History of Pre-AIDS Los Angeles* (New York: Rowman and Littlefield, 2002).

40. Heather McClure, Christopher Nugent, and Lavi S. Soloway, *Preparing Sexual Orientation–Based Asylum Claims: A Handbook for Advocates and Asylum Seekers* (Chicago: Heartland Alliance for Human Needs and Human Rights, 1997), 14.

41. Aráujo, "Declaration of Dusty Aráujo."

42. Ibid.

43. Letter from Houston Asylum Office to applicant (January 28, 1998), on file with the International Gay and Lesbian Human Rights Commission, in "Honduras #2" country packet.

44. Natalia C. Walker, "Withholding Rebuttal" (March 2, 1998), on file with the International Gay and Lesbian Human Rights Commission, in "Honduras #2" country packet.

45. Lisa Getter, "Few Applicants Succeed in Immigration Courts," *Los Angeles Times,* April 15, 2001.

46. Quoted in Brenda Sandburg, "Civil Rights Group Assists Asylum Seekers," *Recorder,* January 3, 2000.

47. Lesbian and Gay Immigration Rights Task Force, "Landmark Victory in Lesbian Asylum Case," *Status Report,* no. 2 (2002).

48. Quoted in National Center for Lesbian Rights, "NCLR Helps Romanian Lesbian Win Political Asylum in the United States" (1998), http://nclrights.org/projects/todea.htm.

49. Ibid.

50. Statistics from asylum database provided by Sara Moore of the International Gay and Lesbian Human Rights Commission on November 10, 2003.

51. Shannon Minter, "Lesbians and Asylum," and Nancy Kelly, "Gender-Related Persecution: Assessing the Asylum Claims of Women," *Cornell International Law Journal* 26 (1993).

52. No. A29766772 (IJ, Miami, April 9, 1996), 7, 9. Also quoted in Minter, "Lesbians and Asylum," 13.

53. Lesbian and Gay Immigration Rights Task Force, "Denied Asylum, Gay Indonesian Who Fled for His Life Fights Deportation," *Status Report,* August 2001.

54. See interviews with asylum officers in *Well-Founded Fear,* a film by Shari Robertson and Michael Camerini (New York: Epidavros Project, 2000).

55. Susan Sachs, "Exposing Cracks in Façade of Refuge," *New York Times*, December 19, 1999.

56. Ibid.

57. Fredric N. Tulsky, "Asylum Seekers Face Capricious Legal System," *San Jose Mercury News*, October 18, 2000.

58. Tracy J. Davis, "Opening the Doors of Immigration: Sexual Orientation and Asylum in the United States," *Human Rights Brief* 6 (1999); McClure et al., *Preparing Sexual Orientation–Based Asylum Claims*, 98.

59. McClure et al., *Preparing Sexual Orientation-Based Asylum Claims*, 98.

60. Lesbian and Gay Immigration Rights Task Force, "Asylum Seeker Contends with Deepening Despair," *Status Report*, Spring 1999.

61. Martin F. Manalansan IV, "In the Shadows of Stonewall: Examining Gay Transnational Politics and the Diasporic Dilemma," in *The Politics of Culture in the Shadow of Capital*, ed. Lisa Lowe and David Lloyed (Durham, NC: Duke University Press, 1997), 498.

62. Lambda Legal Defense and Education Fund, "Lambda Legal Urges Appeals Board to Grant Asylum to Gay Mexican Immigrant and Overturn Judge's Ruling That He Could Hide His Sexual Orientation to Avoid Persecution" (2003), http://www.lambdalegal.org/cgi-bin/iowa/documents/record?record=1335.

63. Quoted in ibid.

64. INA § 208(a)(2)(B); 8 *U.S. Code* § 1158(a)(2)(B).

65. Committee to Preserve Asylum, "The Committee to Preserve Asylum's First Mailing to Senators" (1995), reprinted in the appendix to Philip G. Shrag, *A Well-Founded Fear: The Congressional Battle to Save Political Asylum in America* (New York: Routledge, 2000).

66. Quoted in Lesbian and Gay Immigration Rights Task Force, "Peruvian Seeking Asylum Visits Congressman Nadler," *Status Report*, Fall 1998.

67. INA § 208(a)(2)(D); 8 *U.S. Code* § 1158(a)(2)(D).

68. Lesbian and Gay Immigration Rights Task Force, "New Filing Deadline Is Tested in Immigration Court," *Status Report*, Fall 1998.

69. Karen Musalo, J. Edward Taylor, and Nipa Rahim, *The Expedited Removal Study: First Year of Implementation of Expedited Removal* (Santa Clara, CA: International Human Rights and Migration Project, Markkula Center for Applied Ethics, Santa Clara University, 1998), 9–10.

70. Ibid., 12–19.

71. Lesbian and Gay Immigration Rights Task Force, "'Expedited Removal' Begins," *Status Report*, Spring 1997.

72. Musalo et al., *The Expedited Removal Study: First Year*; Karen Musalo, Lauren Gibson, and J. Edward Taylor, *The Expedited Removal Study: Report on the Second Year of Implementation of Expedited Removal* (San Francisco: University of California, Hastings College of the Law, Center for Human Rights and International Justice, 1999); Karen Musalo, Lauren Gibson, Stephen Knight, and J. Edward Taylor, "The Expedited Removal Study: Report on the First Three Years of Implementation of Expedited Removal," special issue, *Notre Dame Journal of Law, Ethics, and Public Policy* 15 (2001).

73. Quoted in Musalo et al., *The Expedited Removal Study: First Year*, 87.

74. Musalo et al., "The Expedited Removal Study: Report on the First Three Years," 33.

75. Thomas Alexander Aleinikoff, David A. Martin, and Hiroshi Motomura, *Immigration and Citizenship: Process and Policy*, 4th ed. (St. Paul, MN: West Group, 1998), 883.

76. See, for example, Amnesty International, *Lost in the Labyrinth: Detention of Asylum Seekers* (New York: Amnesty International, 1999); Human Rights Watch, *Locked Away: Immigration Detainees in Jails in the United States* (New York: Human Rights Watch, 1998); Lawyers Committee for Human Rights, *Refugees behind Bars: The Imprisonment of Asylum Seekers in the Wake of the 1996 Immigration Act* (New York: Lawyers Committee for Human Rights, 1999); Women's Commission for Refugee Women and Children, *Liberty Denied: Women Seeking Asylum Imprisoned in the United States* (New York: Women's Commission for Refugee Women and Children, 1997).

77. Lesbian and Gay Immigration Rights Task Force, "Detained by INS: Issues Facing Gay Lesbian and HIV+ Individuals," *Status Report*, Summer 1999.

78. Lesbian and Gay Immigration Rights Task Force, "'Expedited Removal' Begins."

79. Stanley Mailman and Stephen Yale-Loehr, "As the World Turns: Immigration Law before and after Sept. 11," *New York Law Journal*, October 22, 2001. An updated version of the article is available at http://www.twmlaw.com/new/immlaw.html.

80. Mathew Purdy, "Bush's New Rules to Fight Terror Transform the Legal Landscape," *New York Times*, November 25, 2001.

81. Marisa Taylor, "Refugees Face New Scrutiny: More Screening, Proof Needed after Sept. 11," *San Diego Union-Tribune*, June 23, 2002.

82. International Gay and Lesbian Human Rights Commission, "Asylum Documentation Program Update," *Outspoken* 9, no. 1 (Fall 2003).

83. Mark Mardon, "Gay Pakistani in SF Seeks Asylum," *Bay Area Reporter* 33, no. 8 (February 20, 2003); Dave Ford, "Homeland Insecurity," *San Francisco Chronicle*, June 22, 2003.

84. International Gay and Lesbian Human Rights Commisson, http://www.iglhrc.org.

85. National Center for Lesbian Rights, http://www.nclrights.org; Lambda Legal Defense and Education Fund, http://www.lambdalegal.org.

86. Lesbian and Gay Immigration Rights Task Force, http://www.lgirtf.org.

87. John Leland, "Gays Seeking Asylum Find Familiar Prejudices in U.S.," *New York Times*, August 1, 2001.

88. Lesbian and Gay Immigration Rights Task Force, "Denied Asylum, Gay Indonesian Who Fled for His Life Fights Deportation," *Status Report*, August 2001.

89. Crenshaw, "Mapping the Margins."

90. See, for example, Jill M. Bystydzienski and Steven P. Schacht, eds., *Forging Radical Alliances across Difference: Coalition Politics for the New Millennium* (London and New York: Rowman and Littlefield, 2001).

CHAPTER THREE

Well-Founded Fear

*Political Asylum and the Boundaries of
Sexual Identity in the U.S.–Mexico Borderlands*

Lionel Cantú Jr. with Eithne Luibhéid and
Alexandra Minna Stern

Between 1999 and 2002, Cantú served as an expert witness in five cases involving Mexican men who petitioned for asylum in the United States on the basis of persecution for sexual orientation. The cases were processed in California, and all five men were eventually granted asylum. Cantú's participation as an expert witness reflected his commitment to using his sociological training and university faculty status to challenge inequalities and to assist those with less privilege. Having researched the lives of men who have sex with men in Mexico, and in migrant Mexican communities in the United States, Cantú appreciated the struggles and courage that underlay each application for asylum based on sexual orientation. Yet, he also began to observe a similarity to the process through which these asylum claims were adjudicated. While standardization remains the cornerstone to ensuring equal application of the law, it also meant that individual asylum applicants' experiences were elicited and given meaning within larger institutional structures that Cantú began to question.

Two issues particularly drew Cantú's attention. One issue was that to gain asylum on the basis of being persecuted for one's sexual orientation, the applicant has to prove that being gay is an "immutable" aspect of his selfhood. This tricky undertaking runs the risk of reinscribing essentialist notions of gay identity that scholars have spent decades painstakingly challenging. The second issue was that, as Saeed Rahman has described, receiving asylum requires painting one's country in racialist, colonialist terms, while at the same time disavowing the United States' role in contributing to the oppressive conditions that one fled.[1] These two issues converged because narratives about immutable homosexual or gay identities in Third World countries often provide the means to reinforce and remake racialist and colonialist scripts of U.S. "progressiveness"/Third World "backwardness."

Immutably Gay

Legally and historically in the United States, asylum for gay petitioners is complexly positioned between, on the one hand, a long-held pattern of pathologizing and othering gays and lesbians, and on the other, discourses of providing a safe haven for persecuted people. As described in this volume's introduction, lesbian and gay immigrants historically were excluded from entry into the United States based on multiple concerns including morality, public health, and political affiliation, and even though exclusion was stricken from immigration law in 1990, lesbian and gay immigrants still face structural discrimination. Throughout the period of explicit exclusion, the Immigration and Naturalization Service (INS) and the courts relied on constructions of gay identity as immutable, inherent, and undesirable when policing the national boundaries. For instance, in *Boutillier v. INS*, the Supreme Court argued, "the petitioner is not being deported for conduct engaged in after his entry into the United States, but rather, for characteristics he possessed at the time of his entry."[2]

Ironically, while these formal and informal terms for excluding gay immigrants were being articulated, a counterdiscourse of asylum rights was emerging and, by 1994, applied to lesbians and gay men. Since 1980, asylum has technically been available in the United States to those fleeing persecution on account of one of five criteria: race, religion, nationality, political opinion, or membership in a particular social group. The question was, where did gays fit in? While many could credibly demonstrate persecution, this was not enough; to gain asylum, persecution had to have occurred on account of one of the five criteria. Yet the INS and courts remained reluctant to consider gays and lesbians as "a particular social group."

Randazzo's essay in this volume describes how the move toward recognizing gays and lesbians as a particular social group began in 1986, when a Houston immigration judge barred the INS from deporting a Cuban gay man, Fidel Armando Toboso-Alfonso, based on concerns that he might face persecution for his sexual orientation. When the INS appealed the case in 1990, the Board of Immigration Appeals (BIA) affirmed the prior decision that had argued that gays were a particular social group.[3] In 1993, another immigration judge in San Francisco granted asylum to a Brazilian man, Marcelo Tenorio, based on the same assumption.[4] In 1994, for the first time, the INS granted asylum directly to a gay Mexican man, "Jose Garcia" (pseudonym). Two months later, Attorney General Janet Reno elevated the Toboso-Alfonso case as precedent and affirmed that lesbians and gay men constituted a particular social group for purposes of asylum.

Particularly noteworthy is the fact that these precedent-setting gay asylum cases involved migrants from Latin America. Not only are numbers of Latin American migrants proportionately large when compared to other national origin groups, but also, during the late 1980s and the 1990s, Latin Americans filed the majority of asylum petitions.[5] However, like all political stories, the issue is more complex than sheer numbers. The Toboso-Alfonso case, for instance, was clearly complicated by U.S.-Cuban politics—from a U.S. policy perspective, deporting a Cuban refugee, whatever his sexual orientation, was not expedient during the Cold War. Moreover, elevating the Toboso-Alfonso decision to precedent in 1994 provided President Clinton with an opportunity not only to show support for gay rights,[6] but also to champion human rights in Latin American countries that had been supported by previous U.S. Republican administrations. The exigencies of U.S. relations with Latin America clearly shaped the politics of gay asylum—in ways that demand further research.[7]

While the INS has officially recognized sexual orientation as evidence of membership in a particular social group for purposes of granting asylum, asylum remains difficult to attain. Illustrating these difficulties are statistics estimating that between 1994 and 1997, approximately sixty petitioners were granted asylum on these grounds, but reportedly over one thousand such petitions were filed in the same time frame.[8]

To gain asylum, gays and lesbians must convincingly establish both that they are members of a particular social group and that they experienced or may experience persecution as a result. The legal standards for defining a particular social group are somewhat inconsistent, but *Matter of Acosta* (1985) established a basic framework that guides the courts. *Acosta* defined a particular social group as being comprised by those who share a "common, immutable characteristic" that is either "innate" or arises from "shared past experience." In addition, this characteristic "must be one members of the group can not change or is so fundamental to their individual identities or consciences that they should not be required to change it."[9] Paradoxically, then, the same logic of inherent, immutable identity that used to be deployed to exclude gay immigrants is now required to establish that one is eligible for asylum.[10] Officials require such evidence in part because of exaggerated fears that migrants may falsely claim gay identity in order to become eligible for asylum.[11] While this may happen on rare occasions, the converse—where asylum applicants remain afraid to detail persecution based on sexual orientation—is much more likely.

Racialist and Colonialist Scripts

For an asylum petitioner from Mexico to prove that he is immutably gay, and has been persecuted as a result, is an undertaking fraught with contradictions. Much anthropological and sociological research, especially from the 1970s and 1980s, argued that gay identity as understood in the mainstream U.S. sense did not exist in Mexico. This literature, which continues to be referred to in asylum hearings today, certainly creates difficulties for petitioners who must establish that they are essentially gay. According to scholars, the Mexican sex/gender system is such that only men who assume the "feminized" position during sex with other men are stigmatized as homosexual. Men who assume the "active" position can retain their masculinity and heterosexual status. According to this schema, the quintessential Mexican gay asylum applicant is therefore an effeminate man.

There can be no doubt that effeminate men face discrimination and persecution that may reach life-threatening levels, and their asylum applications should receive the most serious consideration.[12] But the difficulties with the use of these accounts of the Mexican sex/gender system in asylum hearings are that they often reinforce racist and colonialist imagery and relations. Moreover, they may restrict asylum possibilities for those who do not conform to the image of the effeminate gay man.

To understand how the reinscription of racism and colonialism occurs, one must realize that asylum hearings are, as Sherene Razack says, "encounter[s] between the powerful and the powerless, and the powerful are always from the First World and mostly white, while the powerless are from the Third World and nearly always racialized or ethnicized." The asylum process constructs Third World asylum seekers "as either unworthy claimants or as supplicants begging to be saved from the tyranny of their own cultures, communities, and men."[13] To gain asylum, Third World supplicants must paint their countries in racialist, colonialist terms, while disavowing the United States' role in contributing to the conditions that they fled. If the U.S. government decides to "save" the supplicant by granting asylum, this easily reaffirms the notion of the United States as a land of liberty and a bastion of progress.

Cantú particularly noted that when persecution suffered by applicants is attributed to "culture," understood in a reified manner that divorces it from other variables such as race, gender, class, globalization, neocolonial relationships, and unequal U.S.–Mexico ties, these colonialist effects become realized. "Mexican culture" becomes the prism through which the individual is understood and the sole source of problems and repression in Mexico. Neocolonialism, economic exploitation, and other issues become irrelevant.

In the cases for which Cantú served as an expert witness, narratives of the Mexican sex/gender system, reduced to a manifestation of "culture" conceived in ahistorical terms, were consistently produced. In those cases, the courts heavily relied on reports written by Andrew Reding, director of the Americas Project of the World Policy Institute and associate editor of Pacific News Service. Reding has published a series of reports about gays in Mexico: *Democracy and Human Rights in Mexico* (1995); *Mexico: Treatment of Homosexuals* (1997); and *Mexico: Update on the Treatment of Homosexuals* (1999). Significantly, this last report is part of a Question and Answer Series distributed to asylum officials to assist them in adjudicating asylum claims.[14] The report offers an analysis of the legal, political, cultural, and historical factors shaping the lives of gays in Mexico. Reding's reports may be strategic, in the sense of providing clear-cut explanations of cultural difference and oppression that resonate effectively within the logic of the legal system, but some of their implications are troubling.

Relying on prior scholarship, Reding restates the argument that it is not all men who have sex with men, but instead men who assume the feminized role who are stigmatized and persecuted for being gay. He attributes their persecution to a "dominant cultural ideal of hypermasculinity," which he does not situate in material context, but rather treats

as a timeless and hermetically sealed mainstream Mexican cultural characteristic.[15] According to Reding, "the potential for violence against
homosexuals, especially effeminate men and transvestites, is *inherent* in
the culture of machismo" (emphasis added).[16] In the report, culture is
explicitly separated from the political and legal realms, areas where
significant gains have been made for gays, Reding claims.[17] This eviscer-
ated model of Mexican culture is depicted as existing in a temporal sequence that is anterior to mainstream U.S. culture. For instance, he
describes "the strong attachments most Mexicans feel to their families"
as "comparable to those that prevailed in the United States a century
ago."[18] Reding also suggests that "exposure" to U.S. culture can help to
ameliorate "negative" tendencies in Mexican culture. For example, "with
Mexican culture highly resistant to change from within, the primary
force for change is coming from international contact—primarily the
influence of U.S. culture."[19]

In these ways, the United States is discursively constructed as enlight-
ened, progressive, separate from Mexico, and positioned to save Mexican gay men from "the tyranny of their [timeless] cultures, communities,
and men."[20] Mexico, by contrast, emerges as backward and oppressive,
as evinced by its sex/gender system and treatment of effeminate men. In
fairness, Reding does acknowledge that in terms of certain political and
legal issues, Mexico is in advance of the United States in providing for
gays and lesbians.[21] But since "culture" remains cordoned off from law
and politics, these facts do not alter his fundamental narrative of the
United States as the savior of feminized brown men who are persecuted
by macho men, specifically, and Mexican sex/gender systems, generally,
all of which are conceived as manifestations of some sort of essentialized
Mexican culture. The role of the United States in materially contributing to conditions in Mexico—including sex/gender conditions as these
interact with class and race—is not discussed. Neither is the fact that
lesbians and gays in the United States face significant discrimination
and repression—and that Mexican gay immigrants in the United States
must deal with homophobia, racism, and often severe economic exploitation and language barriers. As Cantú's research showed, "in their attempts
to escape from one form of bigotry [homophobia], most of the [immi-
grant] Mexican men I interviewed discovered that not only had they
not entirely escaped it but they now faced another [racism]."[22]

Thus, narratives about Mexican culture generally, and about the treatment of gay men specifically, which are produced in the course of asylum hearings, variously draw on and reiterate racialist, colonialist imagery, particularly through the role that is attributed to "culture." This approach stands in marked contrast to the ways that white middle-class gay sexuality tends to be understood. As Cantú writes,

> Among U.S. gay and lesbian scholars in the late twentieth century, "gay" identities were understood as the socially constructed results of modernization.... This view of homosexuality stood in stark contrast to that of less developed countries. Traditional anthropological explanations of homosexuality point[] to "culture" to explain differences in how homosexuality was defined in "other," that is, non-Western, societies. Culture becomes the mechanism that reified difference and reproduced the imagined distance of "the others" in academic discourse itself.... Why should our understanding of sexual identities in the developing world give primacy to culture and divorce it from political economy?[23]

The grounding of Mexican homosexuality in a model of "culture" that is divorced from social, economic, and political variables has multiple material consequences, including ignoring or naturalizing inequality in relations with Latin America and discrimination toward Latinos in the United States.[24] Moreover, this exclusive focus on "culture" vis-à-vis sexuality both exoticizes and eroticizes Mexicans, an aspect of U.S.-Mexican relations that Cantú had explored in his research on queer tourism in Mexico and its representation in the United States.[25]

The narratives of the Mexican sex/gender system deployed in the Reding report also materially contribute to difficulties for some asylum petitioners because they conflate gender and sexuality in problematic ways and leave little room for the specificity of lesbian experience or the diversities of gay identity that exist in Mexico. The conflation of sexuality with gender (which is conceived in binary terms) is evident throughout the report. For example, "Effeminate behavior elicits far greater levels of social disapproval than does homosexuality [i.e., homosexual acts] per se.... Effeminacy and cross-dressing are serious violations of the masculine ideal. But the greatest transgression is for a man to assume the sexual role of a woman in intercourse."[26] What is problematic in this passage and elsewhere is that the report does not differentiate between being an effeminate man and being a biological female. Yet, Cantú's research makes clear that Mexican men themselves recognize and act on such a distinction:

> Being a joto is not to be a man. Neither a man nor a woman, it is an abomination, a curse. . . . Thus, the relationship of homosexuality to femininity is more complex than a synonymous equation implies. Homosexuality is not only the opposite of masculinity, it is a corruption of it, an unnatural form that by virtue of its transgression of the binary male/female order poses a threat that must be contained or controlled.[27]

These important distinctions, between men who are feminized and biological females, are not made in Reding's report. Thus, the report frequently compares the treatment of effeminate men to the treatment of biological women. This strategy means that his report gives short shrift to lesbians and the specificity of their persecution. It also contributes to the courts' difficulties in understanding how gender and sexuality variously intersect to produce specific kinds of persecution that single-axis analyses cannot capture (see Randazzo's discussion of intersectionality).[28] Finally, this conflation of gender with sexuality, which results in the production of the feminized gay man as the quintessential asylum applicant, does not allow for the variety of Mexican gay identities that exist today. Scholars including Cantú have described the emergence in the 1980s of identity categories such as "internacional" and the growing popularity of the term "gay" in parts of Mexico.[29] These new identities connect to political and economic changes that Mexico is undergoing, including urbanization, economic restructuring, and new transnational links. Their emergence again underscores that sexuality cannot be analyzed simply by reference to a colonialist notion of "culture"; there must be reference to material, political relations. Reding's report erases the range and complexity of these identities. Options for asylum may be reduced accordingly.

Fear, Loathing, and Other Border Tensions

Based on his experiences as an expert witness, and on his sociological research including in-depth interviews with gay Mexican immigrants in California, Cantú posited that even while globalizing forces had multiplied the range of available sexual identities and political projects, the asylum system was generating new, essentializing constructions of sexuality that functioned within strictly nationalist logics, thereby reinscribing borders that globalization had blurred. These contradictions have been paralleled by the United States' management of the U.S.–Mexico border, historically and at present.

Since the 1990s, the contradictory management of the U.S.–Mexico border has been exemplified by policies such as the North American Free Trade Agreement (NAFTA), which further integrated the economies of Mexico and the United States, even while immigration policies attempted to clearly separate the two countries. As Peter Andreas demonstrates, migrants have continued to cross the increasingly militarized U.S.–Mexico border because the logic of economic integration inevitably increased (rather than reduced) such movement and because U.S. employers continued to demand Mexican labor.[30] While militarization of the U.S.–Mexico border cannot, in Andreas's view, stem the migration of Mexicans, it nonetheless fulfills crucial symbolic functions by providing a means to visibly stage displays of state power, sovereign national boundaries, and distinctive national identity—despite, and indeed because of, globalization. Moreover, these displays have legitimated the further extension of violent and dehumanizing practices, which are directed not only at border crossers but also at those within the United States whose belonging remains in question on racial, sexual, and other grounds. Cantú believed that the INS's construction of the effeminate gay Mexican asylum seeker, whose sexuality and persecution were ascribed to essentialized Mexican cultural characteristics, filled an important role in the symbolic production of images of national difference, which mapped onto distinct sovereign territories—that were then defended through violent means. Cantú was particularly concerned to explore how these discursive constructions translated into material practices that affect border crossers.

Future Research Directions

In this essay, Cantú intended to challenge mainstream accounts of asylum as simply the provision of a haven for the oppressed. To him, the asylum system was more complexly double-edged. On the one hand, it offers hope and security to a small number of individuals. On the other hand, through its processes for eliciting, evaluating, and recirculating individuals' testimonies about persecution and suffering, the asylum system remains part of a governance apparatus that generates racist, colonialist images and relations that greatly affect Latin Americans, U.S. Latinos—and Latin Americans who have been granted asylum in the United States. Moreover, these processes shape the general production of knowledge about immigration and globalization.

Inspired by scholars who suggest that efforts to exclude the Chinese laid the foundation for the entire U.S. immigration apparatus, Cantú speculated that shifting U.S. strategies for managing relations with Latin America in the 1980s and 1990s materially shaped U.S. asylum law, policies, and procedures, and he sought to demonstrate that.[31] In terms of chronology, his argument has strong merit because it was only in 1980 that the United States established a standard system for processing and admitting refugees and asylum seekers, through the 1980 Refugee Act.

Using the figure of the Mexican gay asylum seeker to generate a Latin American–focused genealogy of the U.S. asylum system further demonstrates the originality of Cantú's scholarship. Cantú was among a handful of scholars who contributed to the development of tools and theories for studying gay migrants, who remain invisible, insignificant, or even despicable in most scholarship. Relentlessly situating gay migrants' lives in the context of material relations of race, gender, class, sexuality, and geopolitics, Cantú's essay here illuminates with clarity and sympathy the lives, struggles, dignity, and agency of Mexican gay migrants who seek asylum.

Yet, Cantú was no sentimentalist. He had an unerring eye for irony—for example, the irony confronting a Mexican asylum seeker whose testimony garners him legal residence, but also fuels racist and colonialist relations that negatively affect his life (and the lives of his family, friends, and lovers). Cantú also drew attention to the irony of how the U.S. immigration apparatus historically used essentialist constructions to exclude gays and lesbians, but now requires essentializing narratives from gays and lesbians if they are to receive asylum. Cantú also highlighted the incongruity of the U.S. asylum system's production of fixed models of hermetically sealed cultures, even while globalization in general, and U.S.-Mexican relations in particular, have significantly reconfigured cultural and national boundaries.

This essay's provisional and suggestive character invites other scholars to take up the politically and theoretically significant work that Cantú began, but was unable to finish.

Notes

This essay, which Cantú planned to include in the *Queer Moves* collection, interrogates what he called "the birth of the Mexican gay asylee" as a juridical and social category in the United States. Drawing on a draft of this unfinished essay, Eithne Luibhéid and Alexandra Minna Stern describe the main ideas that Cantú was exploring, how they connect to his earlier work, and the research questions they open up.

1. Saeed Rahman, "Shifting Grounds for Asylum: Female Genital Surgery and Sexual Orientation," *Columbia Human Rights Law Review* 29 (Spring 1998): 516–17.
2. *Boutillier v. INS*, 387 US 118 (1967) at 123.
3. Cited in *Hernandez-Montiel v. INS*, 98–70582 (U.S. Court of Appeals, 9th Cir., August 24, 2000), at 10481. The Toboso-Alfonso decision can be found at 20 I&N Dec. 819 (BIA, 1990).
4. *Matter of Tenorio*, A72–093–558 (IJ, July 1993); *Matter of Tenorio*, A72–093–558 (BIA, 1999).
5. For example, according to the *INS Statistical Yearbook* for 2000, "For over a decade, nationals from Central America dominated the annual number of asylum applications filed in the United States. From 1986 to 1992, about half of all asylum applications were filed by Central Americans. By 1993 and 1994, that percentage had fallen somewhat, but it still remained at about 40 percent of the total applications filed. Then, the number of applications from Central Americans surged to new heights in the next two years, well over half of all asylum applications. A sharp decline in cases filed by Nicaraguans was later offset by a sharp increase in cases filed by Guatemalans and Salvadorans. Beginning in 1997, the numbers started a sharp decline, largely due to the termination of a filing period under the terms of the *American Baptist Churches (ABC) v. Thornburgh* settlement. As a result, Central Americans accounted for about 4 percent of the new claims and 9 percent of the total filed and reopened in 2000" (http://www.graphics/aboutins/statistics/00yrbk_ref/RA2000). In addition to high numbers of asylum claims by Central Americans, South Americans also applied for asylum, as did increasing numbers of Mexicans. "The largest number of asylum seekers in 2001 came from Mexico, with 9,178 applying during the year, up dramatically from 3,936 in 2000" (U.S. Committee for Refugees, *World Refugee Survey 2000* [Washington, DC, 2000], 275). See also *Refugee Reports* 22, no. 12 (December 2001): 7, for cumulative U.S. asylum statistics from FY 1989 through 2001.
6. According to Cantú, Clinton needed to show support for gay and lesbian issues after failing to deliver on his promise to end anti-gay discrimination in the military.
7. Cantú intended to develop this argument in greater detail, but did not have time. We hope that other scholars may further expand on this point.
8. Personal interview conducted by Cantú with Julie Dorf, executive director of the International Gay and Lesbian Human Rights Commission, 1998.
9. Cited in Jin S. Park, "Pink Asylum: Political Asylum Eligibility for Gay Men and Lesbians under U.S. Immigration Policy," *UCLA Law Review* 42 (April 1995): 1115, 1124–25. The *Acosta* decision can be found at *In Re Acosta* 19 I&N Dec. 211 (BIA 1985). The *Hernandez-Montiel* decision notes that "the First, Third, and Seventh Circuits have adopted Acosta's analysis," but the Ninth Circuit "suggests a 'voluntary

associational relationship' requirement" that may conflict with Acosta. See *Hernandez-Montiel* at 10477, 10478.

10. It should be noted that the claim that sexual orientation and sexual identity are immutable, and therefore a basis for membership in a particular social group, is not necessarily intended to reiterate the same old essentialist thinking. Rather, as the *Hernandez-Montiel* ruling relates, that claim has been used by many gay rights advocates to critique attempts to forcibly "convert" lesbians and gays to heterosexuality, and to challenge the general denigration and ill-treatment of queers (*Hernandez-Montiel* at 10479). Thus, essentialism in the asylum system needs to be carefully situated in terms of who is using it and for what purpose. This is another aspect of the paper that Cantú did not have time to fully work through.

11. For example, see Arthur Leonard, "Gay Chinese Men Seek U.S. Asylum," *Gay City News* 2, no. 47 (November 27–December 3, 2003), http://www.gaycitynews.com/gcn_248/gaychinese.html; and Marina Jiminez, "Refuge from the Stones," *Globe and Mail,* December 6, 2003, http://www.theglobeandmail.com/servlet/ArticleNews/TPPrint/LAC/20031206/FCCENT66/Focus/. For a detailed analysis of one Romanian asylum seeker's difficulties in establishing his homosexuality to the satisfaction of the British Immigration Appeal Tribunal, see Derek McGhee, "Accessing Homosexuality: Truth, Evidence, and the Legal Practices for Determining Refugee Status–The Case of Ioan Vracìu," *Body and Society* 6, no. 1 (2000): 29–50.

12. Andrew Reding's *Mexico: Update on the Treatment of Homosexuals,* which we will discuss in more detail, importantly notes the significance of class in ensuring that poor effeminate men have particularly limited possibilities for avoiding persecution: "the poor are most vulnerable" (2), and "in all cases the extent to which an individual can lead a fulfilling life as a homosexual depends heavily on that individual's socio-economic status" (16) (Question and Answer Series [Resource Information Center, Immigration and Naturalization Service, U.S. Department of Justice, 1999], http://www.worldpolicy.org/globalrights/sexorient/1999-Mexico-gayrights.html).

13. Sherene Razack, *Looking White People in the Eye: Gender, Race, and Culture in Courtrooms and Classrooms* (Toronto: University of Toronto Press, 1998), 88.

14. According to the document, "Question and Answer Series papers are one means by which information on human rights conditions and/or conditions affecting given groups or individuals deemed 'at risk' within a given country is presented to Asylum and Immigration Officials. Question and Answer Series papers are brief descriptions of conditions in countries based on information provided by the sources referred to above. They are prepared by expert consultants and/or the staff of the Resource and Information Center, Immigration and Naturalization Service, U.S. Department of Justice. Question and Answer papers cannot be, and do not purport to be either exhaustive with regard to the country surveyed, or conclusive as to the merits of any particular claim to refugee status or asylum" (1). Andrew Reding, *Democracy and Human Rights in Mexico* (1995), http://www.worldpolicy.org/globalrights/mexico/1995-mexico.html; Reding, *Mexico: Treatment of Homosexuals* (1997), http://www.worldpolicy.org/globalrights/sexorient/1997-Mexico-gayrights.html; Reding, *Mexico: Update on the Treatment of Homosexuals.*

15. Reding, *Mexico: Update on the Treatment of Homosexuals,* 1. The report carefully details the existence, and cultural difference from the mainstream, of indigenous groups in Mexico.

16. Ibid., 2. Scholarship that interrogates the ways that Mexican culture gets characterized as macho includes Matthew C. Gutmann, *The Meanings of Being Macho: Being a Man in Mexico City* (Berkeley: University of California Press, 1996); and Pierette Hondagneu-Sotelo and Michael Messner, "Gender Displays and Men's Power: 'The New Man' and the Mexican Immigrant Man," in *Theorizing Masculinities,* ed. Harry Brod and Michael Kaufman (Thousand Oaks, CA: Sage, 1994), 200–218. Readers will note how, in this quote from the Reding report, a series of potentially noncommensurate figures—homosexuals, transvestites, and effeminate men—become collapsed into one.

17. Reding writes that despite an "unfavorable cultural environment," significant legal and political gains are being made for gays in Mexico—in some instances, in ways that are more progressive than in the United States (*Mexico: Update on the Treatment of Homosexuals,* 14). See the section of the report titled "Political and Legal Gains," 14–16.

18. Ibid., 4. Reding also writes, "Mexican society remains highly prejudiced against homosexuals who are HIV positive. As was the case in the United States several years ago, AIDS continues to be identified as a gay disease" (18).

19. Ibid., 9. He also writes, "As the influence of foreign cultures—especially the United States—grows in Mexico, attitudes [toward sexuality and gender] are beginning to change" (2).

20. Razack, *Looking White People in the Eye,* 88.

21. See note 17.

22. Lionel Cantú, "A Place Called Home: A Queer Political Economy of Mexican Immigrant Men's Family Experiences," in *Queer Politics, Queer Families: Challenging Culture and the State,* ed. Mary Bernstein and Renate Reimann (New York: Columbia University Press, 2001), 129. See also Lionel Cantú, "*De Ambiente:* Queer Tourism and the Shifting Boundaries of Mexican Male Sexualities," in "Queer Tourism: Geographies of Globalization," special issue, *GLQ* 8, no. 1–2 (2002): 139–66, especially 155–56.

23. Cantú, "*De Ambiente,*" 141–42; see also Cantú, "Entre Hombres/Between Men," in *Gay Masculinities,* ed. Peter Nardi (Thousand Oaks, CA: Sage, 2000), 229. This is another way in which colonialism manifests in the construction and deployment of narratives of sexuality, including in the asylum hearings for which Cantú served as an expert witness.

24. Cantú intended to further elaborate on these consequences, but that work will have to be done by other scholars.

25. Cantú, "*De Ambiente.*"

26. Reding, *Mexico: Update on the Treatment of Homosexuals,* 5

27. Cantú, "A Place Called Home," 120. See also Annick Prieur, *Mema's House, Mexico City: On Transvestites, Queens, and Machos* (Chicago: University of Chicago Press, 1998); and Ian Lumsden, *Homosexualidad: Sociedad y Estado en México* (Toronto: Solediciones/Canadian Gay Archives, 1991).

28. The intersection of gender and sexuality in lesbian persecution, for example, had made lesbian asylum claims more difficult for courts to understand and adequately address. See Shannon Minter, "Lesbians and Asylum: Overcoming Barriers to Access," in *Asylum Based on Sexual Orientation: A Resource Guide,* ed. Sydney Levy (San Francisco: IGLHRC and Lambda Legal Defense and Education Fund, 1996), sec. 1B, 3–16. See also Randazzo, this volume.

29. Cantú, *"De Ambiente,"* 145–46. See also Hector Carillo, "Cultural Change, Hybridity, and Male Homosexuality in Mexico," *Culture, Health, and Sexuality* 1, no. 3 (1999): 223–38.

30. Peter Andreas, "Borderless Economy, Barricaded Border," *NACLA Report on the Americas* 33, no. 3 (November–December 1999): 14–21, 46. See also Saskia Sassen, "Why Migration?" *NACLA Report on the Americas* 26, no. 1 (July 1992): 14–19, 46–47.

31. On Chinese exclusion as the basis for the U.S. immigration apparatus, see Charles McClain, *In Search of Equality: The Chinese Struggle against Discrimination in the Nineteenth Century* (Berkeley: University of California Press, 1994).

CHAPTER FOUR

Sexual Aliens and the Racialized State

A Queer Reading of the
1952 U.S. Immigration and Nationality Act

Siobhan B. Somerville

The relationship between nationalism and sexuality has had a central place within queer studies for more than a decade, but the field has attended less frequently and consistently to the ways that the state itself (rather than the individual citizen or the nation) might be understood as sexualized.[1] This emphasis on the nation may result, in part, from the influence of Foucault, whose formulation of power directs attention away from the state. It may also stem from the traditional ways that the distinctions between the state and nation have been theorized. While it is difficult to find agreement on the precise definitions of these terms, the "state" is usually understood to be a juridical formation or political body with some territorial component. In contrast, "nation," derived from the Latin root *nasci* (to be born), has traditionally been associated with a sense of kinship, a primordial belonging, or, in the words of one theorist, "a psychological bond that joins a people and differentiates it, in the subconscious conviction of its members, from all other people in a most vital way."[2] Recently, Jacqueline Stevens has challenged the distinction traditionally drawn between state and nation, arguing that it obscures the ways that the state is sexualized, particularly through the deployment of state regulations on reproduction and kinship. She argues instead that "the 'state' and 'nation' are two sides of the same familial coin. . . . The family rhetoric of the state-nation is not obscure, metaphysical, or difficult to locate. The familial nation exists through practices and often legal documents that set out the kinship rules for particular political societies." She outlines the stakes of understanding the state as embedded in, not separate from, the sexual: "Once it is understood that the most fundamental structures of the modern state—the rules regulating marriage and immigration—are what enable the state to reproduce itself and what make possible the power relations associated with nationality, ethnicity, race, and family roles, then it is clear that piecemeal approaches to eradicating certain inequalities will not work."[3]

In this essay, I look at one of these "fundamental structures of the modern state"—U.S. immigration and naturalization law—at a moment when it underwent a major transformation via the 1952 Immigration and Nationality Act (INA), also known as the McCarran-Walter Act. Unprecedented in its comprehensiveness and durability, this legislation brought into one central statute the multiple laws governing immigration and naturalization, which, prior to its enactment, had not been organized in any systematic way. While the act has been amended many times since its passage in 1952, its structure remains the same and it still functions as the basic body of immigration law in the United States today. The 1952 INA is perhaps best known for its strident anticommunist rhetoric, instantiated through its sweeping provisions against so-called subversives, reflecting the Cold War characterization of communism as an "alien movement."[4]

The 1952 INA also marked a significant shift in the deployment of discourses of race and sexuality in U.S. immigration and naturalization policies. The language of race had long been one of the primary mechanisms for determining the eligibility of migrants to enter the United States and/or to become U.S. citizens. The 1952 INA, however, removed the explicit language of race in provisions on both immigration and naturalization, substituting "national" origin as the basis for excluding immigrants and stating that "the right of a person to become a naturalized citizen of the United States shall not be denied or abridged because of race or sex."[5] At the same time, the 1952 INA also introduced two sexual categories, homosexuality and adultery, into the laws determining eligibility for citizenship: Congress ensured that a finding of homosexuality could be used to exclude immigrants from eligibility for immigration and naturalization, and also explicitly named adultery as one of many prohibited acts that constituted an automatic bar to the finding of "good moral character" necessary to qualify for naturalization.

Although these new provisions—one effacing race, the other foregrounding sexual acts and identities—were not explicitly linked in either the text of the 1952 INA or in the proceedings that led to its enactment, they were bound together in at least two important ways that I will explore in this essay. First, the concurrent appearance of provisions on homosexuality and adultery in this law was no coincidence. When read together, these provisions suggest that lawmakers brought new scrutiny—and the power of the state—to bear on forms of sexuality that seemed to threaten the normative status of monogamous heterosexual marriage. Second, although this new attention to prohibited forms of sexuality might seem to indicate that sexuality had "replaced" race as one of the primary principles of exclusion, it was, as I will argue here, in fact inseparable from the ongoing contestation over race in U.S. immigration and naturalization policy during this period.

The stakes of these arguments are both methodological and historical. That Congress implicitly linked the figures of the adulterer, the "homosexual," and other "sex perverts" in this legislation underscores the advantages of using queer approaches, which move beyond a narrow focus on homosexuality toward an emphasis on questions of normative and nonnormative sexual identities and practices. Further, my reading of the 1952 INA emphasizes that we need to continually rearticulate queer approaches beyond sexual identity per se, and attend more carefully to the ways in which state practices regarding sexuality have been entwined historically with discourses of race and racialization. Finally, such an approach challenges a tendency in existing scholarship to treat racism and homophobia as analogous, and therefore parallel, discourses in the Cold War period. The legislative history of the 1952 INA suggests that race and sexuality were profoundly woven together in the boundary-making logic of U.S. policies on immigration and naturalization at midcentury. Using a queer approach that is attentive to the imbrication of sexual and racial discourses demonstrates that the INA's construction of sexual aliens was embedded in and maintained a thoroughly racialized model of national citizenship, particularly at a moment when that model appeared to be undergoing such an enormous transformation.

The 1952 INA, of course, was not the first time that U.S. regulations on immigration and naturalization addressed sexual questions. The earliest federal legislation that explicitly linked citizenship and heterosexual marriage was passed in 1855, when Congress declared that a foreign woman who legally married an American man automatically became a U.S. citizen as long as she met other naturalization requirements (including that she be a "free white person," a provision that I will discuss further).[6] The next time that sexual matters were raised in relation to immigration and naturalization was in 1875, when Congress passed the Page Act, the first federal legislation that defined citizenship in negative terms, enumerating specific types of people who were excluded from access to immigration and naturalization, including women "imported for the purposes of prostitution."[7] Although the legislation was ostensibly aimed at the traffic in *all* so-called immoral women, the figure of the prostitute in this law was inherently racialized because it targeted Asian women.[8] The next major revision of immigration procedures, the Immigration Act of 1891, marked the first appearance of another sexual figure, the polygamist, who joined the list of those restricted from immigration and naturalization. Observing that anarchists were also included in the 1891 Act, Nancy Cott notes that, after this legislation, "polygamists and anarchists always appeared in sequence as excludable, deportable, and ineligible for citizenship, as if disloyalty to monogamy were equivalent to overthrowing the government."[9] The privileges and exclusions established with regard to sexual conduct in these nineteenth-century laws have endured through the twentieth century and, with minor changes, remain in force in existing immigration and naturalization law. Marriage to a U.S. citizen automatically confers eligibility for naturalized citizenship on the heterosexual spouse (although now the law applies to both men and women); and, although the explicit anti-Asian language has been removed, prostitution and polygamy still automatically disqualify potential citizens from the "good moral character" requirement necessary for naturalization.

Appearing relatively late in the legislative history of immigration and naturalization, adultery and homosexuality were mentioned explicitly in congressional debates on immigration and naturalization that led up to the passage of the 1952 INA.[10] Legislators apparently imagined adultery and homosexuality in very different ways and demonstrated varying degrees of concern about the need for these new categories of exclusion. As mentioned earlier, adultery was listed as one of the prohibited acts in the list of requirements for "good moral character," a requirement that had been in place since the first naturalization statutes were passed in the 1790s, but which had remained undefined in the law itself.[11] The report of the Senate subcommittee that drafted the 1952 INA did not specifically explain the changes that introduced "adultery" into the law, stating only that "more uniform regulations should be employed by the [Immigration and Naturalization] Service and adopted by the court, to the end that a higher general standard of good morals and personal and political conduct are [sic] established."[12]

While adultery was considered to be a question of morality, homosexuality was constructed as a medical pathology, positioned within exclusions based on medical status.[13] The committee's discussions focused on obscure language inherited from the Immigration Act of 1917, which had listed "persons of constitutional psychopathic inferiority" as one category of "physically and mentally defective individuals" who were excluded from eligibility.[14] In the 1950 report that preceded passage of the legislation, the Senate subcommittee acknowledged that there existed no standard measures for diagnosing this condition and quoted an officer of the Public Health Service who remarked that "[w]e have certain mechanical aids in evaluating intelligence, and we are attempting to get definite yardsticks for establishing the diagnosis of constitutional psychopathic inferiority."[15] Further, the report admitted that, even though the "constitutional psychopathic inferiority" exclusion had not been widely enforced, within the immigration and naturalization system it had been one of the most controversial provisions of the existing law:

> Perhaps because of the difficulty of diagnosis and definition, there have been numerous protests over continuation of this exclusion clause. A number of the appeals to the Immigration and Naturalization Service have been aimed at the diagnosis of "constitutional psychopathic inferiority" by the examining medical officers. The arguments before the subcommittee centered about two points of attack against the provision: (1) that it placed excessive and arbitrary powers in the hands of officials, and (2) the term is vague, undefined, and has not served any useful purpose.[16]

Dismissing the merits of these arguments, however, the subcommittee decided that the exclusion was not "unduly harsh or restrictive." Instead, it altered the terminology slightly and provided a more specific explanation of its intent: "the purpose of the provision . . . will be more adequately served by changing that term to 'persons afflicted with psychopathic personality,'" and "the classes of mentally defectives should be enlarged to include homosexuals and other sex perverts."[17]

For reasons that remain unclear, this explicit reference to "homosexuals and other sex perverts" was eventually dropped when the final bill was drafted, leaving only the vague language of "psychopathic personality." To dispel any perception that it was easing the provisions, the Senate report insisted that "[t]his change of nomenclature is not to be construed in any way as modifying the intent to exclude all aliens who are sexual deviates." The language of "psychopathic personality," it contended, would be "sufficiently broad to provide for the exclusion of homosexuals and sex perverts."[18] Legal scholars have offered various explanations for the omission of the more explicit language of "homosexuality," "sex perverts," and "sexual deviates" in the final version of the legislation. Noting that the acting surgeon general had stated on record that "considerable difficulty may be encountered in substantiating a diagnosis of homosexuality," Robert Foss has suggested that "the Public Health Service wanted to avoid the enactment of a specific statutory exclusion that would make them responsible for trying to figure out who was a homosexual and who was not." He also notes that it may simply have been an example of the persistent legal tradition of treating homosexuality as the *crimen innominatum*—the unnameable crime or "the love that dared not speak its name"—a crime presumed to be so horrible that it was not to be mentioned in English.[19] Its original reasoning aside, after two Supreme Court cases challenging the law in the late 1950s and early 1960s, Congress ultimately did amend it in 1965 by adding the term "sexual deviation" to the list of excludable traits and citing the earlier Senate report to reaffirm the exclusion of homosexuals.[20]

The vague language of "psychopathic personality" in the 1952 INA may account for the apparent lack of public knowledge of or interest in the legislation's exclusion based on homosexuality, as reflected in existing records of the public response to the INA. The National Archives hold approximately 140 letters commenting on the law, from individuals and groups such as the Daughters of the American Revolution, the Jewish Community Relations Council, and the Association of Immigration and Nationality Lawyers, among others. Most of these letters are concerned with the anticommunist or racial implications of the law; none of the letters refers directly to the exclusion of homosexuals (or adultery, for that matter). Anxieties about gender and sexuality do surface obliquely in a few letters addressing the anticommunist aspects of the law. Contemplating the potential repeal of the INA, one woman from Wisconsin, for instance, feared that "emasculation of this Act is given the highest priority by the Communist Party!"[21] Most of the letters, however, express either support for or dismay over the anticommunist measures of the act, suggesting that the letter writers were not aware of the sexual exclusions, or, if they did know about them, they tacitly agreed with the policies or shared congressional reticence about speaking directly about homosexuality on public record.

As the letter from Wisconsin suggests, anticommunist discourse may also have been more readily available to encompass many of the anxieties attached to the figure of the homosexual. On the surface, the new attention to homosexuality in the legislative history of the 1952 INA was consistent with the larger Cold War association between homosexuality and communism as twin threats to national security.[22] Not coincidentally, the same Senate had also recently generated another investigation, titled "Employment of Homosexuals and Other Sex Perverts in the U.S. Government." This document concluded that "homosexuals and other sex perverts are not proper persons to be employed in Government for two reasons; first, they are generally unsuitable" because they "are law violators," social "outcasts," and frequent victims of blackmailers; and "second, they constitute security risks" because their "lack of emotional stability" and "weakness of... moral fiber... [make] them susceptible to the blandishments of the foreign espionage agent."[23]

Like much Cold War rhetoric, then, the 1952 INA implicitly linked communism and homosexuality as characteristics of "undesirable" immigrants, even as it appeared to rewrite the ways that race was deployed in U.S. immigration and naturalization policy. Race had been a central element of the law beginning with the earliest federal statutes on naturalization. The 1790 "Act to establish an uniform Rule of Naturalization" clearly and quite self-consciously restricted naturalization to "free white persons," thus racializing American citizenship at the very moment in which it was codified as a legal status. While the precise meaning of "white" has never been stable in the enforcement of this law, the naturalization process has been embedded historically in an explicit policy of racial exclusion and the logic of white supremacy.[24] After the Civil War, the "white person" restriction of naturalization was challenged, and, although there were efforts to do away with it completely, Congress simply modified it in 1870, when it extended the right to naturalize to "persons of African nativity or African descent," a law that recognized the citizen status of freed African-American slaves but maintained discriminatory immigration and naturalization policies against other racial groups.[25] In the period before World War II, various groups were allowed piecemeal exceptions to these existing rules, including immigrants from the Philippines, India, and China, as well as Asian brides of U.S. soldiers, but the basic language of racial exclusion remained in place until 1952.

In omitting race as a category of exclusion, the 1952 INA might, on its surface, seem to be part of larger challenges to racial discrimination that would continue through the civil rights era, perhaps most clearly articulated in the Civil Rights Act of 1964 and Supreme Court rulings such as *Brown v. Board of Education* in 1954 and *Loving v. Virginia* in 1967. Indeed, the congressional committee that drafted the 1952 INA noted that "[t]he committee feels that denial of naturalization based solely on race is an outmoded and un-American concept and should be eliminated from our statutes."[26] Constructing racism as "un-American" was a persuasive rhetorical maneuver in the context of the Cold War, and the repeal of exclusions based on race was considered by many to be a shrewd advancement of foreign policy concerns. As one immigration officer commented in testimony presented to the Senate subcommittee,

> with the United States assuming a position of political, economic, and diplomatic prominence in the world, such statutes [on racial ineligibility] tend to raise doubts in the minds of the affected groups as to the true nature of a democracy and obviously provide a propaganda theme for those countries with designs of ultimately imposing their peculiar political philosophies upon other countries of the world.[27]

Using a barely veiled reference to communism ("peculiar political philosophies"), this officer deployed a now familiar liberal vision of a "color-blind" democracy as part of the larger anticommunist ideologies that shaped U.S. Cold War culture. To continue explicitly racist immigration and naturalization policies left the United States vulnerable, by this logic, to communist "propaganda" that exposed American racial inequalities and thus undermined the legitimacy of the United States' "democratic" projects in foreign policy.

Yet as a number of scholars have argued, we should be deeply skeptical about placing the 1952 INA within a civil rights trajectory. The removal of the explicit language of racial prerequisites from the 1952 law did not mean that race suddenly became irrelevant to U.S. policies on immigration and naturalization. On the contrary, by mobilizing national origin as the basis of the quota system, the INA continued to have profoundly racist effects on immigration policy.[28] Despite some legislators' claims,

the 1952 INA was "permeated with the doctrine of racial superiority."[29] As
Rachel Buff notes, "Although the law did eliminate restrictions against
the naturalization of Asians as citizens, it implemented national-origins
quotas that applied the 1920s 'Nordic race theory' of immigration restriction. In accordance with Nordic race theory, this law gave preference to
immigrants of northern European backgrounds."[30] Even at the time of
its passage, the racist implications of the INA were widely acknowledged. In a minority report, for instance, other members of the Judiciary Committee contested the claim that the new legislation did away
with racial discrimination. They asserted that the "sources of our national
strength rest squarely on the guiding idea of our form of government,
the idea that every race and every creed among us is equally entitled to
the protection of the American flag." The new legislation did not, they
argued, uphold these goals, pointing out that quotas based on national
origin constituted de facto "racial discrimination against Eurasians and
colonial natives [of the West Indies], and national ancestry discrimina-
tions against Italians, Poles, and Greeks."[31] In addition, President Tru-
man vetoed the bill (a veto that was overturned) because he objected to
the "unfair and discriminatory" system of national origins quotas.[32] Likewise, an editorial in the *New York Times* strongly criticized the bill as
"racist, restrictionist, and reactionary."[33] The INA's removal of racial
categories of exclusion, then, indicates not the end of racialized and
racist immigration and naturalization policies, but rather a recognition
that the explicit *language* of race was losing legitimacy in official constructions of American citizenship.

How then might we account for the simultaneous disappearance of
the overt language of race and appearance of "outlawed" sexual formations such as homosexuality and adultery in the 1952 INA? The exclusions based on homosexuality and adultery, I would argue, were profoundly entangled with the narrative that Congress was writing about
the relationship between race and nation in the 1952 INA. There is nothing in the record to indicate a conscious linkage between the removal of
the explicit language of race and the simultaneous articulation of exclusions based on prohibited sexual categories. Their very congruence, however, suggests an underlying logic that connects these two aspects of the
law. One clue to how these concepts worked in tandem is suggested in
the Senate report of 1950 that preceded passage of the act. In its discussion of the proposed changes, the Senate subcommittee noted that the

original purpose of the "constitutional psychopathic inferiority" clause in 1917 was "to keep out 'tainted blood,' that is, 'persons who have medical traits which would harm the people of the United States if those traits were introduced into this country, or if those possessing those traits were added to those in this country who unfortunately are so afflicted.'"[34] In constructing homosexuality as a matter of "tainted blood," the subcommittee tacitly reinforced an earlier discourse of eugenics; to exclude homosexuals was to invoke the logic of national purification.[35] Although less overtly, adultery was also historically linked to a history of eugenics and models of national belonging in which citizenship was transferred through bloodlines. The term "adultery" refers, after all, to "pollution, contamination, a 'base admixture,' a wrong combination."[36] To adulterate is "to render spurious or counterfeit; to falsify, corrupt, debase, esp. by the admixture of baser ingredients."[37] If monogamous marriage was assumed to produce an unadulterated line of descent, adultery was imagined as the literal pollution of bloodlines through extramarital reproduction, thus scrambling the inheritance of property relationships and status. Further, as Ursula Vogel has pointed out, the legal history of adultery is thoroughly embedded within essentialist and asymmetrical understandings of gender. Because women's bodies were the site of literal reproduction as well as the transmission of family bloodlines, a wife's extramarital sex could potentially adulterate that lineage, while a husband's extramarital sex could not. In the original laws on adultery, "only a wife was capable of committing adultery. . . . The very same act on the part of her husband had no name in the language of the law, as long as he did not violate the marriage of another man."[38]

Although this double standard had long ago disappeared on the face of the law, I would argue that these underlying anxieties about property and pollution animated legislators who drafted the 1952 INA. Just as the provisions regarding homosexuality apparently respond to eugenic concerns about "tainted blood," the explicit naming of adultery registers anxieties over paternity and the transmission of property. Thus, while Congress removed overt references to race in the requirements for American citizenship, it maintained a logic of blood purification by invoking the sexualized figures of the adulterer and the homosexual.[39] When the explicit language of race disappeared, the underlying fantasy of national purification—an unadulterated Americanness—was articulated instead through the discourse of sexuality. Even though the law appeared "race-neutral" on its surface, the 1952 INA's new provisions on prohibited sexual categories, along with those on "national origins," reinforced rather than replaced the racist logic that had anchored U.S. immigration and naturalization policy from its earliest instantiation.

The exclusions based on adultery and homosexuality in congressional legislation were relatively short-lived compared to the prohibitions against other sexualized figures, such as polygamists and prostitutes. By 1979, following the 1973 decision by the American Psychiatric Association to remove homosexuality from its list of mental disorders, the surgeon general announced that the Public Health Service would no longer issue the medical certificates needed for the INS to exclude aliens solely on the basis of homosexuality.[40] Without the participation of the Public Health Service, the existing policy was difficult to enforce. The reference to homosexuality was finally removed in 1990, when Congress undertook another sweeping reform of all immigration legislation; at that time, it deleted any reference to "persons of psychopathic personality" from the law. (However, in the meantime, HIV had been added to the list of communicable diseases used to exclude potential immigrants, in effect re-legitimating the exclusion of many gay men and immigrants of color from entry into the United States. That law remains on the books.) Similarly, in 1981, Congress removed any explicit mention of adultery from the list of disqualifications from "good moral character" in naturalization provisions (although even after its removal from the letter of the law, the exclusion of adulterers has been enforced by the INS under various other guises).[41]

In subsequent years, the underlying blood logic that had organized earlier exclusions has been articulated instead through the prevailing policy of "family reunification" in immigration and naturalization law, the explicit purpose of which is "to principally reunite nuclear families."[42] This policy, a central feature of the 1965 immigration and naturalization reforms, is tied to the somewhat obvious ideological goals of privileging and reproducing a model of the nuclear family. The policy of family unification allowed the law to appear facially "color-blind" even as it was designed to achieve racialized effects, specifically maintaining the existing racial makeup of incoming immigrant groups. The racial dimensions of the family unification policy were not lost on those who designed and supported it, such as Representative Emmanuel Celler, chairman of the House Judiciary Committee at the time. In discussions leading to the passage of the Immigration Act of 1965, Celler reassured Congress that the immigrant pool would remain largely European:

> there will not be, comparatively, many Asians or Africans entering this country.... Since the people of Africa and Asia have very few relatives here, comparatively few could immigrate from those countries because they have no family ties in the U.S.[43]

This statement is astonishing and ironic for a number of reasons, one of which is its denial of the state's own history of actively destroying structures of kinship that might tie the United States to Africa through the technologies of slavery. Celler's predictions for the future, however, were also proved incorrect by the significant increases in the number of immigrants from Asia, South America, and the Caribbean basin in subsequent decades. The policy, however, did have profound effects in another way, placing heterosexual family structures even more squarely at the center of patterns of legal immigration and naturalization. Indeed, as James Smith and Barry Edmonston have argued, as a result of this "family reunification" policy, "compared with native-born [Americans] of the same age, new immigrants are more likely to be married and are less likely to be divorced, widowed, or separated"; "family ties clearly dominate [the reasons for immigration], accounting in 1995 for two-thirds of admissions."[44] The more recent policy of "family reunification" in U.S. immigration and naturalization law has brought to the surface many of the ideological goals that were implicit in the 1952 INA while simultaneously masking the continuing salience of race to U.S. immigration and naturalization policy. Although the legislators who designed the 1952 law did not explicitly link homosexuality and adultery as similar types of prohibited conduct and status, it is not difficult to see how these exclusions fit coherently into a national narrative about normative sexuality: both exclusions reinforce the state's investment in constructing potential citizens as monogamous, heterosexual, and married (or marriageable). The emphasis on monogamy and heterosexuality in immigration and naturalization law can be understood as part of a larger cultural and political emphasis on sexual discipline and the promotion of the nuclear family after World War II, an ideological vision that had economic consequences, since the nuclear family form played a necessary role in restructuring the postwar economy by expanding consumption of household goods and services.[45]

The 1952 INA and its legislative history tell a particular and powerful story about how models of normative sexuality were enlisted to maintain racist structures in the state's production of citizens during the Cold War era. Despite their relatively brief appearance in the legislative texts concerning immigration and naturalization, exclusions based on adultery and homosexuality served a specific purpose for lawmakers, providing an unspoken logic of blood purification in the absence of the explicit language of race. It is important, however, to clarify the kinds of claims that can be made based on these juridical texts: we cannot necessarily conclude that they were representative of understandings of race and sexuality in American culture more broadly. Further, these changes in federal law did not necessarily reflect the formation of sexual or racial subjectivity during this period, nor do they tell us anything about how these laws were negotiated, at times oppositionally, by those who enforced or were subjected to them. These texts do mark certain key shifts in official discourses about what constituted an embodied "American" citizenry and what language was available for representing it. Although the explicit language of race was losing legitimacy in the eye of the law as a means of excluding potential citizens, the language of sexual pathology and pollution became increasingly available for circumscribing the characteristics of the ideal citizen. The appearance of adultery and homosexuality in the legislative history of the 1952 INA seemed to express an anxious desire to maintain a model of nation bound to citizenship through blood, even, or especially, at a moment when the explicit use of race in the articulation of that model had lost legitimacy.

Notes

1. Notable exceptions include Lisa Duggan, "Queering the State," in *Sex Wars: Sexual Dissent and Political Culture*, ed. Lisa Duggan and Nan D. Hunter (New York: Routledge, 1995), 179–93; M. Jacqui Alexander, "Erotic Autonomy as a Politics of Decolonization: An Anatomy of Feminist and State Practice in the Bahamas Tourist Economy," in *Feminist Genealogies, Colonial Legacies, Democratic Futures*, ed. M. Jacqui Alexander and Chandra Talpade Mohanty (New York: Routledge, 1997), 63–100; and Davina Cooper, *Power in Struggle: Feminism, Sexuality, and the State* (Buckingham, England: Open University Press, 1995). For key studies of nationalism and sexuality, see, for example, Lauren Berlant, *The Queen of America Goes to Washington City: Essays on Sex and Citizenship* (Durham, NC: Duke University Press, 1997); Phillip Brian Harper, Anne McClintock, José Esteban Muñoz, and Trish Rosen, eds., "Queer Transexions of Race, Nation, and Gender," special issue, *Social Text*, no. 52–53 (1997); Andrew Parker, Mary Russo, Doris Sommer, and Patricia Yaeger, eds.,

Nationalisms and Sexualities (New York: Routledge, 1992); Elizabeth A. Povinelli and George Chauncey, eds., "Thinking Sexuality Transnationally," special issue, *GLQ* 5, no. 4 (1999); Eve Kosofsky Sedgwick, "Nationalisms and Sexualities: As Opposed to What?" in her *Tendencies* (Durham, NC: Duke University Press, 1993), 143–53; and Lauren Berlant, "National Brands/National Body: Imitation of Life," in *Comparative American Identities: Race, Sex, and Nationality in the Modern Text,* ed. Hortense J. Spillers (New York: Routledge, 1991), 110–40.

2. Walker Connor, "A Nation Is a Nation, Is a State, Is an Ethnic Group, Is a . . . ," in *Nationalism,* ed. John Hutchinson and Anthony D. Smith (New York: Oxford University Press, 1994), 36. See also Clifford Geertz, *The Interpretation of Cultures* (New York: Basic, 1973).

3. Jacqueline Stevens, *Reproducing the State* (Princeton, NJ: Princeton University Press, 1999), 108, xv.

4. S. Rep. 1515, 81st Cong., 2d sess., 1950, 787. This was the same legislation that was used to deport black Marxist intellectual C. L. R. James, who, while imprisoned on Ellis Island, documented his incarceration and registered his protest to the provisions of this law. See C. L. R. James, *Mariners, Renegades, and Castaways: The Story of Herman Melville and the World We Live In,* with an introduction by Donald E. Pease (Hanover, NH: Dartmouth College, University Press of New England, 2001).

5. It is important not to conflate the removal of the language of race with the end of racism in the law. As I will discuss, the provisions continued a racist logic of exclusion even though they avoided the language of race. As Lisa Lowe points out, "Quotas were not specified by national origin, but through racialized ethnic categories such as 'Chinese.' In other words, the McCarran-Walter Act provided that one hundred ethnic Chinese persons enter annually; these Chinese originated from diverse nations." Lisa Lowe, *Immigrant Acts: On Asian American Cultural Politics* (Durham, NC: Duke University Press, 1996), 193n53.

6. Nancy F. Cott, *Public Vows: A History of Marriage and the Nation* (Cambridge: Harvard University Press, 2000), 133. It is also worth noting, of course, that this law was deeply embedded in both gendered and racialized structures of power. Until 1931, an American woman automatically forfeited her U.S. citizenship if she married a foreign man racially ineligible for immigration and naturalization. See Marian L. Smith, "'Any woman who is now or may hereafter be married . . .': Women and Naturalization, ca. 1802–1940," *Prologue: Quarterly of the National Archives and Records Administration* 30, no. 2 (Summer 1998): n11, http//www.archives.gov/publications/prologue/summer_1998_women_and_naturalization_1.html.

7. "An Act Supplementary to the Acts in Relation to Immigration," 43rd Cong., 2d sess., March 3, 1875, 141.

8. See Eithne Luibhéid, *Entry Denied: Controlling Sexuality at the Border* (Minneapolis: University of Minnesota Press, 2002), 31–54.

9. Cott, *Public Vows,* 139.

10. However, other less explicit means were sometimes used to police immigrants suspected of homosexuality beginning in the early twentieth century. See Margot Canaday's forthcoming dissertation, "Good Citizens and the Straight State: Citizenship and Sexuality in the United States, 1917–1952" (University of Minnesota).

11. Act of March 26, 1790, ch. 3, § 1, 1 Stat. 103; and Act of January 29, 1795, ch. 20, §§ 1, 2, 1 Stat. 414. For an extensive discussion of this requirement, see Steven L. Strange, "Private Consensual Sexual Conduct and the 'Good Moral Character'

Requirement of the Immigration and Nationality Act," *Columbia Journal of Transnational Law* 14, no. 2 (1975): 357–81.

12. S. Rep. 1515, 81st Cong., 2d sess., 1950, 701. Apparently, before this legislation, courts had already used adultery fairly uniformly as a bar to the establishment of good moral character, but avoided defining precisely what was meant by the term "adultery," which varied from state to state. See Strange, "Private Consensual Sexual Conduct," 365–66.

13. However, the "good moral character" requirement has subsequently been used to exclude aliens on the basis of homosexuality. See Strange, "Private Consensual Sexual Conduct," 372.

14. S. Rep. 1515, 81st Cong., 2d sess., 1950, 337. Robert J. Foss notes that this category seems rarely to have been invoked for excluding aliens. See Foss, "The Demise of the Homosexual Exclusion: New Possibilities for Gay and Lesbian Immigration," *Harvard Civil Rights–Civil Liberties Law Review* 29 (1994): 447.

15. S. Rep. 1515, 81st Cong., 2d sess., 1950, 341.

16. Ibid., 343.

17. Ibid., 345.

18. S. Rep. 1137, 82d Cong., 2d sess., 1952, 9.

19. Foss, "The Demise of the Homosexual Exclusion," 452, 445.

20. Ibid., 456.

21. Mrs. Gordon Robert Phelps Connor, Wausau, Wisconsin, to Hon. H. Brownell, December 7, 1955, RG 85, Acc. 58-A0734, file 56340/100, box 3344, 17WB, 14/3/01, part I, National Archives and Records Administration, Washington, DC.

22. The Cold War association between communism and crises of masculinity and sexuality has been deftly examined by a number of scholars, including, among others, Lee Edelman, "Tea Rooms and Sympathy, or The Epistemology of the Water Closet," in *The Lesbian and Gay Studies Reader,* ed. Henry Abelove, Michèle Aina Barale, and David M. Halperin (New York: Routledge, 1993), 553–74; Robert J. Corber, *Homosexuality in Cold War America: Resistance and the Crisis of Masculinity* (Durham, NC: Duke University Press, 1997); and Michael Rogin, "Kiss Me Deadly: Communism, Motherhood, and Cold War Movies," *Representations* 6 (1984): 1–36.

23. "Employment of Homosexuals and Other Sex Perverts in the U.S. Government," Interim Report, pursuant to S. Res. 280, 81st Cong., 1950. Reprinted in *We Are Everywhere: A Historical Sourcebook of Gay and Lesbian Politics,* ed. Mark Blasius and Shane Phelan (New York: Routledge, 1997), 243–44.

24. Ian F. Haney López, *White by Law: The Legal Construction of Race* (New York: New York University Press, 1996), 1.

25. Quoted in ibid., 43–44.

26. S. Rep. 1137, 82nd Cong., 2d sess., 1952, 40.

27. S. Rep. 1515, 81st Cong., 2d sess., 1950, 371.

28. See David M. Reimers, *Still the Golden Door: The Third World Comes to America,* 2nd ed. (New York: Columbia University Press, 1992); and Lowe, *Immigrant Acts,* 193n53. On the persistence of policies of racial exclusion, even in the wake of the eventual repeal of national origins quotas, see Eithne Luibhéid, "The 1965 Immigration and Nationality Act: An 'End' to Exclusion?" *positions* 5, no. 2 (1997): 501–22. On the "invention" of national origins and the implications of this policy for the deployment of race in immigration and naturalization law, see Mae M. Ngai, "The

Architecture of Race in American Immigration Law: A Reexamination of the Immigration Act of 1924," *Journal of American History* 86, no. 1 (1999): 67–92.

29. C. L. R. James, *Mariners, Renegades, and Castaways*, 13.

30. Rachel Buff, "Internal Frontiers, Transnational Politics, 1945–65: Im/Migration Policy as World Domination," in *Postcolonial America*, ed. C. Richard King (Urbana: University of Illinois Press, 2000), 137. Buff takes an innovative and insightful approach to the 1952 INA, demonstrating not only how it furthered an isolationist foreign policy, but also how it coincided with and reinforced a federal "Termination policy" toward American Indian land claims within U.S. borders.

31. S. Rep. 1137, part 2, 82d Cong., 2d sess., 1952, 5.

32. "Revision of Laws Relating to Immigration, Naturalization, and Nationality—Veto Message," H. Doc. 520, *Congressional Record* 98, part 6, 82d Cong., 2d sess., June 27, 1952, 8254.

33. "A Wise Veto," *New York Times*, June 26, 1952.

34. S. Rep. 1515, 81st Cong., 2d sess., 1950, 343. The 1917 law added "persons of constitutional psychopathic inferiority; persons with chronic alcoholism," and broader restrictions on aliens with tuberculosis to existing provisions that denied entry to "[a]ll idiots, imbeciles, feeble-minded persons, epileptics, insane persons; persons who have had more than one attack of insanity at any time previously." An act to regulate the immigration of aliens to, and the residence of aliens in, the United States (1917), 39 Stat. 874, sec. 3.

35. Interestingly, the earlier legislation had provided different rationales for exclusion depending on whether the medical condition was physical or mental, a distinction that revealed how eugenic policy trumped economic concerns. Originally, medical exclusions were justified on the grounds that "physical defects" would interfere with the potential immigrant's ability to make a living. However, people considered to have mental defects were not excluded on the grounds that they would not be able to support themselves financially; rather, "the real object of excluding the mentally defective is to prevent the introduction into the country of strains of mental defect that may continue and multiply through succeeding generations, irrespective of the immediate effect thereof on earning capacity." S. Rep. 1515, 81st Cong., 2d sess., 1950, 338. The quote is from S. Rep. 352, 64th Cong., 1st sess., 1916, 5.

36. Tony Tanner, *Adultery in the Novel: Contract and Transgression* (Baltimore, MD: The Johns Hopkins University Press, 1979), 12.

37. "adulterate, *v.*³" in *Oxford English Dictionary*, ed. J. A. Simpson and E. S. C. Weiner, 2nd ed. (Oxford: Clarendon Press, 1989); *OED Online*, Oxford University Press (http://80-dictionary.oed.com.proxy2.library.uiuc.edu/cgi/entry/00003154).

38. Ursula Vogel, "Whose Property? The Double Standard of Adultery in Nineteenth-Century Law," in *Regulating Womanhood: Historical Essays on Marriage, Motherhood, and Sexuality*, ed. Carol Smart (New York: Routledge, 1992), 148.

39. My thinking about these issues has been enriched by discussions with Chantal Nadeau about the "hygienic nation" within a Canadian context, particularly her manuscript, "*Droit de sang, droit de sexe:* Heredity and Queer Politics," presented at the annual meeting of the American Studies Association, Washington, DC, November 10, 2002. See also Berlant's discussion of "hygienic governmentality" in *The Queen of America*, 175.

40. For excellent overviews of this history, see Foss, "The Demise of the Homosexual Exclusion."

41. As recently as 2001, an applicant for naturalization was rejected under the provision of "good moral character" because of a (mistaken) finding of adultery in his past. See Jon Kamman, "Citizenship Denial Called Mix-up over Adultery Claim," *Arizona Republic,* April 27, 2001.

42. James P. Smith and Barry Edmonston, eds., *The New Americans: Economic, Demographic, and Fiscal Effects of Immigration* (Washington, DC: National Academy Press, 1997), 38.

43. *Congressional Record,* August 25, 1965, 21812; quoted in Reimers, *Still the Golden Door,* 74. As Reimers notes, some who opposed the policy also recognized its intent. The Japanese American Citizens League (JACL), for instance, noted that "although the immigration bill eliminated race as a matter of principle, in actual operation immigration will still be controlled by the now discredited national origins system and the general pattern of immigration which exists today will continue for many years yet to come." *Congressional Record,* September 20, 1965, 24503; quoted in Reimers, *Still the Golden Door,* 73.

44. Smith and Edmonston, *The New Americans,* 56, 68.

45. For a detailed discussion of these shifts, see, for example, David M. Lowe, *The Body in Late-Capitalist USA* (Durham, NC: Duke University Press, 1995), 93–103.

CHAPTER FIVE

The Traffic in My Fantasy Butch

Sex, Money, Race, and the Statue of Liberty

Erica Rand

It's obvious to me that the Statue of Liberty is one hot butch. Her outfit, I know, doesn't really suit her. Yet there's something sexy about the way her butchness shows through anyway. You can tell, for instance, despite all that drapery drag, that her hips would never swing side to side. She'd stride or saunter and then plant her feet in that I'll-move-when-I'm-ready way, alert for any encroachment, yet confident that no one would dare to try. Liberty's the kind of butch who makes her muscles evident without ever looking like she's showing them off. Her calves are visibly stunning. Her torch arm, thrusting for over a century now, cannot be anything less than spectacularly endowed. As this photograph with the guy standing small in her flames suggests, she promises to reward any size queen. Those fingers, nicely rough in some places and smooth in others, look strong and flexible holding that torch, which, if you think about it, is one serious power tool—an activist power tool, wielded for liberty. Imagine what else she might be wielding, thrusting, planning. The designer of the New York Liberty's team logo offers one possibility, as Liberty, in characteristic WNBA butch glory, punches her flames-turned-basketball into the air. Once you get into that erotic space, the possibilities abound.

I proffer this vision and invitation against a different direction in butched-up Liberty that has gotten much more play than the likes of mine since the events of September 11, 2001. Liberty, someone suggested to me, had shrunk over the years as vertical majesty migrated to other parts of the New York skyline; it wasn't so big anymore, or such a big

Figure 5.1. Charlie DeLeo, keeper of the flame, on top of the Statue of Liberty's flame, July 1994. Vincent DiPietro, National Park Service.

deal.[1] Now Liberty's taller and tougher to enable her to stand in for, and to avenge, the missing World Trade Center towers, which themselves, it sometimes seems, changed in conceptual size, beginning to loom larger once physically demolished. The most benevolent type of post-9/11 butch Liberty can be seen in a sign purchased from a New York City street vender in late 2001. Designed to hang from a car's rear window, with the plastic diamond shape and suction cup retained from the genre's "Baby on Board" origins, it features the phrase "America Stands Tall" superimposed on an abstracted stars-and-stripes motif and next to an image of the statue. The thick, elongated letters of "Tall," while ironically downscaling the statue, convey the will to endow Liberty with phallic oomph and stature. Two widely circulated cultural products put Liberty's torch arm to more sinister thrusting. In Toby Keith's 2002 lyrics to "Courtesy of the Red, White, and Blue (The Angry American)," while Uncle Sam added names to his list, presumably a hit list, and "Mother Freedom" prepared to ring her bell, "The Statue of Liberty / Started shakin' her fist," each action a herald of revenge against the unspecified enemy who, having "sucker punch[ed]" the nation, must face the consequences: "You'll be sorry that you messed with / The US of A / 'Cause we'll put a boot in your ass / It's the American way."[2] If the boot's destination seems to place Liberty's fist on the path to sexualized revenge, such connections are less understated in an image easily found on the Web since soon after 9/11 that shows Liberty giving the finger, with the text "We're Coming, Motherfuckers" written in the blue sky next to her arm.[3] The finger and the phrasing, suggesting that the (perverted) fucker will become the (still, if differently, perverted) fucked, makes Liberty the symbol and agent of a punishment marked implicitly here, but explicitly elsewhere, in the sodomizing vengeance genre popular at the time, as feminizing, homosexualizing, and consequently humiliating.

How does popular culture contribute to constructing, circulating, and validating normative ideologies of citizenship? As Jasbir K. Puar and Amit S. Rai point out, post-9/11 vengeance imagery in popular culture pointed to contradictions and consistencies, both within and between registers of representation and practice. Made during a period in which the United States was also being depicted as feminist and gay-friendly in relation to Afghanistan, depictions of vengeance as the fag-making or fag-bashing of Bin Laden and others came with a documented increase in violence against queers, especially queers of color, that the visual and textual rhetoric could well be considered to have incited.[4] Worth noting as well is how much that "We're Coming" was on target. "We" were indeed coming, with impending U.S. invasions that depended for popular support partly on the same elision of geographic or political specification—not that more cogent connections would have justified them—on which the legibility of "motherfuckers," "sucker punch," and,

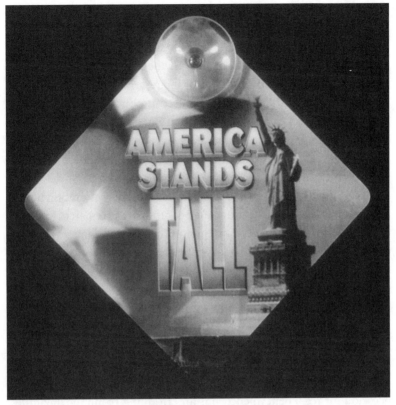

Figure 5.2. "America Stands Tall," decoration for an automobile's rear window, 2001. Photograph: Kathryn Lattanzi.

in fact, "we" depended, too. I note these connections not to suggest direct causality, as if image X propelled action Y, but to suggest ways that "dominant structures, practices, and effects," as Lawrence Grossberg puts it, "circulat[e] around and determin[e] each other."[5] Popular culture demands study, then, because it informs, and informs about, the actions, policies, and practices that inform on popular culture as well.

This essay considers the knotty meanings about sex, gender, sexuality, money, race, nation, migration, and U.S. citizenship that piled up around the Statue of Liberty during an earlier period: the years around 1986. An important year for both the ceremonial and legal construction of U.S. immigration systems and ideologies, 1986 included Liberty Weekend, a three-day extravaganza around the Fourth of July to unveil the statue's centennial restoration. My interest in this topic arose when I noticed the use of sexual metaphor to attach the taint of seedy commerce to the activities of the Statue of Liberty–Ellis Island Foundation, Inc. (SOLEIF), which oversaw the restoration of both monuments. Among various moneymaking strategies, SOLEIF sold sponsorships and product licenses that many viewed as ill-suited to ennoble the statue's image. Stroh's, for $3 million, became the official beer of the restoration; Eveready turned the torch into a flashlight. Other licensed products included the now famous green foam crown, Liberty Edition Harley-Davidsons, and "Spirit of America Air Freshener," in the shape of the statue and "impregnated with a 'fresh citrus flavor.'"[6] In the context of this commercial activity arose a recurring practice, in a wide variety of sources, of describing allegedly dubious fund-raising practices for Liberty's restoration by saying that she had been prostituted. As I continued my research, I came to see this scandal of sex meeting money at the body of immigration's so-called lady as obstructing the view of other matters about sex, money, and race circling around the statue's centennial that really ought to be considered scandalous, but frequently don't seem to be. I consider three in this essay: the Supreme Court's un-Liberty-like ruling, right before Liberty Weekend, to uphold state antisodomy laws challenged in *Bowers v. Hardwick;* the story of a twelve-year-old refugee who couldn't keep her prize in a Statue of Liberty essay contest because its cash value threatened her family's eligibility for public assistance, an irony spun as the occasion for regal benevolence, not for critiquing economic inequities; and the burial, under official rhetoric linking Liberty to "tempest-tost" immigrants through Ellis Island, of the likelihood that honoring the abolition of slavery was one inspiration for the statue.

My approach to the statue, then, involves queer moves in content. Looking at the place of sexualities in various constructions of U.S. citizenship that were staged around Liberty Weekend, I argue that this meaning making cannot be studied without attending to sexual issues marked both queer and (purportedly) straight, as well as to their involvement with economic and racial hierarchies. I also use analytic and expository strategies that enact what can be termed "queer moves." One problem with presenting a relatively linear argument about how meanings knot and pile up is that the form of the argument belies its content. This essay, while nonetheless advancing an argument that, I hope, readers can follow easily, attempts to tweak the linear flow with variations in some features of academic writing that ordinarily remain standard. The tone changes, as does the relation to sources, the degree of investment or detachment, and the play of invention and analysis. Thus, for instance, a fictional scenario that imagines Liberty taking charge of her own relation to sex work abuts a more formal exposition of ideological premises involved in picturing Liberty in sexual commerce.

In addition, by offering extended comments on a few topics in the mix around Liberty's restoration instead of trying to catalog them exhaustively, I intend to advocate for an approach that, instead of arguing for one particular reading of an icon—Liberty *is* a hot butch—or a fixed list of indispensable referents, excavates the foundations, conditions, ingredients, contexts, and alternatives to such meaning making. Henry Giroux suggests that perhaps more significant than how audiences interpret cultural products may be the way that "some ideas, meanings, and messages under certain political positions become more highly valued as representations of reality than others—and, further, how these representations assume the force of ideology by making an appeal to common sense while at the same time shaping political policies and programs that serve very specific interests."[7] As Susana Peña documents in her essay for this volume, which concerns gay men who came to the United States from Cuba during the Mariel boatlift, policies and programs are only part of the issue. Regimes of visibility and silencing, promulgated by the state, the media, individuals, and communities, make histories that affect people's lives in extremely varied ways, from defining criminality to internalizing codes of behavior.[8] The making of national histories is the subject of this essay.

Butch Lubrication

Since I began the essay by contrasting my taste for Liberty's erotic charms to dominant habits of using her butchness to endorse sexualized violence, I want to emphasize before proceeding that I am far from the only person to associate her with erotic pleasures. Of course, takes on Liberty are often hard to read. Who's to say what's going on when people extol the Lady? What does it mean, for instance, that when the game show *Family Feud*—"100 people surveyed, top five answers on the board"—asked people in 2000 to name something associated with the statue, 58 chose the "torch" ahead of "New York" (15), "freedom" (10), "Lady Liberty" (6), and "Ellis Island" (5).[9] Does it mean that 58 people see that flaming torch like I see it, or that the few who conceived of her as one glorious female saw a Lady above all? Yet among numerous indirections in expression are hints of Liberty's turned-on fans. Terms like "in love" or "my girlfriend" that might reflect erotic fantasy come up not infrequently in immigrant narratives, and little eruptions occur in odd places. In the quite staid *Dear Miss Liberty*, a collection of letters sent with donations for the restoration, the author of a prose poem suddenly tells his "beautiful Lady" that "Your freedom is the sweetest, most succulent fruit that any being of this earth could ever hope to pick."[10] In *The Cat Who Escaped from Steerage*, a children's novel about immigration through Ellis Island, the grandmother mistakes Liberty for a woman indecently on display in her nightgown.[11] Although the scene's humor hinges on the idea that grandma, entrenched in the Old World and frequently confused lately, is offended by the slightest hint of sexual display (an idea underpinned, no doubt, by stereotypes of old people as nonsexual), I like to think of her instead as hip to Liberty's erotic charge.

Liberty has other queer fans, too. In *Icky and Kathy Find Liberty* (1999), a short film by Kathy High, pubescent twin girls, turned on by the Statue of Liberty, masturbate together. A cartoon at the beginning of *Betty and Pansy's Severe Queer Review of New York* invites readers to "Take Liberty From Behind." Depending on how/if one codes anal pleasure—does it have a bit of a fag aura no matter who's doing it?—this could be seen as one confirmation from another direction of my sense of Liberty's sex/gender queerness.[12] (I realize here that one might also interpret "take" to imply nonconsensual force, but, given its common appearance also to describe or demand consensual sex, I want to leave room here for a reading of anal penetration to signal other than the rape, degradation, and punishment that it designates in the examples I cited earlier. Homohatred cannot be permitted to evacuate possibilities of pleasure.) Another sex/gender queering comes from a queer punk T-shirt that I heard about, which pictures Liberty showing a penis under that dress with the title "America's Hardcore."

Yet I tend to find my erotic appreciation of Liberty as butch to be far to the side of common readings. Many people apparently mistake her lack of feminine wiles for sexual disinterest, abstinence, or, at least, decorum; viewing her as matron, mother, or spinster ("Miss Liberty"); drawing, it seems often, on the unhappy traditions in which those lack sexual content. Others register her masculinity without knowing quite what to do with it. A few immigrants believed when told that the statue represented Christopher Columbus.[13] A more recent observer, noting her lack of "feminine qualities," called her "gender neutral," "an armed non-woman with whom men would certainly prefer not to mess."[14] Marvin Trachtenberg, whose monograph on the statue was revised for the centennial, also imagined her ready to take on manly men, although it's unclear whether he envisioned her as comrade or lover. Boldly claiming to know what "the nineteenth-century eye would undoubtedly have imagined beneath *Liberty*'s thick antique drapery," he saw viewers envisioning "a characteristic academic nude...large boned, massively curved, substantial and severe, with few traces of delicate femininity, altogether a fit companion for the iron men who dominated the age." To illustrate his hypothesis, Trachtenberg reproduces a painting of a naked woman, representing Truth, who stands with her weight shifted so that one hip juts dramatically out to the side.[15] What could he be thinking? Liberty doesn't move her hips that way.

Knowing that few see what I do doesn't diminish my appreciation. Erotic taste is diverse; that's good. Besides, watching others flail around, I can simply revel in my talents as a connoisseur of butch. I also understand the challenge of getting beyond Liberty's dress-like garb as well as ubiquitous cultural directives to keep the scary unruliness of sex from tainting models of political virtue, or what Linda Zerelli well calls "the risk of the female body set loose in the public sphere."[16] (To these ends, Liberty was deliberately designed with the disheveled, décolleté barricade-charger in Delacroix's famous *Liberty Leading the People* [1830] as an antimodel.) For those who know that Liberty's sculptor Frédéric-Auguste Bartholdi modeled her, at least partly, after his mother, Charlotte, other taboos may be at work.

For Sale

Nor is my sense of Liberty as a commanding activist babe shaken by something that would seem to shake others: the knowledge that time with Liberty or her image can be purchased, a phenomenon frequently described when it is criticized, particularly around the restoration, in terms of prostitution. In 1983, early into the restoration project, Michael Kinsley, a *New Republic* commentator, punctuated his argument that tax dollars instead of corporate dollars should fund it by asking, "Who wouldn't pay a dollar a person to keep Miss Liberty from becoming a high-priced tart?" Two years later, Garnet Chapin, then a recently fired former employee of the Department of the Interior who had worked for the director of the National Park Service as liaison to the Statue of Liberty/Ellis Island project, imagined her working the streets. Commenting on unseemly competition among corporations for sponsorship spots, he said, "If she's sold to the highest bidder, it's not unlike a whore who's being pimped on the sidewalk." A *Wall Street Journal* piece, commenting on corporate sponsors using her image in advertising, argued more vaguely that "The price for survival should not be her virtue."[17] In the left press, the *Nation* also hinted at sexual sales in titling an exposé on the restoration financing "The Selling of Miss Liberty," sacrificing feminist basics (shouldn't the *Nation* by 1985 be addressing Liberty as "Ms."?) to invoke a maiden turned out.[18]

One more direction in prostitution metaphors involves a dirty joke played for serious. Trachtenberg, derisively labeling feminists "perhaps the most unthinking" of all the statue's appropriators, counts among what makes Liberty an unsuitable icon that "for a fee she is open to all for entry and exploration from below."[19] Barbara A. Babcock and John J. Macaloon revived Trachtenberg's point in the early 1990s. While they criticized Trachtenberg's attack on feminists in their essay "Everybody's Gal" (named after Reagan's term for Liberty), they nonetheless grant "the reality" of the access situation that he describes, noting that, as a result, "it is possible to view Liberty as a prostitute, although she seems to be a mother."[20] Unlike Trachtenberg, Babcock and Macaloon don't seem to think that working as a prostitute affects one's feminist credentials. But their conceptual space to remain generous toward Liberty, while also seeing her as open for business, depends, further reading suggests, on understanding Liberty to be without agency where money for her services is involved. They pick up on this theme later when they go on to describe their own feminist interpretive project as something of a small consolation for collective helplessness in the face of female victimization: "Clearly, we cannot control the traffic in women, and it is obviously futile to struggle against female objectification, but we can do something about the interpretation thereof."[21] They also borrow another writer's term, "statuary rape," as a lead-in to a paragraph on the trying of "her dignity . . . in the name of raising money to repair the ravages of time and to celebrate her birthday."[22]

Meanings about sex and money pile on, inform, and alter meanings about sex, money, and more. They also depend on what's already available—in the air, in the media, in the archive, in various sense-making contexts. The motif of Liberty turned prostitute came easily, it seems, to many people, and made it into a wide variety of print sources. Consequently, it came to me easily later; not looking for it at all, I found it all over. I also found repeated coverage of the related matter about those who would pull Liberty into the realm of the trashy by making unseemly use of her image or bringing tasteless extravagance and inappropriate entertainment to her party, like three hundred Jazzercizers and two hundred Elvis impersonators.[23]

My goal here isn't to condemn these texts. I could hardly do so unhypocritically—I can't resist the material either. I'm fascinated by the decisions made by Hamilton Projects, SOLEIF's licensing representative, which turned down requests to license Statue of Liberty lingerie, whips and chains, pet collars, toilet seat covers, caskets, guns, knives with blades over three inches long, and a pictorial tribute in a pornographic magazine to "Love in America," but did approve snuffboxes, barbecue grills, fishing rods, shower curtains, dart boards, and swizzle sticks.[24] These lists virtually compel promiscuous dissemination and invite luxuriating in what remains to be imagined: the objects, many now out of production; the rationale for inclusions/exclusions, alternately obvious and odd; the people deciding. Liberty on the patio with snuff but no kink—or was the kink on the patio for the people in licensing? In 1985, Mrs. America (the kink on the patio?) rode with Liberty's old torch and a giant picture of her head formed in flowers on the Hilton Hotels float in the Tournament of Roses parade.[25] The details of Liberty put out for profit can support the conjuring of many scenarios.

But some of them are more common than others. Interestingly, uses of the Liberty-turned-prostitute motif, despite coming from various political positions, nonetheless turn on certain shared conceptions. Trachtenberg's sarcastic attribution of Liberty's spread-skirt policy to her own bad politics and Kinsley's warning that Liberty could "becom[e] a high-priced tart," which suggests a woman needing rescue from her own bad impulses, both envision Liberty participating in sexual commerce perhaps by choice, but if so unthinkingly. The others all invoke Liberty as a victim, acted upon only—abused, pimped, trafficked. Why not imagine a scenario more like the following:

> Liberty wants to treat herself to some body work and a big party for
> her 100th birthday. Thinking about how to raise money, she considers
> the options available to a woman with limited vocational training or

credentializing degrees: "I need to protect my hands and wrists if I want to keep holding that torch, so jobs with repetitive chores like typing and minute assembly work are out. I don't want to work in the snack shop downstairs. Maybe I'll go back to sex work. I know I'm good at it. Besides, last time I chose this form of labor, I found it enjoyable on the best days, and, on many of the worst, more tolerable than my earlier job in the sweat shop. This pays better, too. If I can't make what I want that way, I'll model for ads. I hate standing around under those lights, but I can make a bundle in a few hours."

That scenario, I admit, involves selective labor realism. Besides throwing in an anachronistic allusion to repetitive stress injury, I had Liberty knowledgeably assess the job possibilities she was rejecting within a range constricted by gender and class oppression, yet did not require her to articulate how those would affect the work she chose to pursue. But my point is partly that all the sex talk above is selective, even when invoking purportedly literal truths. The "reality" simply is not that "for a fee" some "she" is "open to all." For one thing, such a statement evades the fact that the fee just to get to Liberty Island, now $10 per adult and $4 per child, prohibits access to all. It also obscures the additional resources required, which vary according to location, work flexibility, transportation needs, field trip money, and so on, as well as the social and economic inequities that differential access to them may indicate. Nor was the reality ever that all people, once at Liberty Island, had equal access to the inside. After the events of September 11, 2001, the National Park Service closed the statue's interior to all visitors. Before that, entry was effectively limited to people who could deal with waiting in line outside, possibly for several hours and in difficult weather; getting all the way up in her required the ability to climb stairs.

If open access to Liberty is not factually true, neither is it metaphorically as transparent as "the reality" would suggest. While their meaning is presented as obvious, all the scenarios I cited depend on both metaphorical transfers and ideological premises. The metaphorical transfers: entering a representation of a woman is like entering a woman; selling the image of a statue of a woman is like selling the statue of a woman is like selling the sexual services of a woman; the statue, being inanimate, is like a helpless person. The selectivity of metaphor-making stands out here when one considers that the statue, weighing over 450,000 pounds, might well be imagined as a person who could dictate the terms in any interaction—it takes a lot of work to view this huge figure as wholly victimized. The ideological premises: the sale of sexual services is generally bad, dirty sex paid for with dirty money; it degrades the person providing the services and/or is permanently transformative (once a prostitute, never again, or simultaneously, Miss Liberty); it's more degrading and transformative than any other sort of labor one might perform no matter what the working conditions; one would have to be forced or deluded to do it, or, at least, to do it and remain a sympathetic figure worthy of aid if circumstances warrant it; it's more about morality than labor rights.

I wrote my own tale of Liberty's entry into sexual commerce to highlight, by proceeding from some contrasting assumptions, the connective work required to make sense of the ones I cited. This work generally goes without saying partly because it entails the marshalling of certain dominant attitudes about sex work. Some of these attitudes have found life in immigration laws. Laws against the immigration of prostitutes date back to 1875, and in 1910 prostitution became one of the first and only crimes for which an immigrant could be deported at any time after arrival; one could enter the United States at age two and be deported twenty (or sixty) years later. As Wendy Chapkis points out in her discussion of the recent Trafficking Victims' Protection Act of 2000, current laws still pit sexual agency against virtue. The definition of which migrants are covered under the act depends precisely on valuing lack of sexual agency or foreknowledge; no matter how badly one might have been misled or treated, any consent to enter the sex industry disqualifies migrants from assistance.[26]

But while these attitudes may be widely intelligible and easy to grab, that doesn't make applying them to Liberty's money matters a simple production. Besides depending on ideas about sexual commerce, images of Liberty defiled by certain commercial transactions turn on various understandings about gender, sex, and sexuality, about various economic players and practices, about the nation for which the Statue of Liberty is meant to stand. Is Liberty a hot butch or Lady Liberty, and what constitutes either of these? Is Lee Iacocca a hero or a slimeball? Is it OK to have an official hot dog (Oscar Meyer) of the restoration? Is government funding cleaner than private funding? What makes them dirty? Are they ever clean? Is sex ever? Are women ever? When?

Can personifications of U.S. ideals ever be conceptualized as having sexual agency—for free or otherwise? Lauren Berlant, who sees a "porno-graphic structure" as well as sometimes sexual content in the political deployment of female icons, existing to be used as desired, suggests that gender-coded passivity, partly projecting as immobility in the case of the Statue of Liberty, is key: "when the body of the woman is employed symbolically to regulate or represent the field of national fantasy, her positive 'agency' lies in her ability to be narrativized."[27] (Or as Mobil Cor-poration puts it in an essay-style Liberty Weekend ad titled "Confessions of a Lover," which portrays Liberty as something of a high-toned serial monogamist with exacting standards: "She is a silent figure, yet based on eloquence.")[28] Maybe, then, to the extent that Liberty's gender func-tions as a stable ground for narration—which, I have argued, is not always the case—metaphorical habits work against interpreting Liberty, or her allegorical sisters, as grabbing the sex that serves her for pleasure or profit.

One might argue, however, slightly differently, that such gender-coded passivity concerning figures like Liberty is a metaphorical habit that re-quires work to sustain. Jacqui Alexander points out that because the state uses the heterosexual nuclear family physically to reproduce and ideologically to legitimate itself, and because "loyalty to the nation as citizen is perennially colonized within reproduction and heterosexual-ity," women's sexual agency and erotic autonomy, frequently "cathected onto the body of the prostitute and the lesbian," carry a threat to the national order.[29] Writing about state practice in the Bahamas during the last decades, Alexander demonstrates the complex work of the state to censure and contain such autonomy, even sometimes within the alleged purpose of bolstering women's rights within the heterosexual family.

In the United States, one example among many supporting the appli-cability of Alexander's point lies in the early and continuing legislation I cited against the entry of prostitutes. Another, from the period of Lib-erty's restoration, can be found in the Immigration Marriage Fraud Amendments (IMFA) passed in November 1986. The IMFA was designed to curtail a practice that the INS alleged but ill-demonstrated to be huge by which immigrants contracted marriages with U.S. citizens solely to take advantage of spousal reunification policies that enabled them to bypass quota restrictions and shortened the waiting period for citizen-ship.[30] The congressional hearings on the IMFA repeatedly reaffirm "the value placed on [heterosexual] marriage and the unity of the nuclear family" (4) in immigration law without ever justifying why benefits should accrue to people who can demonstrate such ties. They imply in the process that people who don't have them are less desirable or less worthy neighbors and appropriately disadvantaged in seeking long-term residence or citizenship. The hearings also recapitulate the opposition that underpins much immigration policy between virtuous women who violate social and sexual norms only as victims without agency—lured into marriages by "smooth-talking aliens" (14)—and evil women who manipulate sexual and social arrangements for their own profit.

How these categories and the issues at stake are racialized, ethnically marked, and economically specified comes through in the report's examples. One involves "sham marriages between illegal Pakistanis and welfare mothers" (16). A derisive expression for women needing economic assistance, connoting profligates or fools in sex and thrift who sometimes deliberately reproduce for a bigger government allotment, the term "welfare mothers" could also safely be expected to call up images of black women despite statistics to the contrary about who received Aid to Families with Dependent Children. Another example concerns a woman, a U.S. citizen of Indian descent, who enters into an arranged marriage "in keeping with the common practice in India," as Alan Simpson, the senator running the hearings, glossed the situation. She then discovered that her husband, a resident and citizen of India, married her only to bring over his own family and "build the empire," a phrase Simpson reiterates several times to underscore the horror of such an invasion. While both parties in this case might be described as racially and ethnically similar, Simpson's comments imply that we might view the wife's distress over "the empire" to signal the whitening and civilizing effects of U.S. citizenship. Asians, he explains, in one of many allusions by various hearing participants to the notion that "immigration marriages often barely resemble the common interpretation of a nuclear family" (10), have a different understanding of family than the "'cohesive family' or 'nuclear family'" in the minds of the "American citizen" (42–44).[31] Consenting to an arranged marriage, but horrified and victimized by her husband's empire building, the woman is marked by her relation to family formations as both Asian and not Asian, alien and citizen, although her hold on the latter terms seems much less stable—hardly surprising given dominant racial politics in which U.S. citizens with darker-than-labeled-as-white skin, regardless of links by birth or tradition to areas outside the United States, frequently struggle to exercise the rights of citizenship. Her status is further enhanced, however, I would argue, by her apparently comfortable premarital economic status. This arranged marriage is not for love, but it is not (ostensibly) for money either. The disinterest of the IMFA's architects in poor women may be seen in the disastrous consequences of its enforcement provisions for immigrant women rendered vulnerable to abuse by economic dependence on their husbands; the law has already been amended several times to try to lessen this effect.[32]

As the IMFA hearings underscore, oppositions that separate good women who support the nation from those—threatening virtually by definition—who act as independent sexual agents depend on values and practices concerning sexuality, economics, race, and ethnicity. While I have been focusing in this section especially on Liberty's gender, in the next sections I consider incidents and issues around the statue that indicate how the traffic in Liberty both occludes and depends on homophobic, classist, and racist structures.

Bad Party

On June 30, 1986, just before Liberty Weekend, the Supreme Court issued its decision in *Bowers v. Hardwick*. The decision upheld the rights of states to criminalize what the decision called "homosexual sodomy," although the Georgia law upheld by the Court indiscriminately banned all acts involving "the sex organs of one person and the mouth or anus of another."[33] (As Janet Halley points out, heterosexuals are excused from the verdict primarily by silence, the decision's refusal to mention them.)[34] Now, a national ruling against the right of adults to engage with each other in private consensual sex acts clearly has relevance to the weekend's themes of freedom, rights, and liberty, especially since the United States was being promoted in conjunction with Liberty Weekend as the primary place to enjoy them. Indeed, Chief Justice Warren Burger oversaw a ceremony designed to signal just that—several days after his absolutely superfluous concurring statement to the *Bowers* decision, added solely, he said, "to underscore [his] view that in constitutional terms there is no such thing as a fundamental right to commit homosexual sodomy."[35] On July 3 at Ellis Island, he administered the oath to several hundred immigrants from about one hundred countries, representing thirty-one states, which they recited simultaneously with tens of thousands connected by satellite TV or audio hookup from forty-one other sites, including the Orange Bowl.[36] The verdict itself got major coverage, and if writers covering the weekend needed a nudge to note the gross irony of its timing, activists provided it. On July 4, thousands of people, estimated at six thousand by the *Advocate,* marched in protest from Greenwich Village to Battery Park, the site of some Liberty Weekend festivities. Signs like "Miss Liberty? You Bet I Do" and "Lady Liberty, Light the Torch for Us, Too" made the connections visible.[37]

Yet the case's relevance to Liberty Weekend received little attention in the mainstream press. Articles in the *New York Times* about protests against the verdict cited less pointed connections,[38] and few articles devoted to Liberty weekend mentioned it at all. After being reminded of the verdict's timing by a text on gay activism that I was reading outside the context of this project,[39] I searched the LexisNexis database for July and August 1986 using the keyword "Liberty" along with either "gay," "Hardwick," or "sodomy." I found only six articles, four of which appeared in one paper, the *Los Angeles Times.* Of the six, only one, in the *Times* Opinion section, is an article about the case, which, without mentioning Liberty Weekend specifically, explains the "subtle cruelty of the timing" involved in releasing the verdict just before Independence Day.[40] The others, which very briefly mention the demonstration against the verdict in more general accounts of Liberty Weekend, show little interest in the liberties under assault. None use the key terms "consenting," "private," or "adult" that are necessary, especially given the homophobic conjurings commonly evoked by putting "homosexual" and "sodomy" together, to convey the decision's reach and limits. Two don't even mention antisodomy laws: the *Toronto Star* misleadingly mentions "yet another Gay Pride demonstration" among the downtown spectacles and amusements, while a *Los Angeles Times* piece lists "monitor[ing] a gay-rights demonstration" among police tasks for the weekend, along with finding lost children, responding to accidents, and "coax[ing] drunk spectators off rooftops."[41] Far from addressing or even naming the protestors' charges alleging state-sanctioned anti-gay bigotry, the writer portrays a social landscape in which police function as benevolent agents of the benevolent state, saving children and drunks from themselves and the public from gay activists. And while two articles cite activist invocations of liberty, all nonetheless present the protests primarily as evidence of the general social good: "The crowd was tolerant"; "Police said the protest was broken up peacefully."[42]

These snippets, among other omissions, fail to indicate that all was not peaceful toleration; David Deitcher writes in *The Question of Equality* that "revelers responded to the estimated six thousand queer activists in their midst by bloodying a few noses," "hurling...verbal abuse," and tossing a few firecrackers at them. Nor, of course, do they question whether the protest not disrupting the party should be considered good news.[43] LIBERTY SHOCKER: HIGHEST COURT CALLS CONSENSUAL SEX AT HOME ILLEGAL BUT PEOPLE PARTY ON ANYWAY. Where is that headline? The *New York Times* did run an editorial called "Crime in the Bedroom" against the decision on July 2. But it declined to mention Liberty Weekend, an omission that can be called commission given the editorial under it about the symbolism of the Fourth of July's tall ships and fireworks and, even more relevant, an editorial one day later that, in praising the Supreme Court decisions upholding affirmative action and the voting rights act, calls them an important civics lesson for Reagan on Liberty Weekend.[44] Apparently, the lesson of *Bowers v. Hardwick* is supposed to be that (homo)sex belongs off to the side of Liberty. Of course, that dismissal defines her as well.

Sweet Poverty

Ought-to-be-scandals about money also appear as tidbits of good news in the literature on Liberty's restoration. Four letters in *Dear Miss Liberty* explain small contributions in terms of financial problems related to aging: can't find work, cost of retirement home, life on fixed income made more difficult by job-related loss of vision, and "you understand. I am now 91," as if it should go without explanation that old age brings hard economic times.[45] In the context of the volume, in which the primary criterion for inclusion is clearly "heartwarming," these statements come off as evidence of love for the statue, not as evidence of inexcusable inequities.

Another story about economic inequity that gets folded into touching sentiment concerns a twelve-year-old girl named Hue Cao. A refugee from Vietnam, she was Hawaii's winner in the nationwide state-by-state essay contest on "What the Statue of Liberty Means to Me," a contest named, to add one emotion tugger to another, after Christa McAuliffe, the schoolteacher killed in the explosion of the space shuttle *Challenger*. After Hue Cao won, it turned out that she couldn't keep her prize, a $9,000 new car, because having resources above $1,500 would make her family ineligible to continue receiving public assistance. Moved by the story, the state committee auctioned off the car and started a scholarship fund for her with the money. President Reagan congratulated her personally by phone, someone else bought her family a 1980 white Skylark valued at $1,499, and a rich donor paid for her family to stay at a fancy hotel on Liberty Weekend. Then, introduced by Henry Winkler, "the Fonz" from TV's *Happy Days*, she read her essay at the unveiling ceremony.[46]

Unlike the protests about *Bowers v. Hardwick,* which received only brief, trivializing mainstream press coverage in relation to Liberty Weekend, Hue Cao got a lot of media coverage. The issue here is what kind. Like the image of Liberty as a prostitute, which, regardless of a dominant interpretive trend, could be spun in various and divergent ways, the tale of Hue Cao is interesting partly for the range of economic analyses it could easily support. For example, it might well be interpreted to epitomize the gross inequities of capitalism. Some people struggle to subsist, while some have the money to put up others in expensive hotels (or earn $23.6 million a year in compensation, as Iacocca did from Chrysler in 1986).[47] Or it might be seen to highlight the failure of Reaganomics, which gave tax cuts to the wealthy in 1981 and 1982 on the theory that the benefits of economic opportunities for rich people would "trickle down" to everyone. The situation of being too poor to accept free stuff beautifully illustrates the structural barriers to this hypothesized flow of resources that the term "trickle down" implies to be natural. The spectacle of a heroic refugee on welfare also intrudes into the cast of characters put forth for Liberty Weekend. As the historian Mike Wallace points out in his essay on immigration history at the two sites, the Reagan/Iacocca reading of immigration history presented for the occasion has immigrants—including those who might now be characterized as refugees—making it on their own, with the implication that currently struggling residents of the United States, new migrants and otherwise, should be able to pull themselves up without aid, too.[48] During the year when the Immigration Reform and Control Act, which Reagan signed on November 6, 1986, inscribed several measures to restrict immigrants' eligibility for public assistance,[49] Hue Cao's situation advances the notion, with the emotional nudge of melodrama, not just that public aid for new residents is appropriate but also that current policies to dispense it may be too stingy.

That this interpretation didn't make it to the daily newspapers can be attributed to a number of factors. One, which should not be minimized or belittled, is Hue Cao's own interpretation of her current situation, represented in her prize-winning essay:

> My family and I are from Vietnam. After the war ended, the Communists took over and they were very cruel, stern and ill-tempered. They took away our freedom, and worst of all, they could kill anyone. . . . In 1979, we escaped on a small fishing boat, and I remember how crowded it was before a Navy ship saved us. The Americans provided us with food, shelter and clothing. We wanted to live in America, a land where there is liberty and justice. Every time we saw a picture of the Statue of Liberty, my mother would tell us that *she* is America. America is a place that lends a hand to those in need.[50]

Hue Cao's sense of herself as fortunate is certainly justified and completely understandable, if also ideologically convenient for right-leaning political-economic interpretations. Her linking of communism, privation, and indiscriminate murder on the one hand, and America, relief from need, and freedom on the other, lines up nicely with the common misconception that capitalism is the required economic system of democracy. It obviously appealed to Hawaii's contest judges, who picked it over two thousand other entries.

In addition, dominant themes of Liberty Weekend, besides the one that I mentioned above about immigrants most appropriately struggling to make it, beckon away from interpreting Hue Cao's story as an illustration of inequity. The idea, dramatized in the big naturalization ceremony, that the United States stands in relation to other countries only as a place of shelter from them or a model of freedom for them also finds expression in narrations about Hue Cao, which offer no clue that the United States had any role in Vietnam other than to receive its refugees. The idea that rich people make up with gifts for what the government withholds fits right in with restoration rhetoric, too. At the time, the restorations were touted as the epitome of Reagan's public/ private partnership idea. Tours and texts about both Ellis Island and Liberty Island still frequently explain that "no tax dollars" went into the restorations—with no hint, usually, that the value of privatizing the care of national monuments might be contested, not least because, as a number of people have argued, sponsorship affects the histories told.[51] In addition, although a portion of the restoration donation narrative, far greater than the portion of the restoration money, concerns poor people sending their pennies, much of the funding narrative builds on the idea that sufficient resources for the social good lie in the benevolence of rich people and corporations willing to step in where the government can't, won't, or thinks it shouldn't have to. Add in the obfuscating pathos that often attends gifts from the rich to the poor—as if small windfalls could be a solution to problems caused by inequitable distribution of resources—and it's easy to see how the wonderful fortune bestowed on one fortunate individual might be the winning spin.[52]

I have suggested some ways in which the tale of Hue Cao as an appropriately struggling newcomer to a humane state resonates with a number of dominant Liberty Weekend narratives. It is also built on the dominant account of the statue as a beacon for migrants, which itself depends on the way that discourses about the Lady keep sliding away from the color of skin.

Green Woman, Race Matters

Actually, the statue was in between two green phases on Liberty Weekend, with the first hundred years of copper patination cleaned off and the next batch waiting on the weather. But green suits her quite well on one level because much race talk around the Statue of Liberty hangs out in the company of lines like "I don't care whether you're white, black, red, blue, green, or yellow" that posit colorblindness as a virtue. One example of that position in literal proximity to Liberty occurs in the *New York Times* editorial I mentioned earlier about Reagan getting a "civics" lesson from the Supreme Court on affirmative action and voting rights: "America not only aspires to be a color-blind society, it remains committed to achieving it." Yet if, as this editorial also admits, seeing race is key to fighting racism—one reason among many that one might question blindness to race as the ultimate goal—statue talk is all the more notable for the skin talk that seems repeatedly to get dismissed.

I say dismissed rather than missing deliberately because it certainly exists and is often easy to find. As Juan Perea points out, race issues appeared early in the statue's history, during the initial fund-raising and inauguration when people protested that Liberty hardly raised her torch for everyone. In 1885, for instance, Saum Song Bo, in "A Chinese View of the Statue of Liberty," criticized appeals to Chinese people in the United States for contributions to the statue's pedestal fund given the denial of liberty to Chinese people inherent in the Chinese Exclusion Act of 1882, which prevented most Chinese people from entry, and the harsh treatment of Chinese people in the United States.[53]

Related comments attended Liberty's centennial. In *Enacting Political Culture: Rhetorical Transformations of Liberty Weekend*, David Procter documents, and unadeptly evaluates, extensive commentary in the black press about whether blacks have been included or excluded in the freedoms extolled as American on Liberty Weekend.[54] The issue also got enough mainstream publicity that David Wolper, who produced the extravaganza—and whose previous credits include *Roots, Welcome Back Kotter*, and the L.A. Olympics—was called on to stress that "blacks, too, were immigrants to this country." Jim Haskins, the "Vice Director, Southeast Region of SOLEIF" and author of many books on black history, some for children, including, in 1986, *The Statue of Liberty: America's Proud Lady*, also took on the charges. He showed more respect than Wolper, however, for those who argued that it was negligently thoughtless, at best, to declare the United States a nation of immigrants, a rhetorical move that subsumes forced transport for slavery under voluntary immigration. In a June 1986 piece in *U.S. News and World Report*, Haskins admits a basis for why "some black leaders" declined to support the restoration campaign from the position that "blacks came through the back doors of America—the slave markets of New Orleans and Savannah—not Ellis Island," and notes the "common saying among blacks that she has always had her back to us." But, he states, the abolition of slavery may be part of what inspired Edouard de Laboulaye, the prime mover behind Liberty, to propose the statue. Besides, he suggests, tweaking some much-memorized phrasing from "The New Colossus," Emma Lazarus's poem about the statue, even though "the newest Afro-Americans—Haitians, West Indians, Africans and the wretched refuse of other black countries' teeming shores," are now likely to come through Kennedy Airport, not via boat, those who saw the statue from the plane "must have felt the same swelling of hope as did the shipbound immigrants from Europe."[55]

Hey, black countries have teeming shores with wretched refuse now, too, just like the Europeans did before. In arguing that the poem can newly be applied to black immigrants, Haskins points to something frequently camouflaged by the unmarked language ordinarily used to describe Liberty as the welcomer of immigrants: how race-specific are both this dominant device for explaining the statue's meaning as the "Mother of Exiles" welcoming "huddled masses" and the dominant explanation itself. The racial specificity comes partly from a third link, Ellis Island, that gets attached to the statue and the poem to form a mutually explaining triad. Ellis Island functioned as an immigrant processing, detention, and deportation center from 1892 until 1954, although most of the processing dwindled off after the immigration exclusion laws of 1924. More than twelve million immigrants passed through Ellis Island, primarily immigrants from Europe who were then (e.g., German, English) and/or are now (Irish, Russian, Jewish) generally considered white. It is connected to the statue geographically, as a neighboring island in New York Harbor; administratively, as part of the Statue of Liberty National Monument; and by the massive subsequent publicity around their connection during their restorations in the 1980s, when the founding of SOLEIF linked their financial fates as well. It is connected to the poem, and through it back to the statue, by the much publicized idea that the "huddled masses" in the poem refer to Ellis Island immigrants, although the poem actually preceded the immigration station by a decade, and the statue was not consistently or happily seen to welcome immigrants. Thus, while connections between the statue, the poem, and a certain set of predominantly white immigrants had been well established by the time SOLEIF promoted them in the 1980s, and while people regularly break into a few lines from the "New Colossus" to explain either the statue or the immigration station, articulations of the monuments as a poetically linked unit work to cement a shorter and less fixed conjunction than they often purport to reflect.[56]

If the race content of tying the statue to immigrants depends partly on the particular immigrants referenced through the dominant statue-poem-Ellis trope, it also derives from that triad's erasure of the other referent that Haskins mentions as a possible motivation for Liberty's commission: the desire to commemorate the abolition of slavery. Interestingly, Haskins describes this motive as merely possible in *U.S. News* (suggesting, perhaps, some editorial hedging on the paper's part). In *America's Proud Lady*, he names it a definite motive, but one that, he notes, "Most people do not realize." He repeats the statement on his current Web site, although he distances himself from two further claims about the statue's racial inspirations that have recently found wide circulation through an anonymous e-mail: that the original Statue of Liberty was black, which, the e-mail claims, can be verified by looking at two early clay models in the Museum of the City of New York; and that the statue was commissioned to honor, as the e-mail puts it, "the part that Black soldiers played in the ending of Black African Bondage in the United States." This argument is attributed to the book *The Journey of the Songhai People,* which the e-mail incorrectly seems to claim that Haskins wrote when it was actually written by members of an Afrocentric organization, the Pan African Federation Organization.[57]

I can only gesture here to the cultural politics involved in the debate over the race origins of Liberty. Their complexity can begin to be indicated by noting that the misattribution to Haskins, identified in the e-mail as a "member of the National Education Advisory Committee of the Liberty-Ellis Island Committee, professor of English at the University of Florida, and prolific Black author," effects a huge change in cultural and intellectual context. The text now appears to come from a black man credentialed by the (white-dominated) mainstream rather than operating outside it. (That relocation did not, however, deter one of the e-mail's most dismissive and widely quoted commentators, Barbara Mikkelson, coeditor of the Urban Legends Reference Pages, from invoking suspect Afrocentrism to denigrate the theory. Using a now standard device for discrediting claims about neglected black history, she identifies among its supporters the controversial promoter of Afrocentrism Leonard Jeffries, then chair of the Black Studies Program at City College of New York, and reminds readers of his anti-Semitism and other apparent manifestations of unreasoned prejudice.)[58] Important, too, is that the cultural politics have financial stakes. When it comes to the Statue of Liberty, whose heritage are resources being marshaled to honor?[59]

What I want to emphasize here, however, begins from the following observation: evidence of significant and by now longstanding, if circumscribed, attention to the black Statue of Liberty appears in Haskins's annoyed comment on his Web site about the Museum of the City of New York receiving inquiries for "the past dozen years," and in Mikkelson's essay, which locates Jeffries's enthusiasm in 1991. By 2000, the e-mail had generated enough publicity that the National Park Service agreed to look into it, ABC News and an AP story had spread it in the mainstream press, and McDonald's saw enough of a market for the image to put coloring books with a black Statue of Liberty in some Happy Meals.[60] And no matter how plausible one deems the argument about the black soldiers or the black model, there's really no reason to question whether Laboulaye, an active member of the French Anti-Slavery Society, saw the abolition of slavery as one reason that he wanted to present a statue to the United States. Information is also readily accessible that the statue was not originally about immigrants.

Thus, every immigrants-only reading of the statue needs to be understood in relation to the absence of readily available and credible material tying the statue to slavery. This absence constitutes just one element in the racial profiling of those on whom Liberty smiles, which may change in various contexts, depending on matters such as the racing of immigrants, often perceived as dark themselves, and on other circumstances. On December 20, 2001, for instance, the day Liberty Island reopened after the events of September 11, Al Roker said on *Today* that the statue "welcomed immigrants on the way to Ellis Island from 1890 to 1954," a description in notable contrast with Katie Couric's identification of "Lady Liberty" on the recent Fourth of July episode of *Today* as a "symbol for millions of immigrants." Couric had vaguely suggested Liberty's continuing and general welcome, although interestingly the remark introduced a story about white U.S. parents adopting Siberian children. Roker's comments, in contrast, implied that the welcome of immigrants ended after Ellis Island closed, and consequently before subsequent influxes of non-European migrants, who are now increasingly labeled dark and dangerous on the surface of discourse and policy. Clearly, with the *Today* scriptwriters, telling omissions that whiten the statue concern the particular migrants presented as well as the absence of abolition.

Return to Scandal

I suggested earlier that the scandal of Liberty as a hooker stood in the place of other matters about sex, gender, and money that ought to be considered scandalous but frequently aren't. I want to end by suggesting that the struggle over whether the statue is fundamentally white or black—or "colorless," as Mikkelson chastised "Jeffries and others" to realize—covers something that is often is considered scandalous, but shouldn't be: the reality of racial mixing. Liberty's history, like much about race, isn't simply black or white, for a number of reasons. For one thing, people beyond those designated by the terms "black" and "white" are involved; I have indicated several instances, like connections made to the Chinese Exclusion Acts and the case of Hue Cao, where people and issues beyond those categories are involved. One of my points in this essay is that such matters, like the disparity in sexual rights re-inscribed by *Bowers v. Hardwick,* contribute to constituting the mean-ings of Liberty, rather than remain to the side of them. Another exam-ple comes from Liberty's sculptural parentage. Whether or not a black model posed at any stage, it remains known, if, significantly, unheralded, that Liberty most immediately descends from a proposed statue com-memorating the opening of the Suez Canal that Bartholdi, in the late 1860s, tried to get the khedive Isma'il Pasha of Egypt to commission. The models for *Egypt Carrying the Light to Asia,* a colossal figure of an Egyp-tian peasant woman in traditional dress holding a lantern, look not quite white but quite like the statue.

Few paths to and around Liberty are mono-raced, and it's not just because whites and blacks, slaves and immigrants, people of European descent and people of African descent—the groups often set in opposi-tion to each other in debates about Liberty—cannot be presumed wholly distinct. They also move in relation to each other (and to others, of course). To give just one example, I turn to a conversation with a Statue of Liberty scholar who, trying to hand me a tip, said, "Emma Lazarus's father made his money in sugar refining and you know that money's not clean," referring to the dependence of the sugar economy on the plan-tation labor of slaves. Although I got little response when I said, "That's really interesting. So why didn't *you* write about this?" the answer, I pre-sume, lies in the ugliness that might result from calling a Jewish poet-hero a virtual slaveholder.[61] I understand wanting not to be the messen-ger, although I also want to put this information forward with some complicating questions about matters including the perceived racial iden-tity of Jews and whether Jews or their money ever are considered clean. Those questions, of course, are akin to the ones that I suggested earlier regarding the underpinnings of claims about Liberty's virtue, both be-cause they take on some related topics, like about when dirt appears to define people and money, and because the answers to them depend on understandings about gender, sex, and sexuality, each, as with Liberty, constituted in talk and telling silence about issues of race.

I have sought, throughout this essay, to identify some of these understandings and silences that contribute to dominant meaning makings about Liberty. Yet my purpose is not to propose one reading that results from adding these specific particulars to the mix, although I do indeed want to add them. When people regard Liberty and her big party weekend, I want these to be as easy to come by as the comments I found all over about Liberty as a victimized prostitute: the gendering of immigrant worthiness, the heterosexualizing of citizens in Chief Justice Burger's trip from Bowers to Ellis, the situation of being too poor to accept the benefits that allegedly trickle down from the rich, and the antislavery activism of Liberty's gift makers. At the same time, in bringing up this somewhat idiosyncratic collection of topics circling around the statue, I hope just as much to argue for the queerness, but hardly the uniqueness, of meaning making in general. Liberty might not be everyone's fantasy butch, but what she is depends on a complex of views and practices that bring gender, sex, money, and race to bear on immigration narratives.

Notes

1. Thanks to James Clifford for introducing this point about the statue changing size at a colloquium at which I presented this material. The colloquium was sponsored by the Center for Cultural Studies at the University of California, Santa Cruz, April 2002. I also thank the other participants at this event and at other forums where I presented this material, including Bates College, Bowdoin College, University of Southern Maine, and the conference "Sexuality, Migration, and the Contested Boundaries of U.S. Citizenship" at Bowling Green State University. I am grateful, too, for Lionel Cantú's enthusiasm and encouragement, and for the close reading and invaluable suggestions offered by Eithne Luibhéid; this essay and much more in my life have been much enriched by getting to know and work with them. Thanks to Jason Goldman, Penelope Malakates, Julia Getzel, and Alex Wenger for research assistance; to Sallie Hackett, for help with manuscript preparation and much else; and to Sallie McCorkle for coming on many trips to my fantasy butch and being a fantasy butch in the flesh.

2. Toby Keith, "Courtesy of the Red, White, and Blue (The Angry American)," on the CD *Unleashed* (Dreamworks, Nashville, 2002); lyrics Tokeka Tunes (BMI).

3. Although I haven't been able to date the image precisely, it appears on one Web page that gives the date of its last update as October 16, 2001 (Current Events Humor Archive, http://kd4dcy.net/rthumor, accessed November 7, 2003). Searching "Statue of Liberty" plus "Osama" yields numerous sites with the image.

4. Jasbir K. Puar and Amit S. Rai, "Monster, Terrorist, Fag: The War on Terrorism and the Production of Docile Patriots," *Social Text* 20, no. 3 (Fall 2002): 126. See this essay, too, for a description of other representations in this genre.

5. Lawrence Grossberg, *We Gotta Get out of This Place: Popular Conservatism and Postmodern Culture* (New York: Routledge, 1992), 63.

6. Paula Span, "Liberty Trash," *Washington Post,* June 27, 1986, D1; F. Ross Holland, *Idealists, Scoundrels, and the Lady: An Insider's View of the Statue of Liberty–Ellis Island Project* (Urbana: University of Illinois Press, 1993), 68, 86. Actually, SOLEIF was supposed to be carrying out the decisions of the Statue of Liberty–Ellis Island Centennial Commission, a government advisory committee of the Department of the Interior appointed by Reagan (and headed by Lee Iacocca). However, SOLEIF was the major player of the two. According to Roberta Brandes Gratz and Eric Fettman, by 1985 the commission, which was packed with celebrities and business people rather than restoration experts, had hardly met and never touched its staff budget ("The Selling of Miss Liberty," *Nation* 241, no. 15 [9 November 1985]: 469). On the relation between the foundation and the commission, also see Holland.

7. Henry A. Giroux, *The Mouse That Roared: Disney and the End of Innocence* (Lanham, MD: Rowman and Littlefield, 1999), 8.

8. Susana Peña, "Visibility and Silence: Mariel and Cuban American Gay Male Experience and Representation," in this volume.

9. Aired on March 14, 2001.

10. Al Robb, "Lady Liberty," in *Dear Miss Liberty: Letters to the Statue of Liberty,* ed. Lynne Bundeson (Salt Lake City: Peregrine Smith Books, 1986), 71.

11. Evelyn Wilde Mayerson, *The Cat Who Escaped from Steerage* (New York: Charles Scribner's Sons, 1990), 46.

12. *Icky and Kathy Find Liberty* is part of the Icky and Kathy trilogy; *Betty and Pansy's Severe Queer Review of New York* (San Francisco: Bedpan Productions, 1994), vi.

13. In Coan's *Ellis Island Interviews,* Estelle Miller recalls seeing the statue from the ship at age thirteen in 1909: "Nobody knew what it was. One man said, 'Don't you know? That's Columbus.'. . . So we thought it was Columbus. For years I thought that" (221). Theodore Spako, age sixteen when immigrating in 1911, recalled questioning a cabinmate who made the same identification, "Listen, this don't look like Christopher Columbus. That's a lady there" (277–78).

14. Kathleen Chevalier, quoted by Neil G. Kotler, in "The Statue of Liberty as Idea, Symbol, and Historical Presence," in *The Statue of Liberty Revisited,* ed. Wilton S. Dillon and Neil G. Kotler (Washington, DC: Smithsonian University Press, 1994), 13.

15. Marvin Trachtenberg, *The Statue of Liberty,* rev. ed. (New York: Penguin Books, 1986), 104. The painting is *Truth* by C.-V.-E. Lefebvre, 1859.

16. Linda Zerelli, "Democracy and National Fantasy: Reflections on the Statue of Liberty," in *Cultural Studies and Political Theory,* ed. Jodi Dean (Ithaca, NY: Cornell University Press, 2000), 180.

17. Michael Kinsley, *New Republic,* December 19, 1983; Garnet Chapin, in "Taking Care of Miss Liberty," *20/20,* aired December 12, 1985; Richard Cohen, *Washington Post,* September 28, 1985. All cited in Holland, *Idealists, Scoundrels, and the Lady,* 84, 181, 85.

18. Roberta Brandes Gratz and Eric Fettman, "The Selling of Miss Liberty," *Nation* 241, no. 15 (November 9, 1985): 465–76.

19. Trachtenberg, *The Statue of Liberty,* 195–96.

20. Barbara A. Babcock and John J. Macaloon, "Everybody's Gal: Women, Boundaries, and Monuments," in *The Statue of Liberty Revisited,* ed. Dillon and Kotler, 90.

21. Ibid., 94.

22. Ibid., 92; Rattan Davenport, "Statuary Rape," *Social Anarchism* 13 (1987): 32–33. Babcock and Macaloon obscure by omission that their source, calling anarchists to trash "icons of the state religion," implies a stance toward rape metaphors of which I doubt they would approve.

23. Martha Grove and Deborah Whitefield, "N.Y. Singing Red, White, and Bucks to Miss Liberty," *Los Angeles Times*, June 29, 1986, sec. 1, p. 1 (LexisNexis, July 18, 2000).

24. Paula Span, "Liberty Trash," D1; Maureen Dowd, "The Statue as Souvenir," *New York Times*, sec. 6, part 2, p. 8 (LexisNexis, July 18, 2000).

25. Hall, *Idealists, Scoundrels, and the Lady*, 126–27, illustration facing page 36. Iacocca was the grand marshal of the parade.

26. Jane Perry Clark, *Deportation of Aliens from the United States to Europe* (New York: Columbia University Press, 1931), 53, 63–69; Wendy Chapkis, "Soft Glove, Punishing Fist: the Trafficking Victims' Protection Act," in *Regulating Sex: The Politics of Intimacy and Identity*, ed. Elizabeth Bernstein and Laurie Schaffner (New York: Routledge, 2004).

27. Lauren Berlant, *The Anatomy of National Fantasy: Hawthorne, Utopia, and Everyday Life* (Chicago: University of Chicago Press, 1991), 27–28.

28. *New York Times*, July 3, 1986, A31.

29. M. Jacqui Alexander, "Erotic Autonomy as a Politics of Decolonization: An Anatomy of Feminist and State Practice in the Bahamas Tourist Economy," in *Feminist Genealogies, Colonial Legacies, Democratic Futures*, ed. M. Jacqui Alexander and Chandra Talpade Mohanty (New York: Routledge, 1997), 64–65.

30. Immigration Marriage Fraud Amendments of 1986, Public Law 99–639, 100 Stat. 3537, codified as amended at 8 *U.S. Code* (1994) §§ 1154, 1184, 1186a. On the inaccuracy of the data cited by the INS, see James A. Jones, "The Immigration Marriage Fraud Amendments: Sham Marriages or Sham Legislation," *Florida State University Law Review* 24 (1997): 679–701, 698–700.

31. U.S. Senate Committee of the Judiciary, Subcommittee on Immigration and Refugee Policy, *Hearing on Immigration Marriage Fraud*, 99th Cong., 1st sess., July 26, 1985.

32. On how IMFA provisions for ensuring the authenticity of marriages have made immigrant women vulnerable to abuse and the (insufficient) attempts to remedy the law, see Jones, "The Immigration Marriage Fraud Amendments"; and Michelle J. Anderson, "A License to Abuse: The Impact of Conditional Status on Female Immigrants," *Yale Law Journal* 102 (April 1993): 1401.

33. *Bowers v. Hardwick*, 478 United States 186 (1986). The Georgia antisodomy law in question criminalized all acts involving "the sex organs of one person and the mouth or anus of another" (Ga. Code Ann. 16-6-2(a) [1984]). Indeed, as Justice Blackmun wrote in his dissent, the state's code, which, until 1968, defined sodomy as "the carnal knowledge and connection against the order of nature, by man with man, or in the same unnatural manner with woman" (Ga. Crim. Code 26–5901 [1933]), may actually have been revised in 1968 to include heterosexual acts, such as "heterosexual cunnilingus," that had been ruled exempt in previous cases (Blackmun, dissent, footnote 1). However, the decision of *Bowers v. Hardwick* ignored the scope of the actual statute. Its primary finding was that "The Constitution does not confer a fundamental right upon homosexuals to engage in sodomy."

34. Janet Halley, "The Construction of Heterosexuality," in *Fear of a Queer Planet: Queer Politics and Social Theory,* ed. Michael Warner (Minneapolis: University of Minnesota Press, 1993), 91–92.

35. Chief Justice Burger, concurring.

36. Sara Rimmer, "Nation Rekindles Statue of Liberty as Beacon of Hope; Across U.S., a Ceremony for History," *New York Times,* July 4, 1986, A1 (LexisNexis, July 17, 2000); Bob Drogan, "Chief Justice Leads Massive Swearing In of New Citizens," *Los Angeles Times,* July 4, 1986, sec. 1, p. 1 (LexisNexis, July 17, 2000). Rimmer states 100 countries participated; Drogan states that it was 109.

37. Peter Freiberg, "Supreme Court Decision Sparks Protests: 'New Militancy' Seen in Angry Demonstrations," *Advocate,* August 5, 1986, 12.

38. William H. Blair, "City's Homosexuals Protest High Court Sodomy Ruling," *New York Times,* July 3, 1986, B5; Alan Finder, "Police Halt Rights Marchers at Wall St.," *New York Times,* July 5, 1986, A32.

39. Deborah B. Gould, "Sex, Death, and the Politics of Anger: Emotions and Reason in ACT UP's Fight against AIDS" (Ph.D. diss., University of Chicago, 2000). As both Gould's text and the *Advocate* article point out, demonstrations against the verdict, which occurred before the advent of ACT UP stepped up the pace of demonstrations and civil disobedience on queer rights issues, stood out also by size and visible anger.

40. John Rechy, "A High Court Decision and a Sense of Betrayal," *Los Angeles Times,* July 6, 1986, sec. 5, p. 1 (LexisNexis, July 26, 2000).

41. Michael Hanlon, "4 Million Liberty-Lovers Take Over Streets of New York," *Toronto Star,* July 5, 1986, A3 (LexisNexis, July 26, 2000); Maural Dolan and Siobhan Flynn, "Coast Guard Kept Scrambling; N.Y. Waters Roiled but Streets Peaceful," *Los Angeles Times,* July 5, 1986, sec. 1, p. 8 (LexisNexis, July 26, 2000).

42. Elizabeth Mehren, "Joyous Creature Roams N.Y.," *Los Angeles Times,* July 5, 1986, sec. 1, p. 1 (LexisNexis, July 26, 2000); Cass Peterson, "Celebrating Liberty Weekend in Manhattan Not for Claustrophobics," *Washington Post,* July 5, 1986, A15 (LexisNexis, July 26, 2000); Jay Sharbut, "Battery Park Hosts Show of Its Own," *Los Angeles Times,* July 7, 1986, sec. 6, p. 1 (LexisNexis, July 26, 2000).

43. David Deitcher, "Law and Desire," in *The Question of Equality: Lesbian and Gay Politics in America since Stonewall,* ed. Deitcher (New York: Scribner, 1995), 150. Deitcher also includes a report that police went out of their way to avoid arresting even protestors who tried to get arrested, suggesting how narratives about "keeping the peace" need to take account of the intended beneficiaries—here, it seems, the festivities' corporate and government sponsors, not the protestors.

44. "Crime in the Bedroom" and "Day of Sail, Night of Fire," *New York Times,* July 2, 1986, A30; "The Right to Remedy, Affirmed," *New York Times,* July 3, 1986, A30.

45. Bundesen, *Dear Miss Liberty,* 18, 52, 31, 33.

46. "Girl Wins Freedom Essay; Family May Lose Benefits," *San Diego Union-Tribune,* May 22, 1986, A17; Peter Rowe, "Happy Ending," *San Diego Union-Tribune,* May 27, 1986, E2; Holland, *Idealists, Scoundrels, and the Lady,* 222–23; Michael Hanlon, "U.S. Puts On the Ritz for Liberty," *Toronto Star,* July 4, 1986, A15.

47. Peter Wyden, *The Unknown Iacocca* (New York: William Morrow, 1987), 17.

48. Mike Wallace, *Mickey Mouse History and Other Essays on American Memory* (Philadelphia: Temple University Press, 1996), 57–58.

49. According to Aristide R. Zolberg, "Reforming the Back Door: The Immigration Reform and Control Act of 1986 in Historical Perspective," in *Immigration Reconsidered: History, Sociology, and Politics,* ed. Virginia Yans-McLaughlin (Oxford: Oxford University Press), 334 § 201 (h) of the act states that in most cases "an alien [who] was granted lawful temporary resident status" is ineligible for any federal assistance programs for five years.

50. Hue Cao, "A New Life," *Los Angeles Times,* June 29, 1986, magazine section, 15 (LexisNexis, June 22, 2001).

51. Besides Wallace, *Mickey Mouse History,* see, for instance, Lynn Johnson, "Ellis Island: Historical Preservation from the Supply Side," *Radical History Review* 28–30 (1984): 164–67.

52. This queen-for-a-day economics is hilariously parodied in the 2000 movie *Bring It On* when the cheerleaders from an underfunded "inner city" school full of black and Latino kids need money to attend the national cheerleading championships. Refusing the corporate philanthropy that a rich white cheerleader from the predominantly white public school has squeezed for them from her dad, they get their money during "Wish Day" on the *Pauletta Show,* Pauletta being in appearance and style a parody of Oprah; they know that their economic power lies, at best, in determining who gets to be the hero of their weepy PR moment (*Bring It On,* Beacon, 2000). There's also a good implicit subplot here about disproportionate public school funding and schools' increasing reliance on inequitably available local private resources, but it is hampered by relegating discussions of race to code phrases like "inner city" and scenes where race issues are meant to seem so obvious that they go without saying. They need some saying.

53. Saum Song Bo, "A Chinese View of the Statue of Liberty," *American Missionary* 39, no. 10 (October 1885), quoted by Juan Perea, "The Statue of Liberty: Notes from Behind the Gilded Door," in *Immigrants Out! The New Nativism and the Anti-Immigrant Impulse in the United States,* ed. Perea (New York: New York University Press), 52–53.

54. David E. Procter, "The Struggle for Identity: Black America's Liberty Rhetoric," in *Enacting Political Culture: Rhetorical Transformations of Liberty Weekend* (New York: Praeger, 1991), 35–56. It's worth noting that Procter mentions *Bowers v. Hardwick* only in a footnote about the protest (unfortunate but apt, considering the tendency to keep the decision from touching the holiday).

55. Wolper is quoted by James M. Banner Jr. in "The Wrong Symbol," letter to the editor, *New York Times,* June 15, 1986 (LexisNexis, July 18, 2000); "The Torch Shines for Blacks," *US News and World Report,* June 16, 1986, 65 (LexisNexis, July 18, 2000); *The Statue of Liberty: America's Proud Lady* (Minneapolis: Lerner Publications, 1986), 12.

56. On the history of the poem's relation to the statue, which burgeoned in the 1930s and 1940s, see John Higham, *Send These to Me: Immigrants in Urban America,* rev. ed. (Baltimore: The Johns Hopkins University Press, 1984), 77–79.

57. Jim Haskins, "Jim Haskins, From my Viewpoint," http://web.clas.ufl.edu/ users/jhaskins/ (May 13, 2002). This widely circulating e-mail is reproduced at http://urbanlegends.about.com/library/weekly/aa020900a.htm. The author of the e-mail was possibly intending not to misattribute the book, but to repeat the book's statement, which the e-mail author virtually copies directly, that Haskins had made

the argument, in a place significantly unspecified by the book's author or authors. See Calvin R. Robinson, Redman Battle, and Edward W. Robinson, *Journey of the Songhai People* (Philadelphia: Farmer Press, Pan African Federation Organization, 1987), 160–63. Edward Robinson, or PAFO, is sometimes identified as the sole author. Although the e-mail implies, again not necessarily intentionally, that perhaps only the comment about Haskins comes from *The Journey of the Songhai People,* everything following that comment is also almost a copy from the book.

58.   Barbara Mikkelson, Urban Legends Reference Pages: History (Statue of Liberty), http://www.snopes.com/history/american/liberty.htm (last updated February 14, 2000). Of course, the very labeling of this theory as an urban legend also involves a race-coded dismissal. On the use of Jeffries to denigrate claims about black history and African American studies in general, see Manning Marable, "Beyond Racial Identity Politics: Toward a Liberation Theory for Multicultural Democracy," in *Privileging Positions: The Sites of Asian American Studies,* ed. Gary Y. Okihiro, Marilyn Alquizola, Dorothy Fujita Rony, and K. Scott Wong (Pullman: Washington State University Press, 1995), 322–23.

59.   This question becomes quite complicated due to the fund-raising tactics of SOLEIF. As some critics suggested, many people who donated with the intention of contributing to the statue's restoration might be surprised to learn that most of the money raised went to Ellis Island. Less than a third of the $277 million that Iacocca announced on July 1, 1986—SOLEIF formally named its total as $305.4 million in March 1987 and declared "$450 million (and counting!)" on its Web site in 2001—went to restore the statue. See Holland, *Idealists, Scoundrels, and the Lady,* 98; "About the Foundation," The Statue of Liberty–Ellis Island Foundation Web site, http://www.ellisisland.org/Eiinfo/about.asp (May 30, 2001). Figures vary about what money went where. *Ellis Island and Statue of Liberty Magazine,* which is less a periodical with changing articles than a booklet published with changing advertisements, states in its tenth edition that of more than $295 million raised, $86 million went to the statue (Des Moines, IA: American Park Network, 2000), 57.

60.   "Theory Shakes Up Lady Liberty," *Lewiston Sun-Journal,* February 8, 2000, A1. The ABC News story, by Geraldine Sealy, appeared on the same date (http://more.abcnews.go.com/sections/us/dailynews/statue000208.html).

61.   For several reasons on which I cannot elaborate, I have chosen to respect this author's wish not to be associated with the topic. That Moses Lazarus, Emma's father, was in sugar refining is noted generally without any elaboration in biographies of her. See, for instance, Eve Merriam, *Emma Lazarus: Woman with a Torch* (New York: Citadel Press, 1956), 10. A study of Lazarus's other poetry suggests complicated imagined relationships of Jews to people of other diasporas, partly forged in trying to write against the ideological conditions producing the Russian pogroms, the refugees of which occupied much of her activism.

PART II

Queering Racial/Ethnic Communities

CHAPTER SIX

Visibility and Silence

Mariel and Cuban American
Gay Male Experience and Representation

Susana Peña

I was a young girl when the Mariel boatlift occurred. After one man drove his truck into the Peruvian embassy in Havana in early 1980, a series of events unraveled that led to the mass migration of 125,000 Cubans to the United States. The political leader whom they had fled, Fidel Castro, invited Cuban Americans to come pick up their relatives in Cuba's Mariel Harbor. Cuban Americans arriving at Mariel to pick up their family members were required to take other Cubans back to the United States. Faced with a public relations nightmare of tens of thousands of Cubans desperate to leave their country, Castro began a disparagement campaign in which he labeled the migrants *escoria*, lumpen proletariat, *antisociales*, prostitutes, and homosexuals.[1] Ironically, the echoes of the Cuban government's insults were heard among Miami's Cuban American population as it became evident that the Mariel migrants were blacker, poorer, and less educated than previous Cuban immigrants.[2] Compared to previous Cuban immigrants, Mariel immigrants tended to be a much younger group. Seventy percent were men, whereas previous gender ratios were close to even; and a large percentage of those arriving were single males, whereas in the past families were the norm.[3] Approximately 10 percent of the migrants were black; in previous migrations only about 2 to 3 percent were black.[4] Also, Mariel refugees had fewer relatives already living in the United States and received less assistance from those family members than did previous Cuban migrants.[5]

Just as this dramatic series of events and the immigrant crisis that Miami confronted transformed Miami and its Cuban American community, my own neighborhood, the southern part of Miami Beach, was equally transformed.[6] Before Mariel, my neighborhood was known as a retirement community for mostly Jewish elderly who lived in low-rent and increasingly dilapidated apartment units. After Mariel, queens or transvestites became a common presence in my neighborhood, doing something I had never seen before: wearing women's clothing during the day. I remember how "obviously gay" men became a regular fixture at department stores, both as clients and employees, their mannerisms and talk marking them as "other" even if they did not wear women's attire. My grandmother, who worked at a women's clothing store, would regularly report that yet another man had insisted on trying on a dress in the dressing room.

Shortly after Mariel, my neighborhood became known mostly for a surge in crime rate and was considered a dangerous and unsavory place to live. Twenty years later, however, the southern part of Miami Beach, now christened South Beach, had gone from being a "dangerous" place to being a trendy, gay, entertainment hub, to an incarnation as a more fully gentrified neighborhood hosting several Starbucks, Gap franchises, trendy restaurants, fashion designer boutiques, and a deco-modern-styled cineplex.

When I began my study of Cuban American gay male culture in Miami, I assumed a direct, if not causal, relationship between the concentration of gay-identified Marielitos in South Beach and the subsequent transformation of that area into South Florida's most prominent gay neighborhood. A mass migration, stigmatized in part because of male homosexuals, had to impact the culture, identities, and possibilities of Miami's gay Cuban American population. Instead, what I found as I interviewed Cuban American gay men was a palpable silence about Mariel, especially about homosexuality and Mariel. This article draws on a larger ethnographic study of Cuban American gay male culture and grapples with the tension between the visibility of gay men who came during Mariel and the silences and silencing strategies that have surrounded their generation in Cuba and the United States. I examine the strings of visibility and silence that envelop this historic moment.

I address several dimensions of visibility in this article. In the first section, I discuss attempts by the Cuban state to identify and control male homosexuality between 1959 and 1980. I focus on the ways this official effort increased the visibility of male homosexuality, the way it directed attention to *visible* markers of homosexuality, and, finally, how this identification influenced the generation of men who arrived in the United States via Mariel. Key to this element of visibility is the systematic nature of state identification of male homosexuality.

In the second section, I refer to the role the media plays in how or whether a minority group is seen. I examine how U.S. media coverage silenced the issue of homosexuality in relation to the Mariel migration. Focusing on the *Miami Herald*'s coverage, I analyze how the gay Mariel issue was framed and how this framing led to the elimination of this issue from the mainstream media.

In the final section, I refer to the development of a visible, public gay male culture in Cuba and Miami. Visibility in this case refers to distinguishing markers that indicate one's homosexuality to others. I discuss some of the ways that the Mariel generation affected Miami's Cuban American gay male culture. In Cuban and Cuban American histories, "obvious homosexuality" has included a wide range of gender transgression since effeminacy has been equated with male homosexuality. Forms of gender transgression include dressing in women's clothing and subtleties in speech, fashion, and cultural tastes. Like both Martin F. Manalansan and Horacio N. Roque Ramírez in this volume, I am interested in the ways in which gay men contest state discourses through everyday practices. Similar to Roque Ramírez's claim that gay Latino men's cultural practices in San Francisco were a way of claiming "queer cultural citizenship," I argue that the gender transgressions of a portion of Mariel gay men were a way of claiming public space, revaluing identity, and challenging dominant discourses of Cubanidad in Miami.

The State

Cuban men who came to the United States during Mariel lived their early lives during one of the most repressive eras of the Cuban revolution. An oppressive set of state policies, enforcement, and political discourse around masculinity, homosexuality, and the nation elevated male homosexuality into a public, official visibility and played a formative role in the lives of the gay men who came during the Mariel migration. These men, molded by the state practices that identified and controlled male homosexual behavior, in turn impacted Miami's gay worlds.

A set of laws indirectly and directly targeted Cuban homosexuals. For example, the Ley de Peligrosidad, or Law of Social Dangerousness, was used to punish Cuban homosexuals, among others. This law targeted a wide range of "antisocials" using a concept of precriminality. Violators were not arrested because they committed an illegal act but rather because they were deemed to have a high potential to violate laws.[7] Although the law against social dangerousness did not specifically identify homosexuals as one of its targets, reports indicate that in the period prior to Mariel visibly gay men were often arrested and charged under this law.[8] As Lumsden points out, "in Cuba, *antisocial* has been a code word for allegedly ostentatious homosexuality, amongst other forms of 'deviant' behavior."[9]

In 1979, the targeting of visible male homosexuality was made explicit. In addition to criminalizing gay sexual acts in public and sex with minors, Cuban laws made "public ostentation" of homosexuality illegal. For example, Article 359 of the Legal Code criminalized anyone who "(a) scandalously dedicates himself to practicing homosexual acts or makes public ostentation of this conduct or importunes others with the requirements of this nature."[10] According to the 1979 Penal Code, public ostentation of homosexuality was punishable by sentences of three to nine months.[11]

The day-to-day enforcement of these laws took a variety of forms in the period prior to the 1980 Mariel boatlift: detainment of homosexuals in reeducation camps, individual arrests, and *recogidas* or street sweeps of "ostentatious" homosexuals.[12] The street sweeps mainly targeted "public displays of homosexuality," and men were reportedly singled out because their "dress and hair styles were deemed inappropriate . . . [or their] mannerisms were effeminate."[13] Rafael,[14] who left Cuba during the Mariel migration, characterized life in Cuba prior to 1980 in the following way:

Allá nos divertíamos, éramos muy perseguidos, pero ya convivíamos con la persecución. Ya era muy normal que te arrestaran, te metieran en un calabozo, te soltaran a la semana o los 28 días, y salir a la calle. Era como una rutina, una cosa muy normal.

[In Cuba we had fun, we were persecuted, but we lived with the persecution. It was already very normal for them to arrest you, stick you in a cell, and let you out in a week or 28 days, and then return to the street. It was already routine, a very normal thing.]

Rafael's experiences were part of a longer history; between 1965 and 1967, gay men were detained in reeducation camps known as Unidades Militares para el Aumento de Producción (UMAPs, Military Units for Increased Production). Even in the most severe period of enforcement, Leiner reminds us, private homosexual expression was never the main target of the Cuban state. Rather, "even during this period of the camps and public arrests, the major concern, as it had always been, was with the public display of homosexuality."[15] Paul Julian Smith has referred to the enforcement of these laws as a "trial of visibility" in which men were arrested for appearing homosexual.[16] For all practical purposes, these sets of laws and their enforcement criminalized "looking gay."

It is important to note that these state discourses and practices targeted male homosexuality, as opposed to female homosexuality. The visibility of gay men (and the difficulties inherent in that visibility) contrast markedly with the invisibility of Cuban lesbians (and the difficulties inherent in that invisibility). Leiner argues:

> The relegation of women as secondary, lesser "others" is . . . apparent in the almost total absence of lesbianism from official and social concern over homosexuality. . . . From the machismo point of view, lesbianism simply does not matter much. It does not seriously challenge machismo as long as women have no acceptable social choices other than marrying men.[17]

The targeting of male homosexuality is partially explained by the masculinist rhetoric of the Cuban revolutionary government that articulated a relationship between productivity, ideal socialist values, and a critique of bourgeois capitalism through the creation of the "New Man."[18] This New (needless to say, masculine and heterosexual) Man would be the product of hard work and socialist training and would provide the future of the revolution. Men who transgressed these gender boundaries were therefore associated with a betrayal to the revolution. Fidel Castro clarified this point in the late 1960s:

> We would never come to believe that a homosexual could embody the conditions and requirements of conduct that would enable us to consider him a true Revolutionary, a true Communist militant. A deviation of nature clashes with the concept we have of what a militant Communist must be.[19]

As evidenced by this statement, in the early phase of the revolution the male homosexual was defined as outside of the "true" revolutionary process.[20]

The persecution of homosexuals, and in particular visible homosexuals, is not unique to revolutionary Cuba. Yet, as René Cifuentes has written, "Even if our strong Catholic and machista tradition makes us into an easy breeding ground for homophobia, never [before] has a [Cuban] president taken an official stance on the subject."[21] Cifuentes points to the explicitness of the state's targeting of homosexuals as one factor that distinguished the 1960s from previous historic periods. Likewise, Emilio Bejel remarks that "what was truly extraordinary about the situation at the time was not the homophobic positions themselves, but their convergence, extremism, and institutionalization."[22]

Also distinct is the way the issues of gay rights and homosexual persecution figured prominently in international debates about the success and failures of the Cuban revolution. For example, Allen Young notes that the UMAPs were closed in part due to pressure from the left in the United States and in Western Europe. He documents the left's "silence" or unwillingness to fully challenge Castro's homophobic policies.[23]

The irony is that while the state hoped to eradicate visible male homosexuality and hence make it invisible, state labeling and control strategies themselves made homosexuality more visible. José Quiroga captures the irony of the Cuban state's focus on the visibility of male homosexuality:

> The revolution itself rendered the issue of homosexuality visible in the first place—visible in the sense of its being transparent to the society as a whole. As early as 1962 . . . the Cuban Revolution already indexed homosexuality as a condition that needed to be extirpated in order to fulfill an economic and political program that in turn became affixed to the nationalist ideology.[24]

Emilio Bejel further argues that with the institutionalization of homophobia in Cuba's revolutionary government, "homosexuality became a more obviously constitutive part of the very concept of the Cuban nation."[25]

Although homosexuality in general was stigmatized, the revolutionary state identified specific manifestations of homosexuality as problematic: visible manifestations of effeminacy or transgressions of accepted masculinity. These external markers of effeminacy assumed to be associated with male homosexuality were central to the identification of male homosexuals. Although gender-transgressive male homosexuality was heavily policed both in practice and in discourse, this state identification also contributed to the cultural presence of male homosexuals. That is, identifying male homosexuality as a problem made it visible. When contrasted with the practical invisibility of lesbians, the political nuance of this situation comes into focus. Whereas female homosexuality was defined almost by a complete silence in dominant narratives, male homosexuality had a cultural presence. This negatively marked hailing reinforced a subject position from which Cuban gay men would articulate a series of challenges to Cuban, U.S., and Cuban American communities.[26]

Media Representation and Silence

When Cubans began to arrive in the United States in 1980 as part of the Mariel migration, their reception was mediated in large part by media representations that forewarned of the danger of this migrant group.[27] In the early phases of the Mariel migration, national mainstream media avoided the topic of gay men among the Mariel entrants, even while the gay press (including the *Sentinel*, the *Blade*, and the *Advocate*) reported on the story.[28] In a *Columbia Journalism Review* article, Michael Massing notes that although hundreds of articles were published in mainstream newspapers looking at the Mariel crisis from different angles and focusing on different groups within the migration, writers and editors did not write about the gay presence, despite their own awareness of this population.[29]

Massing quotes editors and reporters from *Newsday*, the *New York Times*, and the *Boston Globe* who were aware of the gay presence among Mariel migrants, were aware of segregated homosexual barracks in re-settlement camps,[30] and/or observed same-sex couples walking hand in hand at the camps. They did not, however, identify this visible gay presence as a "story," even though focus on the gay Mariel migrants could have shed light on interesting questions about the boatlift: Were the gay migrants' reasons for leaving Cuba different from those of the rest of the migrants? How did the resettlement process at improvised camps work for stigmatized members of the migration? Would the Immigration and Naturalization Service enforce its ban on homosexuals entering the country?[31] Massing argues that one reason reporters and editors did not pursue this story was the "unavailability of reliable data."[32] The theme of unreliable data would emerge again and again in the silencing of the gay Mariel story.

When discussion of the gay Mariel migrants did appear in the mainstream press, it was quickly silenced. On July 7, 1980, *Washington Post* reporter Warren Brown published a story about the gay presence after he received a government leak stating that twenty thousand gay people remained in the camps.[33] Brown had previously seen gay men and women during his visits to Fort Chaffee and Eglin Air Force Base, but said that he "kind of ignored it."[34] He only reported the story after receiving the leak. His report that half of the inmates that remained in the camps were gay and awaiting sponsors in order to be released was picked up by the newswire and reprinted on top of the *Miami Herald*'s front page under the headline "20,000 Gay Refugees Await Sponsors."[35]

The next day the *Herald* ran another front-page story reporting that this figure of twenty thousand homosexuals was greatly exaggerated. The story cited various camp representatives who claimed that the number of homosexuals within the migration or in their individual camps was much lower. The focus of this semiretraction centered around the number of homosexuals present on the boatlift—how many gay men actually did come during Mariel? The reports cited in this second article were not consistent or complete. Interviewees gave widely different numbers and/or only discussed information about one of many camps or agencies that handled the Mariel migrants. For example, Judy Weiss from Fort Chaffee asserted that only 94 of the 10,000 Cubans who had passed through her camp were known to be gay; Bruce Brockway reported 900 homosexuals in Fort McCoy. Brockway estimated that 6,800 of those who were being detained in all of the camps were gay; Larry Mahoney of FEMA estimated this number at 4,000.

The question of how many gay men came to the United States during Mariel will probably never be answered. First, these stories focused on the Mariel migrants who remained in camps, and in that way ignored the possibility of other gay men and women who had joined family members and were no longer detained. Second, while there might be some data about the number of people who admitted being homosexual to the Immigration and Naturalization Service or the number who were segregated into "gay" sections of the camps, this represents only a portion of gay Marielitos and excludes those who would lie about their orientation or who would not be classified by their appearance as gay. The impossibility of quantifying the significance of the gay Mariel migration provided a successful means of muting this issue in mainstream newspapers. By focusing on this unanswerable question, other questions were neglected and the "story" of gay Mariel remained relatively uncovered.

Ten years later, in April 1990, *Miami Herald* staff writer Elinor Burkett drew the public's attention to gay men who came to the United States during Mariel. Her human interest story, rather than simply reporting a number of gay migrants, provided in-depth accounts of the migration of ten gay men who left Cuba to come to the United States. The story documented forms of persecution in Cuba, the motivations of gay men coming to the United States, the types of life this particular generation of gay men developed, and the dramatic impact of AIDS on their generation.

The story highlighted the presence and life of the Mariel gay generation and how their ways-of-being shocked gay men (Cuban and not) who had been living in Miami before 1980. Burkett discussed the visible gay cultures in resettlement camps and throughout the city:

> In the late summer of 1980 in Miami, everyone was noticing the gay men of Mariel. They were showing up everywhere, not exactly unobtrusively.
>
> Driving by the refugee Tent City under the I-95 overpass in downtown Miami, you could not miss the men in high heels and makeup, the men strolling with parasols, the men holding hands and kissing.
>
> Customers at women's clothing stores in Little Havana were left speechless as their countrymen in the next dressing room tried to wiggle into size 10 dresses and lace camisoles.... The more sedate majority went openly, unabashedly public with their homosexuality.... The less sedate went kind of berserk. They were flagrant, outrageous. Even Miami's gay population was appalled.
>
> When the men from Mariel arrived at Miami Beach's Arlequin Club, the old-time Latin transvestites complained loudly about the brazen newcomers who were cheapening the craft by cross-dressing not just onstage, but offstage, too.[36]

Burkett not only discussed these gay men openly, she celebrated them. Her account paints a vivid picture of what I remember seeing as a young girl growing up in South Miami Beach, an area in which many Mariel immigrants came to live. These visible Mariel gay men had an impact at the street level, on daily life. Although gender-transgressive Mariel gay men were not the first to cross-dress in Miami, as Burkett's account indicates, they did push the boundaries of acceptable behavior even within gay and drag worlds. They were considered controversial precisely because they were public and visible in the context of everyday life, rather than limiting this behavior to specifically "gay" or "drag" settings.

Burkett's article was met with much the same hostility and protest as Warren Brown's 1980 article that first announced the presence of the gay Marielitos. The *Miami Herald* published reactions to Burkett's article from two commentators. The first reaction, signed by Rene V. Murai, chairman of the Facts About Cuban Exiles (FACE) group, which promotes positive and accurate representations of Cuban Americans, was published on April 13, 1990.[37] The second article was authored by Alejandro Portes and was adapted from a report he authored for FACE.[38] We can imagine that Portes's response was likely included because he was a prominent sociologist, immigration expert, and Cuban American academic. Published more than a year after Burkett's gay Mariel article, Portes's response received its own headline, subheadline, and his own byline.

Portes begins his attack on Burkett by focusing on the numbers of gay men she cites in her article, a scenario almost identical to that played out in 1980. Portes refutes two "numerical assertions" made by Burkett. He rejected the claim that 70 percent of the Mariel migrants were young men and that 30,000 of the migrants were male homosexuals. Portes notes that a much smaller percentage of the Mariel migration were young men, defined as ages 18 to 35. Burkett most likely used the figure of 70 percent because that was the percent of male migrants; however, Portes does not point this out in his article. Although he recognizes the difficulty of estimating a gay population, Portes cites available figures about marriage rates of the Mariel immigrants and characteristics of the different phases of the boatlift to contradict Burkett's figures and to explain the source of her inflation. Although Portes attacks Burkett's unreliable figures, his figures relating to the number of married men and adult males are equally unreliable in that they assume that only unmarried adult males could be gay, excluding married gay men and gay minors.

Portes also argues that the media was responsible for the misleading overestimation of the homosexual male population because there was more media coverage of the second phase of the Mariel migration. This second phase coincided with "stepped up efforts by the Cuban government to discredit the refugees by forcing an increasing number of 'antisocials' to board the ships," and people who arrived during the second phase were more likely to be held in camps. This media focus "included the spectacle of blatant male homosexuality." Therefore, Portes argues that the focus on male homosexuals was due solely to the media's general tendency to portray this more "deviant" portion of the Mariel migration. He does not mention that this focus on the second phase of the boatlift completely excluded all gay men who had been reunited with families in the first phase, therefore possibly underestimating the size of the whole gay migration.

In fairness to Portes, he correctly points out that the media played a pivotal role in shaping Anglo-Americans' and Cuban Americans' negative opinions of Mariel migrants. In his article he is trying to counteract a common tendency in relation to perceptions about Marielitos, which was to generalize the experience and characteristics of one group of the migrants onto the 125,000 men, women, and children who arrived in 1980. However, his concern with how the overestimation of the gay Marielitos might stigmatize the whole Mariel population is problematic.

Portes states that because of the slanted media portrayal "it was difficult to remember that the majority of new refugees—including those in the first phase and many detained in the camps—were just ordinary persons seeking a new way of life in the United States." The implication here is that the "ostentatious" homosexuals dying of AIDS that Burkett interviewed were not "just ordinary persons." Portes continues his critique:

> When a quarter of any given group is portrayed as socially deviant, the entire group is tainted by extension. By advancing these figures, unsupported by reliable evidence, the author transformed a "human interest" story concerning the personal misfortunes of some Mariel refugees into a general statement about the common path followed by many members of this group—a homosexual career that ends with AIDS and death.[39]

Portes is concerned that the stigma associated with blatant male homosexuality was generalized to all the Mariel migrants. The point that Portes misses, or is blind to, is Burkett's goal to destigmatize this population by speaking openly about them (rather than silencing them) and by giving weight to their pursuit of liberty, to their challenges to the Cuban state and to Miami's exile values, and to their own transnational culture of resistance. For Portes to say that what Burkett writes about is only the "personal misfortunes of some Mariel refugees" is simply inexcusable. Sexuality is not a personal matter, and we know that "misfortunes" such as disease and stigma are socially distributed in particular ways. Burkett's article revealed a great deal about state persecution in Cuba, cultural views about homosexuality, the myth of the American (gay) dream, and the local impact of the AIDS epidemic. Although her figures might not have been accurate, the thrust of her article was not really about the number of gay men who came on Mariel but rather their impact on Miami. Portes clings to a quantitative high ground as a way of avoiding asking questions about the sociological significance of the gay Mariel migration.

The visibility of Mariel gay men after 1980 made the numbers game played out in the media almost irrelevant because even if there were few gay men, as some reported, it was clear that those few had an impact on street culture, on drag, and on Cuban Americans. The conflicting accounts about their numbers make Burkett's account and my childhood memories important; if an official story could not be told about the impact of the gay Mariel generation because of the lack of substantiated figures about the size of the population, what was left was images of a fleeting subculture that impacted a city's daily life.

Mariel and Cultures of Visibility in Miami

I have been discussing the ways the Cuban state and U.S. media contributed to the visibility and silencing of a particular generation of Cuban gay men. Now, I shift the discussion and try to reconstruct the ways the Mariel migrants changed Cuban American gay culture. I am interested in the ways a politics of visibility can be gleaned from this generation.

Gay Cuban artists and intellectuals who arrived during Mariel played a role in increasing the visibility of male homosexuals. Although we might include in this category a number of visual artists and writers, perhaps no gay Marielito cultural agent has influenced North American gay knowledges more than Reinaldo Arenas. With the posthumous publication of his autobiography, Arenas unveiled to the world the intricacies of Cuba's gay and same-sex worlds. His detailed story of his own persecution and that of other prominent gay men and his active denunciation of the Castro regime's policies against homosexuals forced right-wing Cuban exile groups to confront, if not embrace, the issue of homosexual persecution and gay rights.[40]

Intellectual and political culture is only one way gay Mariel changed Miami's gay worlds. A promiscuous and visible gay Mariel culture developed in Miami's urban worlds. Some interpreted the development of this culture as a result of the perceived gay freedom available in the United States. As this argument goes, Mariel gay men were more extroverted in the United States because they believed this was the land of unrestrained gay freedom. A man who arrived in the United States via Mariel explains his initial perceptions of gay life in the United States:

> Como es natural uno llega, se deslumbraba por el simple hecho de que hubiera una discoteca para hombres gay na'mas, que tu entraras y todo el mundo era gay, y no venía la policia a recojer a todo el mundo y llevárselo. Ya eso era un cambio tremendo.

> [Naturally, when you get here you are blown over by the simple fact that there's a disco exclusively for gay men, that you go in and everybody's gay, and that the police don't come and pick everybody up. Just that is a tremendous change.]

Although the slackening of certain types of persecution of homosexuals and the rupture with parents caused by the migration created new opportunities for gay expression for some gay men, it is important to note that defiant sexual cultures had been developing within Cuba prior to Mariel. Arenas is particularly helpful in describing this culture:

> There was another powerful homosexual scene in Havana, underground but very visible. . . . I think that in Cuba there was never more fucking going on than in those years, the decade of the sixties, which was precisely when all the new laws against homosexuals came into being, when the persecutions started and concentration camps were opened, when the sexual act became taboo while the "new man" was being proclaimed and masculinity exalted. . . . I think that the sexual revolution in Cuba actually came about as a result of the existing sexual repression. Perhaps as a protest against the regime, homosexuality began to flourish with ever-increasing defiance. . . . I honestly believe that the concentration camps for homosexuals, and the police officers disguised as willing young men to entrap and arrest homosexuals, actually resulted in the promotion of homosexual activities.[41]

It was the combination of the perceived freedom in the United States and the defiant cultures that had been developing in Cuba that created the context for the immigrant gay culture that developed in 1980s Miami.

What was that immigrant gay culture like? When I ask René, a fifty-year-old Cuban man who lived in Miami before and after 1980, what the Mariel time was like for gay Cuban men in Miami, he first tells me about radical changes in Miami's sexual life:

> Oh my god, era así. Yo podía recojer seis personas en las carpas, en la cuidad de las carpas o en el Orange Bowl. El sexo era tan, tan, tanto sexo, tanto, tanto, tanto, tanto, tanto, como esta cuidad nunca ha visto.

> [Oh my God, it was like that. I could pick up six people in the tents, in "Tent City," or in the Orange Bowl. The sex was so much. There was so, so, so, so, so, so much sex, like this city had never seen.]

René tells me that Mariel made Miami more sexually open. I ask him to clarify how he thinks the Mariel migration changed Miami's sexual life. He explains:

> R: Por ejemplo el cruising, en las áreas abiertas, en la calle, etc. Los gay américanos se volvieron loco. Hacían cola...con el carro para rocojer gente.
>
> SP: Por qué era sexualmente más abierto?
>
> R: Era porque eran sexualmente más divertidos, creo yo. Porque los américanos son mucho menos extrovertidos en el sexo. O sea, ellos pueden estar sintiendo mucho...tu te das cuenta de que ellos terminaron ya...tu no te habías enterado. O sea, eso paso y nadie te avisa, ni nada no. En Cuba se decia, la gente decia "a mi hay que gritarme el palo." El palo es el sexo, y es esa cosa de decir lo que sientes en el momento que estas teniendo el orgasmo, de gritar, de decir, que se yo, y yo creo que eso a los américanos lo enloquecía. Los américanos son tan frios, tan aburidos.

> (R: For example, cruising in open areas, in the street, etc. Gay Americans went crazy. They would get in line...in their cars to pick people up.
>
> SP: How was it sexually more open?
>
> R: I think it was because they [Mariel gay men] were sexually more fun. Because Americans are much less sexually extroverted. They could be feeling a lot...you realize they've finished...and you hadn't noticed. I mean, that [ejaculation] happened and no one tells you or anything. In Cuba there's an expression, *a mi hay que gritarme el palo* [you have to scream your orgasm at me]. *El palo* is sex, and it's about saying, yelling, saying what you feel in the moment you're having an orgasm, I don't know. I think that drove the Americans crazy. Americans are so cold and boring.]

The concept of *gritar el palo* reveals one irony about the interrelationship between visibility and silence: it is men arriving from a country in which public displays of homosexuality and public sex were so persecuted, and where tightening material conditions made privacy a luxury, who embody this notion of announcing one's orgasm. I see in the yelling, in the announcement of ejaculation, the direct response to systematic efforts to muffle homosexuals and underground sexual cultures. The silencing and the screaming, the persecution and the defiant announcement of sexual pleasure seem to depend on one another.

In Miami, not only did underground sexual cultures flourish as René described, but a more visible gender-transgressive street culture developed. There is scattered evidence of this subculture. Burkett's article contains one eloquent set of testimonies. Another, Miñuca Villaverde's low-budget documentary *Tent City*, which chronicled the experiences of a group of Mariel refugees being held in an improvised camp, captures a fleeting glimpse of the gender transgressors being held at a temporary resettlement camp under Interstate 95.[42] Arguably, the locas/queens did more to increase the visibility of homosexuality in Miami than anyone else. What was most persecuted in Cuba during the 1960s and 1970s was the public display of homosexuality. Given that male homosexuality was associated with effeminacy, a wide array of gender-transgressive behavior was believed to demonstrate one's sexuality. Dressing in women's clothing would be the most obvious, but men reported being singled out for letting their hair grow out too long or wearing tight pants or a colorful shirt. Speech patterns, mannerisms, and the people one associated with could be cause for suspicion and apprehension. It was precisely these types of expressions that blossomed in Miami's Mariel gay world. Drag and transvestitism were reinvented by young, poor immigrants who grew out their hair and then peroxided it and wore housedresses out on the street during the day. They created a visible gay Mariel culture in Miami in the 1980s, concentrated in neighborhoods like South Miami Beach and Southwest Miami. Clearly, not all gay men who migrated during Mariel participated in this segment of gay culture. More accurately, a small minority of the gay men who came during Mariel identified with this subculture. Yet, the men who did choose the gender-transgressive path added a new face to Cuban Miami and helped create the gay Miami that exists today.

Although I am focusing here on expressions of effeminacy, I believe the politics of visibility is related primarily to masculinity and maleness. I argue that these gender-transgressive practices became political strategies of resistance in everyday life in part because of the targeting of these practices by the Cuban state. Likewise, the visibility politics intrinsic in the changes in sexual culture and gender-transgressive street culture rely on the relative access of men to public space.

Fear of Effeminacy and Silence

Luis, a respondent who was a young elementary school-aged boy during 1980, describes his memory of gay Mariel men:

> [I remember] seeing, you know, flamboyant, gay, you know, they weren't necessarily drag queens or transsexuals, I mean they were very effeminate gay men with brightly colored, brightly dyed orange hair. They were expressed in a more feminized way, but they weren't necessarily trying to pass as women specifically. Maybe in a place where gender roles are a lot more specific, they feel that in order, if ... they're not going to pass as straight men who happen to have sex with other men, then they're going to express their gay way by looking more feminine, and some were like drag queens or transsexuals. ... If anything maybe I felt like a fear, maybe there was a part of me that, that part of me that was trying to fight with what I had been accused of my whole life was like: I didn't want to be associated with that; I didn't want to be that; that was not what I was, even though I had maybe a subconscious fear that that's what I was being told I was.

The first adjective Luis uses to describe the gender-transgressive gay men of Mariel is "flamboyant." Even in his childhood observations, Luis could recognize the transgressions of feminized "ostentation" that were stigmatized in Cuba as well as in Miami. In Luis's account, we see both how he interpreted Mariel gay expressions as a boy through his own emerging notions of sexuality and gender and the ways that he interprets the feminized notions now. As a boy who was beginning to suspect his own attraction for men, Luis confronted the new models of gay life as embodied by "feminized" Mariel men with fear rather than identification. The Mariel gay men transgressed gender and class definitions of appropriate behavior. As Luis confronted the gay men with only a partial understanding that he too might be gay, he wanted to distinguish between his type of gay and their type of gay. As a young adult looking back on Mariel, we see him try to place the need for feminine expression

in a historical context, distinguishing between Mariel gay men's "feminized" expressions and the emulation of women, and trying to place these
"feminized" expressions in a cultural context that defines them as gay.

Luis articulates a vivid picture of one sector of gay Mariel and of
his relationship to it. Within the context of my interviews, this type of
explicit discussion of gay Mariel is unusual. The *Marielenas*, as one respondent referred to the gay men who came on the Mariel boatlift,
slipped out of most men's accounts. Men rarely mentioned this sector
of Mariel unless directly asked. Given the dramatic impact Mariel had on
all aspects of life in Miami in general and on gay life specifically, I was
surprised by the silences that enveloped gay Mariel.

Although most men did not discuss the impact of gay Mariel in any
sustained way, they did describe their distance from visible expressions
of male homosexuality in the form of effeminacy. For example, Martín
was quite explicit about his dislike of femininity.

M: I don't necessarily hide being gay, but I don't want to be the
stereotype of the horrible gay Cuban queen.
SP: Which is what?
M: Which is awful. It's awful. You'll know it when you see it. I guess in
their worst form, I find them overtly effeminate. I find them inclined
to put on airs of grandeur where none exists, I think. I find them un-
educated.... I think they're low class. They tend to be very vicious....
I can't really relate to them because I just find that they have a whole
world of their own, and they remind me to an extent of women.

Martín describes his distancing from effeminacy in particularly ethnic
terms. It is not only that he fears being a "queen," but he fears being a
"Cuban queen" in particular. This "queen" image clearly also has class
connotations. Martín describes queens as "low class," and I argue that
his image of the low-class Cuban queen is typically associated with gay
men who arrived on the Mariel boatlift. Therefore, I associate this distance from a class-marked effeminacy with an unspoken distancing from
Mariel gay expressions and as a result of the fear of being identified
with their forms of gay expression.

Cuban American gay men's silences about Mariel and their distancing
from effeminacy are related to their strategies for balancing gay and family lives. For most of the Cuban American gay men I interviewed, respectability and acceptance in their families, their residential communities,
and/or their jobs required a quite different mask than that worn by the

locas of Mariel. Most of the men I interviewed achieved respectability by not being identifiable as gay outside of gay communities. A masculine normative identity and image, as opposed to a queen or effeminate image, provided the ability to move in and out of different social worlds and social roles.

In this article, I have identified the forces that affect visibility, the methods of social control used to make that visibility invisible, and the ways that different groups of gay men of Cuban descent have constructed lives and cultures within these contexts. The events surrounding the Mariel migration demonstrate the complicated interrelationship between visibility and silence. The same strategies that were employed by Castro's government to silence homosexual expression actually made male homosexuality more visible. At the same time that a consciously and visibly identified group of gay men were establishing their lives in the United States, the media and fellow Cuban Americans weaved a web of silence around their lives and their place in Cuban Miami.

It is ironic (although not unusual) that the tactics of Fidel Castro's revolutionary government and those of the Cuban American exile community share so much in common. Silencing strategies were used by the Cuban state, in U.S. media debates, and in today's gay Cuban American community in an attempt to eliminate gender transgression. The issues of silencing and visibility meet on the terrain of gender behavior and its relation to perceived homosexual behavior. Effeminacy was targeted by the Cuban state; the same "ostentatious" expressions of homosexuality finally caught the eye of a few journalists who were quickly scorned for their lack of numerical data; and it is the fear of being associated with effeminacy that underlies the interviews I conducted with Cuban American gay men.

Notes

This research was assisted by a fellowship from the Sexuality Research Fellowship Program of the Social Science Research Council with funds provided by the Ford Foundation and by the University of California's President's Fellowship.

1. *Escoria* translates loosely to "scum." *Antisocial,* which literally translates to "antisocial," is a catchall term often used to refer to "ostentatious" homosexuality (Ian Lumsden, *Machos, Maricones, and Gays: Cuba and Homosexuality* [Philadelphia: Temple University Press, 1996], 83).

2. After Mariel, a whole scholarly debate emerged about the true nature of the Mariel immigrants, addressing questions such as: What percentage were really "undesirables"? Were these immigrants really different from previous Cuban migrations? How did these migrants fare economically compared to previous migrations? For more on this debate, see Benigno E. Aguirre, "Cuban Mass Migration and the Social Construction of Deviants," *Bulletin of Latin American Research* 13 (1994): 155–83; Robert L. Bach, Jennifer B. Bach, and Timothy Triplett, "The Flotilla 'Entrants': Latest and Most Controversial," *Cuban Studies* 11–12, no. 1–2 (1981/1982): 29–48; Gastón A. Fernández, "Comment—the Flotilla Entrants: Are They Different?" ibid., 49–54; Eduardo A. Gamarra, "Comment: The Continuing Dilemma of the Freedom Flotilla Entrants," *Cuban Studies* 12, no. 2 (1982): 87–91; Mark F. Peterson, "The Flotilla Entrants: Social Psychological Perspectives on Their Employment," ibid., 81–85; Alejandro Portes, Juan M. Clark, and Robert D. Manning, "After Mariel: A Survey of the Resettlement Experiences of 1980 Cuban Refugees in Miami," *Cuban Studies* 15, no. 2 (1985): 37–59; Alejandro Portes and Leif Lensen, "The Enclave and the Entrants: Patterns of Ethnic Enterprise in Miami before and after Mariel," *American Sociological Review* 54 (1989): 929–49. For an analysis of Mariel as a moral epidemic, see Benigno E. Aguirre, Rogelio Sáenz, and Brian Sinclair James, "Marielitos Ten Years Later: The Scarface Legacy," *Social Science Quarterly* 78 (1997): 487–507.

3. Thomas D. Boswell and James R. Curtis, *The Cuban American Experience: Culture, Images, and Perspectives* (Totawa, NJ: Rowman and Littlefield, 1983), 56.

4. Bach, Bach, and Triplett, "The Flotilla 'Entrants'"; Portes, Clark, and Manning, "After Mariel."

5. Portes, Clark, and Manning, "After Mariel."

6. During 1980, Miami also confronted mass migration from Haiti, race riots after an all-white jury acquitted four white officers in the killing of a black man, and a racially charged English-only election campaign. For a discussion of these events, as well as the Mariel migration and its effect on the city of Miami, see Alejandro Portes and Alex Stepick, *City on the Edge: The Transformation of Miami* (Berkeley: University of California Press, 1993).

7. Luis Salas, *Social Control and Deviance in Cuba* (New York: Praeger, 1979), 153.

8. Debra Evenson, *Revolution in Balance: Law and Society in Contemporary Cuba* (Boulder: Westview, 1994), 159.

9. Lumsden, *Machos, Maricones, and Gays*, 183.

10. Salas, *Social Control and Deviance in Cuba*, 153.

11. It is interesting to note that when the legal code was revised in 1987, the language of this law was changed, and references to "public ostentation" of homosexuality were omitted. However, "homosexual behavior that causes a 'public scandal,' either because it contravenes public decency or because it entails sexually importuning another person" was still considered illegal, and the penalties were increased to three to twelve months (Lumsden, *Machos, Maricones, and Gays*, 84).

12. Marvin Leiner, *Sexual Politics in Cuba: Machismo, Homosexuality, and AIDS* (Boulder: Westview, 1994); Lumsden, *Machos, Maricones, and Gays*; Allen Young, *Gays under the Cuban Revolution* (San Francisco: Grey Fox, 1981).

13. Leiner, *Sexual Politics in Cuba*, 31.

14. All names have been changed unless noted otherwise. All translations by the author unless otherwise noted.

15. Leiner, *Sexual Politics in Cuba*, 31.

16. "For in Cuba . . . the trial of visibility was enforced as a criterion for measuring the degree of 'social pathology' exhibited by gay men" (Paul Julian Smith, "Cuban Homosexualities: On the Beach with Néstor Almendros and Reinaldo Arenas," in *Hispanisms and Homosexualities,* ed. Sylvia Molloy and Robert McKee Irwin (Durham, NC: Duke University Press, 1998), 256.

17. Leiner, *Sexual Politics in Cuba,* 23.

18. For more on Che Guevara's description of the "New Man," see Che Guevara, "Socialism and Man in Cuba," in *Che Guevara and the Cuban Revolution,* ed. David Deutschmann (Sydney, Australia: Pathfinder, 1987). For an analysis of Guevara's conceptualization of the "New Man" in the context of his larger political trajectory, see Carlos Tablada, *Che Guevara: Economics and Politics in the Transition to Socialism* (Sydney, Australia: Pathfinder, 1987).

19. Lee Lockwood, *Castro's Cuba* (New York: Vintage, 1969), 107.

20. Castro later softened his official stance on homosexuality, and the degree of systematized persecution of homosexuals later decreased in Cuba (Lumsden, *Machos, Maricones, and Gays*). However, this article highlights the historical conditions experienced by gay men arriving during Mariel. State practices toward male homosexuals in revolutionary Cuba prior to 1980 were severe, and it is this historical condition that framed the experiences of gay men arriving at that time.

21. "Si bien nuestra tradición católica y machista nos convierte en un terreno fácil a la fertilización de actitudes anti-homosexuales, nunca un presidente había tomado una actitud oficial al respecto." Cifuentes here is commenting on a speech Fidel Castro made during the First Congress on Education and Culture (René Cifuentes, "Los Parametros Del Paraiso," *Mariel* 11, no. 5 (Spring 1984): 12.

22. Emilio Bejel, *Gay Cuban Nation* (Chicago: University of Chicago Press, 2001), 96.

23. Young, *Gays under the Cuban Revolution,* 27, 78–88.

24. José Quiroga, "Homosexualities in the Tropic of Revolution," in *Sex and Sexuality in Latin America,* ed. Daniel Balderston and Donna J. Guy (New York: New York University Press, 1997), 134–36.

25. Bejel notes, "this time of great homophobic furor in Cuba brought signs of the homosexual specter never before seen: works and personal projects by writers and artists in which homosexuality occupied a central role" (Bejel, *Gay Cuban Nation,* 103).

26. My use of identification follows Stuart Hall's reworking of Louis Althusser. See Stuart Hall, "Ethnicity: Identity and Difference," *Radical America* 23, no. 4 (1989): 9–20.

27. In this section, I focus mostly on the *Miami Herald* because I am especially interested in the mainstream media coverage in the Miami area. I discuss articles that deal specifically with homosexuality, not those that just mention homosexuals as part of a list of "undesirable" elements of the new migrants.

28. Michael Massing, "The Invisible Cubans," *Columbia Journalism Review* 19 (1980): 49–51; Young, *Gays under the Cuban Revolution.*

29. Massing, "The Invisible Cubans."

30. Resettlement camps were established for Mariel migrants awaiting sponsors. Camps were established in Fort Chaffee, Eglin Air Force Base, and Fort Indiantown Gap.

31. Massing, "The Invisible Cubans," 49.

32. Ibid., 50.

33. Warren Brown, "Cuban Boatlift Drew Thousands of Homosexuals; Thousands of Refugees from Cuba Are Homosexual," *Washington Post,* July 7, 1980.

34. Massing, "The Invisible Cubans," 50.

35. Warren Brown, "Gay Refugees Await Sponsors," *Miami Herald,* July 7, 1980.

36. Elinor Burkett, "The Price," *Miami Herald,* April 1, 1990, 14.

37. Rene V. Murai, "Rebuttal to Tropic Article on Mariel Gays," *Miami Herald,* April 13, 1990.

38. Alejandro Portes, "Homosexuality among Mariel Men," *Miami Herald,* September 8, 1991.

39. Ibid., 4C.

40. Reinaldo Arenas, *Before Night Falls,* trans. Dolores M. Koch (New York: Viking, 1993).

41. Ibid., 105–7.

42. For scripts and stills from *Tent City,* see Jorge Gutiérrez Ulla, ed., *Dos filmes de Mariel* (Madrid: Editorial Playor, 1986).

CHAPTER SEVEN

Migrancy, Modernity, Mobility

Quotidian Struggles and Queer Diasporic Intimacy

Martin F. Manalansan IV

I was sitting in a cramped apartment in Queens, New York, in the spring of 1992 after talking for more than an hour with Roberto, one of my informants, when he suddenly blurted, "Look around you, this is not the glamorous life that people back in Manila think I have. They all believe I live in a brownstone or a spacious house on Fifth Avenue—like the ones in the movies and TV. They don't know the daily drama I have to go through here just to make it. Although if you ask me whether I would exchange the struggle here with a cushy life over back in the Philippines, never darling, never!"[1]

The complicated twists and turns of Roberto's declaration reveal a particular dimension of gay life that is often missed if not ignored in queer scholarship—the daily life struggles and experiences of queer immigrant men of color. This essay focuses on my ethnographic fieldwork research with Filipino gay immigrant men living in the New York City area. I use the term "gay" as a provisional term and intersperse it with "queer" as a rubric and to signal the cultural dissonance queer immigrants experience with identity categories and cultural practices.

I conducted research from 1990 to 1995 focusing on the various strategies of identity articulation and self-formation of Filipino gay immigrants. My fieldwork involved over a hundred informal interviews and countless observations in various sites such as bars, households, and streets, but the whole project is built around fifty life history interviews of Filipino gay immigrants who have a median age of thirty-one and have lived in the United States from two years to thirty years.[2]

I am interested in the ways the seemingly mundane activities of daily life construct a vital arena in which to investigate various underexplored issues, specifically the connections between everyday life, intimacy, and diasporic queer identity formation. While there has been an emerging body of scholarship in recent years around the travails and travels of gay identity and peoples within a globalizing world, most of these works have concentrated on social movements that provide panoramic snapshots of people and communities on the verge of universal queer comradeship. While the works of Barry, Dyvendak, and Krouwel and Altman[3] have ably analyzed global efforts of queer social movements that are demanding rights and creating viable communities in various parts of the world, they have overemphasized collective and organized acts with little or no regard to how queer subjects apprehend and negotiate the cultural products of these transnational movements of ideas, technology, and people.

Following Appadurai's reworking of locality,[4] I am interested in the interscalar connections between the lived locality and the larger seemingly more expansive sites of the city, the nation, and the global. More important, this essay is a response to the overvalorization of circuits and flows in the study of queer globalization and transnationalism; it highlights how queer subjects mediate these processes[5]

While heavily influenced by the body of lesbian and gay community research, my work departs from it by centering on the seemingly private and banal aspects of queer people's lives. While most ideas about queer community and identity formations are based on organized public enactments of gayness and lesbianness, the focus on the everyday reveals not only the inadequacy of conventional narratives where self and community progressively unfold, it also points to the complexities of various intersections and borderlands of race, gender, class, and sexuality in diasporic and immigrant groups. The everyday also troubles, if not resists, the conventional time-space binary by expressing the ways in which memory is spatialized and space is entangled with intimate habits, routines, personal histories, and deviant chronologies.[6] Moreover, influenced by the works of the social theorist Michel de Certeau and the feminist sociologist Dorothy Smith,[7] I take the everyday as a crucial "problematic" and as a site of tactical maneuvers for creating selves and forging relationships for marginalized groups, particularly diasporic queers everywhere. In other words, the focus on the quotidian life unveils the veneer of the ordinary and the commonplace to lay bare the intricate and difficult hybrid negotiations and struggles between hegemonic social forces and voices from below.

This essay documents a specific instance, a case or moment if you will, that grounds the cultural, political, and historical specificities of Filipino diasporic gay men's experiences within the uneven yet hegemonic power of global capitalist expansion. These men's experiences are anchored to the Philippines' long enduring political, cultural, historical, and economic connections to the United States and being part of the intensification of movement of labor and capital in the late twentieth century.[8] Yet this contextual anchoring is a backdrop to the creative tensions between these men's individual predicaments and larger social forces.

Everyday life is a site for critically viewing and "reading" modernity.[9] Unlike traditional historiography, which depends on grand narratives of "famous men" and great events, the narrative of everyday life reveals the rich intricacies of the commonplace. Everyday life intersects and engages with the intimate, the private, and the search for home in modern life. While these three sites are not necessarily equivalent to each other, I would argue that they meet at critical junctures, especially in the displaced lives of queer immigrants.

Intimacy, according to Lauren Berlant, is a crucial yet ambivalent practice in modern life because of its connections to domesticated and normative forms of relationships and spaces such as home, family, and privacy.[10] If home, privacy, and domesticity are vexed locations for queer subjects, particularly those in the diaspora,[11] then it follows that queers' struggles toward finding, building, remembering, and settling into a home, as well as the displacements brought about by migration, create a sphere of what has been called diasporic intimacy.[12] Diasporic intimacy constitutes these struggles that showcase the different ways in which the state, public life, and the "world" outside intrude on and permeate these seemingly bounded, private, and domestic spaces of home and how diasporic subjects confront them. The process of creating diasporic intimacy can be achieved either through counterpublic cultural productions[13] or through more mundane routes that translate and transform "the habitual estrangements of everyday life abroad."[14] Therefore, I suggest that everyday life is the space for examining the creation and rearticulation of queer selves in the diaspora.

My analysis of the everyday is shaped by my understanding of biyuti and drama, which are two emic concepts or idioms typically used in Filipino gay slang or what is called "swardspeak." Swardspeak, as I describe in earlier essays,[15] is an argot that showcases the hybrid cultural engagements of Filipino gay men; the syntax and lexicon of this speech style include Tagalog, Spanish, and English words in a virtual linguistic amalgam. More important, language as exemplified by swardspeak is one of the more crucial spaces for diasporic queers to inhabit particular positions and selves. The deployment of these linguistic concepts of biyuti and drama in the analysis aims to create the lenses through which Filipino gay men's voices, images, and ideas are filtered.

While biyuti and drama betray their provenance from the English language, their deployment in everyday discourse reveals their complex and intricate articulation with various issues of race, gender, class, sexuality, and nationality. "Biyuti,"[16] which may in fact refer to aesthetic experiences and features, also points to a particular notion of the self as highly mercurial and plastic. "Biyuti" is deployed in such situations as a daily greeting: "Kumusta na ang biyuti mo ngayon?" or "How is your biyuti today?" The closely related notion of drama refers to a theatricalized notion of the self and everyday life. Depending on the context, drama can refer to occupation, sexual orientation, health, or daily travails: "Ano ang drama mo ngayon?" or "What is your drama today?"; or conspiratorially when two Filipino gay men are speaking about another person's business, "Ano ba ang drama niya?" or "Now what is this guy's drama?"

The idioms of biyuti and drama are not mere instances of linguistic mimicry between the queer colonized and the gay metropole. Biyuti is not a literal appropriation of American gay camp aesthetics. Rather, Filipino gay men's worldview resonates with cultural practices of what is called Island Southeast Asia, which includes the Philippines and Indonesia. The play of surface, the logic of managing "turbulent hearts,"[17] and the presentation of the self in daily life are not products of the modern or postmodern West but are actually embedded in premodern rituals and ideas in Southeast Asia.[18]

This essay analyzes how these notions are deployed in everyday life situations and how they may illuminate the predicament of Filipino gay immigrant men as diasporic subjects. Through my ethnographic forays into queer everyday life, I seek to arrive at what Gayatri Gopinath termed "a more nuanced understanding of the traffic and travel of competing systems of desire in a transnational frame."[19] I present pivotal vignettes of two Filipino gay immigrants that provide the fulcrum for the mobilization of other narratives. These narratives are glimpses into the ways in which space, time, and selfhood are engaged with and confronted by Filipino gay men in the diaspora.

The Story of an Apartment

The first vignette is about Alden, a middle-aged Filipino gay man, and focuses on his apartment in Greenwich Village. Unlike most cinematic and televisual unreal renderings of the spacious and sophisticated New York City apartment, the small studio apartment will strike many New York City natives as typical, with nothing to really distinguish or mark it as different from other apartments of this type in the city. The living, sleeping, and eating/cooking quarters are situated within a space of twenty by thirty feet.

The furniture exuded a slightly worn quality that Alden acknowledged to be emblematic of a kind of bohemian lifestyle of the "old" Village that is slowly being eroded by the influx of straight white yuppies into the expensive condos and townhouses. Having lived in the same apartment since the early seventies, Alden is one of the lucky few in the city to be in a rent-stabilized apartment, paying a mere four hundred dollars a month to live there.

This apartment, Alden contends, is not just a place but also a story—the story of his life in America. Alden came to America in 1971, and he first lived with a female cousin in New Jersey. His parents thought that it would be important to have somebody to look after him and to serve as a surrogate parent. However, when he arrived at his cousin's house, the cousin declared that she was not about to be responsible for Alden. She admonished Alden to become more self-reliant, since that is what was needed to be able to succeed in America. He was expected to carry his own weight and pay part of the rent. Alden was dismayed at first, but after a while he admitted that it was "a different drama" that he had to learn.

He moved out after six months and stayed with a couple of Filipino men whom he knew from the private school he attended in Manila. After a few petty quarrels about rent, Alden moved out. He found this apartment after a few weeks of searching. He said that finding something on his own was a turning point. For him, it marked a distancing from his way of life in the Philippines where he lived in a big house with his parents, grandparents, unmarried sibling, and several maids. He shared a room with his brothers until he was seventeen. Getting his own room allowed him to create a world for himself. Remembering that moment, he looked around his present studio and said, "When I got my room [at seventeen], I did a full interior decoration. I went crazy and I made it really fabulous. . . . [My mother came into my room and then] she told me to throw out the loud curtains and throw pillows. . . . She said it looked like a [cheesy] dance hall. Here [in my Greenwich Village apartment] I can put in whatever I want. Look at that Herb Ritts poster [of a naked man]. I would not even think of putting that up back home; my mother would upbraid me."

Alden's apartment studio was a study in contrasts. Right across from the wall with the poster of a naked man is a corner he dubbed alternately the "guilt corner" or his "Filipino corner." This corner was in fact a wall filled with photographs, mainly of family members in the Philippines. Occupying the central part of this wall, right next to the television set and VCR, was an altar. He proudly showed me several religious images and statues his mother made him bring to America, mostly antiques that were owned by his great-grandmother. The religious figures included a crucifix, the Virgin Mary, and the Infant Jesus of Prague. When I asked him why he called this his "guilt corner," he said that sometimes life in America can get so frenetic and stressful that he sometimes forgets to call his family back home. After an extremely busy week at work, he would sit on his sofa and stare at the pictures and statues and suddenly feel guilty, then make his weekly overseas call to the Philippines. After a series of sexual encounters, the power of the corner would also befall him, and he would suddenly feel the impulse to pray and would try to become, as he said facetiously, "virtuous" again.

His apartment consists of two parts or sides, the American side with the poster and sofa and the Filipino side with the altar and family pictures. He said that by crossing the room, he traverses two boundaries of his two selves. "This part of the apartment is like the Philippines. So I only need to sashay to the other side, and I am back in America. This is how I feel, always going back and forth even if I have not actually gone home."

Alden still lives in his studio apartment to this day. He does not plan to move because of the rather prohibitive prices of new apartments in the city. When I last visited him in December 1995, a full year after our interview, he had replaced the Herb Ritts poster of the naked man with prints of French impressionists. He reasoned that he was getting old and Herb Ritts was quite passé. The altar was still there on the opposite wall. It still held the same arrangement of religious figures, except for a small bud vase with a yellow rose. Alden reminded me that his aunt was ailing back in the Philippines and he was praying for her.

Everyday Routes to Gay Modernity

Let us move both literally and figuratively from Alden's apartment to another vignette and another dimension of the everyday. Our move is from the meanings of mundane spaces to the meanings of banal activities—chores or routines. Roldan, a forty-year-old informant, arrived in the United States during the early eighties. I followed his daily activities for two straight weeks and off and on for several months. I kept a diary and recorded his daily, weekly, and monthly activities. The following are highlights of the two-week detailed record I made of his daily life. I knew him for five years before I asked him to allow me a voyeuristic view of his activities.

Every day Roldan got up early. He spent most of his weekdays at work and his weekends doing chores around his apartment in Queens. On Wednesday of the first week, after breakfast and putting on his office garb, he looked at the mirror and said, "Nobody would guess who is under this suit and tie. They might think I am a Wall Street executive or a successful career girl [he giggles]—oh, I really need more coffee—I must still be dreaming. People will take one look at me and say—immigrant—fresh off the boat." He then twirled around the mirror: "You know, people in the office treat me a little differently." When I asked him what he meant by a different treatment, he said, "it is difficult to say—you know my biyuti is Asian (Asiatika), so you never really know whether they think right away that I am effeminate or if they think I am gay because I am a thin frail-looking Asian . . . who knows?"

When I pressed further about this issue, he said, "When I used go to bars in the Village or Chelsea, I felt left out—you know I don't look good in a tight T-shirt. But then, when another Filipino gay friend told me about these cross-dressing bars—all of a sudden I found a different world where these gorgeous white men found me attractive." Roldan then revealed how he started to regularly go to cross-dressing bars in

Manhattan every weekend. He said, "I used to think that I came to America to be gay, but then I realized that I came to America to be a real bakla." In this statement, "bakla" is a broad Tagalog rubric that encompasses cross-dressing, hermaphroditism, homosexuality, and effeminacy. He was referring to the fact that he always perceived gayness and gay culture as rooted both in the United States and ultramasculine images and practices. He was reflecting on the fact that he has become more of the bakla than the gay man he thought he was going to be in America because of his weekend leisure activities.

At the same time he was talking about this, Roldan talked about the dangers of being a cross-dresser in public. He was afraid of getting caught and thrown in jail. He was not worried about the embarrassment such a situation may potentially cause but about how such an incident might jeopardize his stay in America. I have known for a long time that Roldan was an undocumented immigrant. He confessed to me about his status in this way: "You know my biyuti is TNT." "TNT" is an acronym used in Filipino queer language or swardspeak and literally means "always in hiding."

He was proud of the fact that no one in the office knew about his immigration status. In fact, he once worked in a personnel department, and one of his duties was to check on the paperwork regarding job candidates' eligibility to work in the United States. Despite this irony, Roldan talked about the difficulty of being in such a legal limbo. He once considered a green card marriage but backed out. When I asked him why he backed out, he answered, "Do you think my biyuti can pass INS scrutiny? I don't think so, sister! One look at me and they will say—oh a big fag, a big bakla!" I countered that maybe the authorities may just see him as another slim Asian man. He said, "Oh, there is too much risk to do that drama, too much . . . I am too afraid." Then he paused for a second and said, "Well, you may be right. I know through the bakla grapevine that there is this . . . [he mentions a famous female impersonator in the Philippines] who was in a green card marriage. Darling, he is now a U.S. citizen. Oh well, he is used to the stage—I am not . . . or maybe I am not always on stage." Then he laughed, this time a little sadly.

He mentioned how he really cannot risk being caught in this situation. He has a family in the Philippines who are dependent on his monthly financial remittances. One weeknight, during the two-week period, Roldan received an urgent phone call from his mother. The phone call was unusual since they always talked on weekends. After talking to her for thirty minutes, Roldan hung up the phone with an irritated facial expression and breathed a long sigh. I asked him if anything was wrong. He said that his mother had just informed him that his youngest sister, whom he was sending to one of the most exclusive private schools in Manila, wanted to get married. She was seventeen years old. Roldan's mother wanted him to talk to the sister to convince her to continue her studies. Roldan was fuming mad, not only at his sister, but also at his mother who expected him to play surrogate father via an overseas phone call. Besides, he said, his father was still alive, but because of his vital role of being provider, he was by default given authority over specific family issues.

He made it clear to me that his family was not poor but middle-class. The money and goods he regularly sends back enable his family to be more comfortable economically, especially during the troubled times in the Philippines. He said that he was looking forward to the day when his responsibility would end. After saying this, he shook his head and admitted that his previous statement was in fact wishful thinking. Then in a voice of surrender he said, "ganyan talaga ang drama—that is how the drama goes."

His weekends, apart from his jaunts to the cross-dressing bars, also included attendance at Sunday mass. He once took me to a church in Greenwich Village with a large Filipino congregation. As part of the service, slips of paper that people dropped in a box near the altar were taken out and read. These slips of paper contained petitions for God's intervention in mundane situations. There were petitions for better health and safe trips back to the Philippines, but there was a significant number of petitions about receiving the green card or passing the nursing licensure examinations. Roldan said, "You can't really mistake this drama for anything but Filipino."

Staging Queer Diasporic Lives

These two vignettes provide an affirmation of the view that immigrants, particularly those from the Third World, "always perceive themselves onstage, their lives resembling a mediocre fiction with occasional romantic outbursts and gray dailiness."[20] Moreover, as Shohat and Stam have argued, these immigrants—or as they call them, "hybrid diasporic subject[s]"—are "confronted with the 'theatrical' challenge of moving, as it were, among diverse performative modes of sharply contrasting and ideological worlds."[21] In other words, citizenship for queers of color and diasporic queers—like Filipinos and those Latino immigrants and exiles that Roque Ramírez and Peña examine in this volume—is not a birthright nor is it about the romance of dissidence; instead, it is about survival and making it.

Diasporic queers in particular refuse the assimilative framework; they not so much carry with them the baggage of tradition but rather are in constant negotiation, or—to use the idioms of biyuti and drama—selfhood and belonging are framed in the process of cultural translation and transformation. The concept of biyuti and drama partakes of this negotiated space between tradition and modernity as queer immigrants move or "sashay" between local, national, and global spaces. Their deployment by Filipino immigrant men living in New York City points to the kind of negotiations that create an "imperfect aesthetics of survival"[22] as well as a counternarrative to the prevailing view of the immigrant route as a movement away from tradition in the homeland and settling into an assimilated modern life in the land of settlement. Moreover, these idioms constitute what can be considered an alternative form of modernity.[23] The bakla or the Filipino gay man is neither a ludic nor an anachronous figure, but a subject in constant mediation whose modernity is not always dependent on Western mainstream queer culture.

The space of the everyday, as in Alden's apartment, portrays an ironic kind of movement inherent in "settling in." His narrative also portrays the possibility of performance in the global/local stage. That is, the story of his apartment narrates in spatial terms the constant engagements with experiences of emplacement and displacement. While physical distance from his family and the Philippines has allowed Alden to create his intimate, seemingly private local space, the routine intrusions and almost habitual hauntings of familial images, voices, and sentiments of both family and organized religion unravel the locality of his Village studio and showcase its transnational connections.

The Philippine corner and the American wall not only reconstruct national landscapes, but also are spatialized translations of desire and propriety. The grammars of desire and propriety are expressed in the kinds of situational and diachronic movement between guilt and pleasure, and between land of settlement and the homeland. It is perhaps no wonder that Alden, who has not been home, realizes a kind of homecoming when certain sentiments arise after sexual encounters or after missing his usual weekly overseas phone call to his family. The ambivalent and troubled relationship between "being at home" and "homecoming" beset queer immigrants like Alden. As such, they are in perpetual motion, shuttling between settling in and feeling displaced.

Diasporic people today are more than ever faced with creating multistranded relationships with the homeland and their new land of settlement.[24] No longer is assimilation the only fate for the present-day immigrant. Immigrants are compelled and propelled by new developments in technology and by increasing mobility of capital to devise a flexible performative repertoire that increases their survival and success in an increasingly unequal yet global world. Familial ties for both Alden and Roldan—as well as for many of my informants—mark the continuity and discontinuity of the immigrant experience. Phone calls, monetary remittances, and regular trips back to the homeland rescue the queer immigrant from this assimilative fate.

Roldan's mental and physical reflections in front of his mirror on a workday reveal how the routine regimes of race and gender permeate if not infect daily assessment of situations involving confrontations, disputes, and obedience.[25] Roldan's astute observation of the forms of racialization in America and their articulation with gender points to the power of his daily experiences and their impact on identity.[26] Because of this situation, bakla as an identity becomes a possibility in the metropole. While bakla is seen as rooted to the homeland, it becomes a tool to negotiate Roldan's cultural discomfort with mainstream gay public life. Immigration narratives are conventionally and popularly constructed as a linear movement from tradition to modernity, but Roldan's observation of being bakla in America rejects this particular teleology. At the same time, his condition is not a retreat from modernity; rather, it unwittingly destabilizes a monolithic gay identity. Roldan's recuperation of bakla, of alienation to both transgender and gay identity politics, is a result of the kinds of daily barrage of images, ideas, and bodies.

The intimate spaces and routines of the everyday may be seen by many as a kind of retreat from worldliness by an individual or a kind of bounded warm refuge of authenticity from the harsh realities of the public sphere, but, as many of my informants have unwittingly performed, for immigrants and exiles the everyday is an incomplete if not imperfect colonization of the wildness and trauma of displacement.[27]

The everyday is an important arena open to manipulation and intrusion by the state. Roldan's fear of being caught by the INS or other authorities extends to his practice of cross-dressing and his cultural discomfort with gay mainstream practices. His routines are tracked by his own fear of being found out as an illegal alien, while at the same time he consciously accepts his place in the queer cultural world in New York City. He realizes that the script or, more appropriately, the drama of dissimulation is a crucial tactic for his legal, cultural, and physical survival. His marginal status in relation to what are considered authentic forms of citizenship and belonging compels him to refigure his routines and re-create his biyuti in America.

A Cautionary Hopefulness

The narratives of Filipino gay men may suggest a dystopic and rather bleak fate. However, I am dissatisfied with current fashionable skepticism over liberation and its overemphasis on failed dreams and dim futures. I am neither resurrecting a grand narrative of redemption nor positing the notion of the global as modernity's triumph over the local. Rather, the ethnographic examples above recast seemingly static locales, such as apartments and routines, into spaces of fervently mobile fictions, tactics, and strategies. And as such, I am convinced that a cautionary hopefulness is very appropriate at this juncture, since Filipino gay men are creating alternative routes for selfhood and belonging despite the unrelenting forces of globalization and the weight of Western institutions and practices. In other words, we need to look beyond the dizzying and often loud noise of overarching global circuits and flows, such as cyberspace images and other technological marvels, and appreciate these voices from below.

In this regard, I want to highlight the opportunities in the ambivalent and often contradictory nature of the quotidian. As I have demonstrated, the narratives of daily life in Filipino gay men's terms are constituted through the drama of survival and the biyuti of pleasure and belonging. These idioms illustrate the ambivalent yet transformative potential of quotidian engagement. Henri Lefebvre warns against the pitfalls of skepticism over the burden and dreariness of *la vie quotidienne.*[28] Instead, Lefebvre urges readers to look beyond the paralyzing effects of the banal and the routine and to appreciate its changeability and dynamism. Following Lefebvre, I finally submit that the everyday struggles of queer subjects within a globalizing world form a strategic path leading not to a teleologically determined home but rather to other more exciting possibilities.

Notes

This essay is a slightly revised section of a chapter from my book *Global Divas: Filipino Gay Men in the Diaspora* (Durham, NC: Duke University Press, 2003). Versions of this paper have been presented at University of California, San Diego, Critical Gender Studies Program Lecture Series; University of California, Davis, Asian American Studies Lecture Series; University of Illinois, Sociocultural Studies Workshop; University of Washington, Recasting Asia Lecture Series; and Bowling Green State University, Provost's Lecture Series. I am grateful to the following for their support and advice: Deb Amory, Rick Bonus, David Eng, Dara Goldman, Gayatri Gopinath, Judith Halberstam, Allan Isaac, Lisa Lampert, Lisa Lowe, Cathy Prendergast, and Chandan Reddy. Special thanks to Eithne Luibhéid and the late Lionel Cantú for shepherding this project, and to the faculty and students at Bowling Green State University for their questions, comments, and hospitality. This essay is for my parents who, despite having chosen to stay put in the Philippines, have encouraged me to venture forth and follow my itinerant ways.

1. Most interviews were conducted in Taglish or code-switching from Tagalog and English. Names of informants have been changed to protect their anonymity.

2. According to the 2000 U.S. census, Filipinos in the United States number around 1.8 million, second only to the Chinese, who are the biggest group of Asian Americans with 2.3 million.

3. Adam Barry, Jan Willem Dyvendak and Andre Krouwel, eds., *The Global Emergence of Gay and Lesbian Politics: National Imprints of a Worldwide Movement* (Philadelphia: Temple University Press, 1994); and Dennis Altman, "Rupture and Continuity? The Internationalization of Gay Identities," *Social Text* 48 (1996): 77–94.

4. Arjun Appadurai, *Modernity at Large: Cultural Dimensions of Globalization* (Minneapolis: University of Minnesota Press, 1996).

5. Elizabeth Povinelli and George Chauncey, "Thinking Sexuality Transnationally: An Introduction," *GLQ* 5, no. 4 (1999): 445.

6. For an excellent ethnography of immigrant spaces and ethnicity among Filipino Americans in California, see Rick Bonus, *Locating Filipino Americans: Ethnicity and the Cultural Politics of Space* (Philadelphia: Temple University Press, 2000).

7. Michel de Certeau, *The Practice of Everyday Life* (New York: Cambridge University Press, 1984); and Dorothy Smith, *The Everyday World as Problematic: A Feminist Sociology* (Boston: Northeastern University Press, 1987). See also Keya Ganguly, *States of Exception: Everyday Life and Postcolonial Identity* (Minneapolis: University of Minnesota Press, 2001).

8. See the following for critical historiographies of Philippine-U.S. relations: Oscar V. Campomanes, "Afterword: The New Empire's Forgetful and Forgotten Citizens; Unrepresentability and Unassimilability in Filipino American Postcoloniali-

ties," *Critical Mass: A Journal of Asian American Cultural Criticism* 2, no. 2 (1995): 145–200; Epifanio San Juan, "Configuring the Filipino Diaspora in the United States," *Diaspora* 3, no. 2 (Fall 1994): 117–34.

9. Svetlana Boym, *Common Places: Mythologies of Everyday Life in Russia* (Cambridge: Harvard University Press, 1994), 20. See also David Frisby and Mike Featherstone, eds., *Simmel on Culture: Selected Writings* (London: Sage, 1997), for key studies on the everyday and modernity.

10. Lauren Berlant, "Intimacy: A Special Issue," *Critical Inquiry* 24, no. 2 (1998): 287.

11. David Eng, "Out Here and Over There: Queerness and Diaspora in Asian American Studies," *Social Text*, no. 52–53 (1997): 31–52; and Gayatri Gopinath, "Homo Economics: Queer Sexualities in a Transnational Frame," in *Burning Down the House,* ed. Rosemary M. George (Boulder, CO: Westview Press, 1998).

12. Paul Gilroy, *The Black Atlantic: Modernity and Double Consciousness* (Cambridge: Harvard University Press, 1993), 16.

13. Gayatri Gopinath, "Funny Boys and Girls: Notes on a Queer South Asian Planet," in *Asian American Sexualities: Dimensions of the Gay and Lesbian Experience,* ed. Russell Leong (New York: Routledge, 1996). Both Gopinath's and Gilroy's notions of diasporic intimacy focus on the creation of public cultural forms, such as bhangra music or hip-hop, respectively.

14. Boym, *Common Places,* 51.

15. "Performing Filipino Gay Experiences in America: Linguistic Strategies in a Transnational Context," in *Beyond the Lavender Lexicon: Authenticity, Imagination, and Appropriation in Lesbian and Gay Language,* ed. William Leap (New York: Gordon and Breach, 1996); and "Speaking of AIDS: Language and the Filipino Gay Experience in America," in *Discrepant Histories: Translocal Essays in Philippine Cultures,* ed. Vicente Rafael (Philadelphia: Temple University Press, 1996).

16. My spelling of "biyuti" instead of "beauty" is to signal the former's departure from the constrictions of the English word and also to acknowledge the unique pronunciation styles and usage by Filipino gay men. In some cases, the word is shortened to "biyu" or "B.Y." to signal attractiveness.

17. This is from the title of the book by Unni Wikan, *Managing Turbulent Hearts: A Balinese Formula for Living* (Chicago: University of Chicago Press, 1990), which showcases the idiom of self-transformation as crucial in the construction of persons and selves in Southeast Asia.

18. See the following for a theorization of the notion of beauty in the Philippines: Fennell Cannell, *Power and Intimacy in the Christian Philippines* (Cambridge: Cambridge University Press, 1999); and Mark Johnson, *Beauty and Power: Transgendering and Cultural Transformation in the Southern Philippines* (Oxford: Berg, 1997).

19. Gopinath, "Homo Economics," 116.

20. Svetlana Boym, "On Diasporic Intimacy: Ilya Kabakov's Installations and Immigrant Homes," *Critical Inquiry* 24, no. 2 (1998): 502.

21. Ella Shohat and Robert Stam, *Unthinking Eurocentrism: Multiculturalism and the Media* (London: Routledge, 1994), 42.

22. Boym, "On Diasporic Intimacy."

23. In my book, *Global Divas: Filipino Gay Men in the Diaspora* (Durham, NC: Duke University Press, 2003), I develop this idea of an alternative modernity among Filipino gay men in the diaspora.

24. See Linda Basch, Nina Glick Schiller, and Cristina Blanc-Szanton, *Nations Unbound: Transnational Project, Postcolonial Predicaments, and Deterritorialized Nation-States* (New York: Gordon and Breach, 1994).

25. This includes the hegemonic "whiteness" prevalent in gay mainstream cultural images and products.

26. See Lisa Lowe, *Immigrant Acts: On Asian American Cultural Politics* (Durham, NC: Duke University Press, 1996), for an excellent discussion of gender and Asian American citizenship.

27. Boym, "On Diasporic Intimacy," 500.

28. Henri Lefebvre, *Critique of Everyday Life* (London: Verso, 1991).

CHAPTER EIGHT

Claiming Queer Cultural Citizenship

Gay Latino (Im)Migrant Acts in San Francisco

Horacio N. Roque Ramírez

WOMAN 2, *in a marked Uruguayan accent:* Good evening. *(Alejandro and Woman 1 exchange glances.)*

WOMAN 1: Sit down. You're crossing, too? Where do you come from?

WOMAN 2: From Uruguay.

ALEJANDRO: What are you doing so far from home?

WOMAN 2: I wanted to come to the United States with my son, but they wouldn't give us a visa. But then I saw on television that people cross running from Mexico to the United States, so I got tickets to Mexico and to Tijuana, and I told myself, we're going to run like any other Mexican. *(Alejandro and Woman 1 laugh.)*

WOMAN 1: Welcome, then.

ALEJANDRO: Welcome to the adventure.[1]

By the time viewers see and hear the above border-crossing sequence in the 1999 independent, Spanish-language film *Del otro lado* (On/from the other side), they have already followed Alejandro's own "adventures" in Mexico City. Finding himself among strangers while weighing the risks for crossing the U.S.–Mexico border, after the *coyote*, or people smuggler, has deserted them in an isolated mountain in the middle of the night, Alejandro already carries multiple losses during his trip. He has left behind his biological family, his gay male lover, and his tight circle of gay friends in Mexico. Certainly a dangerous adventure for all, Alejandro's own crossing involves leaving queer networks behind. He becomes just another immigrant in flight, but Alejandro's own trek involves the additional burden of negotiating his sexuality as a gay Latino who is HIV-positive and in search of medication to deal with his infection.

While Alejandro has these "invisible" life issues to address in *Del otro lado*, his character also personifies the economic, social, and cultural dislocation of hundreds of thousands of Latinos in the United States—brown bodies disconnected from blood kinships and cultural ties in search of the promise of a better future in the United States. For these immigrants, California since the 1990s literally and figuratively has become a land of selective inclusion: immigrants fill the underpaid labor needs of the state, but are made invisible in the cultural life of its citizenry—politically, linguistically, and otherwise.[2]

Scholars have taken up the question of citizenship and specifically that of cultural citizenship to address Latinos' political claims for inclusion in the United States. This idea of cultural citizenship speaks to claims for excluding and for belonging. Rather than encompassing a notion of citizenship solely as that quality of *legally and officially* belonging to the nation, cultural citizenship speaks to what Renato Rosaldo refers to as the "uneven field of structural inequalities."[3] In this field, domination and marginalization structure society, making some subjects "less equal" than others. But also in this field, those deemed lesser subjects aspire to eliminate such hierarchies and to redefine the meaning of citizenship for everyone. "Cultural citizenship," these scholars argue, offers an opportunity to consider everyday forms for seeking entitlement in the United States:

> [W]hat makes cultural citizenship so exciting is that it offers us an alternative perspective to better comprehend cultural processes that result in community building and in political claims raised by marginalized groups on the broader society. Unlike assimilation, which emphasizes absorption into the dominant white, Anglo-European society, or cultural pluralism, which conceives of retention of minority cultural traits and traditions within U.S. society, but nonetheless privileges white European culture and history and assumes retention of existing class and racial [and gender] hierarchies under the pretense of political equality, cultural citizenship allows for the potential of opposition, of restructuring and reordering society.[4]

Cultural citizenship thus allows for an exploration of alternatives to the dominant model of citizenship based on assimilation, for new possibilities for Latinos—immigrant and U.S. born—to make public communities and claim space and rights as full members of society.

Cultural productions like *Del otro lado* become key sites for understanding how contestations over cultural citizenship operate—not only do they represent such contestations symbolically, but they also provide a literal means to intervene into these issues. Lisa Lowe discusses culture as a critical space for engaging the national discourse of citizenship: "[C]ultural productions emerging out of the contradictions of immigrant marginality," Lowe argues,

> displace the fiction of reconciliation, disrupt the myth of national identity by revealing its gaps and fissures, and intervene in the narrative of national development that would illegitimately locate the "immigrant" before history or exempt the "immigrant" from history.[5]

As direct responses to the exclusionary political and cultural representations of the nation, Lowe continues, Asian Americans generate critical *acts:* "the *acts* of labor, resistance, memory, and survival, as well as the politicized cultural work that emerged from dislocation and disidentification."[6]

Building on these scholars' notions of cultural citizenship and politicized cultural work, I explore in this essay two instances of gay Latino (im)migrant cultural productions in San Francisco. Based on oral history field research and existing archives, I look at the social history and significance of two productions. The first one, the 1984 play *El corazón nunca me ha mentido* (My heart has never lied to me), was an adaptation of Salvadoran novelist Manlio Argueta's *Un día en la vida (One Day of Life)*.[7] Set in 1970s El Salvador, both the testimonial novel and the play related the political and social dislocations in the country that decade. Written and produced in San Francisco by two gay Chicanos from Texas, the play drew attention not only for its sociopolitical engagement, but also for its homoerotic critique of patriarchy. The second cultural production I explore is the film *Del otro lado* (1999). Written in the mid-1990s in San Francisco by two gay Mexican immigrants, the film follows the challenges of a gay male couple in Mexico City and the decision of one of the partners to migrate to the United States as a result of his HIV diagnosis. Exploring the processes of departure, arrival, and exodus for gay Mexican immigrants in the context of AIDS and of economic dislocation in Mexico and the United States, *Del otro lado* is a cultural text of queer social membership and cultural citizenship. Together, these two cultural productions reveal how cultural works provide the means to materially renegotiate citizenship and the importance of reconceiving the very meaning of citizenship itself.

Sexiled Bodies and Their Cultures

Since the 1960s, queer Latinas and Latinos have been part of queer migrations settling in San Francisco.[8] Many have been regional migrants, while others have traveled farther, across international borders. Since the organizing days of the Gay Latino Alliance in San Francisco in the 1970s (one of the first gay Latino organizations in the country), local, national, and international politics have intersected in the lives of queer Latina and Latino activists in the Bay Area. For many of these (im)migrants, their lives in San Francisco have revolved around maintaining old networks of support while establishing new ones in the city's heterogeneous queer communities. These are the sexual migrants Manuel Guzmán has referred to as "sexiles," those queer migrants leaving home/nation as a result of their sexuality.[9]

Queer Latino immigrants have had to contend with exclusionary politics around their immigration status in the country. But they have also had to negotiate their membership in the local queer body, specifically the queer Latina/o community. Despite some of the local rhetoric of diversity and openness, San Francisco has not been an altogether welcoming place for immigrants.[10] Queer and Latino nonprofit service agencies themselves have often informally demarcated services and alliances around immigrant/nonimmigrant social memberships. Although not formalized, these demarcations in practice speak to the limits of community and citizenship for queers marked as immigrants, and for immigrants marked as queer. The negotiations and relations between immigrant and nonimmigrant Latino queers have taken place on two social fields, one political and the other cultural. Their efforts to mark identity, visibility, and space on these fields speak precisely to the notion of cultural citizenship, of collective membership always in contestation.

Given the role organizing has played for many gay Latino immigrants, their cultural work is an excellent space for examining their negotiation of citizenship and social membership in the national and local body. "Culture" in their work speaks to the productions themselves, but also to the depiction and experience of social and community life. To employ Raymond Williams's observation about the social experience of "culture" as a lived present, their productions represent "structures of feeling," "affective elements of consciousness and relationships: not feel-ings against thought, but thought as felt and feeling as thought."[11]

Feeling and thinking about culture and political change were at the center of the lives of the four gay cultural workers producing *El corazón nunca me ha mentido* and *Del otro lado*. All of them had (im)migration histories leading to their work in San Francisco, histories that in turn impacted the content and direction of their work *as* (im)migrants. In 1988 Gustavo Martín Cravioto, one of the writers and producers of *Del otro lado*, fled the economic deterioration of Mexico City and arrived in California at age twenty-two, originally moving into the city of Novato, north of San Francisco. Eventually he helped about fifteen other friends and relatives, gay and straight, to immigrate to the United States. In this regard, his extensive immigration network, extending from Mexico to the United States (and back) was similar to that of many other Latin American immigrants (gay and non-gay), what Roger Rouse has aptly described as a "transnational migrant circuit."[12] Already identifying as gay in Mexico, Gustavo permanently moved to San Francisco in 1992, attracted by the city's gay Latino cultural life and the opportunities it offered.

By the time Gustavo moved to San Francisco, an AIDS service indus-try had already developed in the Mission District, the city's historically Latino neighborhood.[13] Gustavo joined these efforts, volunteering in these and mainstream (white) services responding to the ongoing AIDS crisis. While the epidemic was beginning to level off for white gays, it continued to impact disproportionately gays of color, including a large immigrant class. As Gustavo's volunteering efforts turned into paid posi-tions as an outreach worker, he came into close contact with immigrant and nonimmigrant HIV clients. An immigrant himself, this segment in the city's Latino population needing HIV education and services would remain his priority.

Mario Callitzin, the other writer and producer of *Del otro lado*, was also a Mexican immigrant when he landed in the Bay Area, although with a different family history than Gustavo's. The son of two professionals in Mexico City, Mario moved from this Mexican metropolis to a small town in South Texas in the late 1970s. Immersing into his studies to es-cape the culture shock and racism in the United States, and the "terror" he describes following him since childhood as a result of being harassed as a "sissy," Mario attended Stanford University in the mid-1980s. There feminist, race theory, and anti-apartheid study groups fueled him with more purpose, leading to the birth of what he refers to as "Mario the activist."[14] Although Mario returned to Mexico briefly and joined the gay movements there, he moved back to the Bay Area with his lover, finding the economic challenges in Mexico too overwhelming. By the early 1990s he had joined several San Francisco gay Latino organizations, usually in close connection to the work taking place elsewhere in Latin America and especially in Mexico.

Compared to Gustavo and Mario, Juan Pablo Gutiérrez and Rodrigo Reyes, the producers of *El corazón nunca me ha mentido,* were a different type of migrant when they landed in San Francisco. They were sexiles too, given the intimate connections between their gay selves and the work they sought to carry out in San Francisco. The son of migrant workers from the small Texas town of Westlaco, Rodrigo moved permanently to San Francisco in the early 1970s, part of the large gay migration to the city in that decade. Migrant work had taken Rodrigo and his family throughout the Midwest. With the financial support of one of his white high school teachers, Rodrigo attended Ohio State University, giving him an opportunity to dabble in acting and theater. This first theater experience was the foundation for his experiments one decade later in San Francisco's Mission District as an openly gay Chicano cultural worker. It was not until he got to San Francisco, Rodrigo would recall decades later, that he felt "at home," as a gay Chicano organizing around racial and gay consciousness—simultaneously.

Juan Pablo Gutiérrez, too, was a Texan transplant in San Francisco's Mission District. He arrived in the midst of the AIDS epidemic in the city, in 1985, one decade after the large gay migration had brought tens of thousands of newcomers to the city. A different kind of large migration into the city was taking place in the 1980s, one visible in the Mission District. As revolutionary struggles had triumphed in Nicaragua under the Sandinistas, and ongoing guerrilla warfare challenged U.S.-backed right-wing dictatorships in Guatemala and El Salvador, Central America was sending hundreds of thousands of its citizens to the United States, a visible portion of them to San Francisco's Mission District.

The very trip taking Juan Pablo from Texas to what he would eventually carry out in the Bay Area revolved precisely around Central American and particularly Salvadoran reality. Picking up the English translation of Manlio Argueta's testimonial novel *One Day of Life,* he read it on his way to San Francisco and began to make plans for a possible the-atrical adaptation once he landed. Bringing with him a history of gay Chicano activism in Texas and cultural work throughout the South-west, Juan Pablo had a politicized theatrical sensibility grounded on Chicano experiences. Upon reading *One Day of Life*, his interest turned to the ongoing conditions left behind by thousands of refugees escaping political repression and social deterioration in El Salvador.

As part of a long tradition of cultural and community organizing in the Mission District, Juan Pablo, Rodrigo, Mario, and Gustavo brought to their respective cultural stages (im)migration experiences and the politics of their specific (gay) exodus.[15] How they engaged gender and sexuality in these politicized cultural creations was itself a manifestation of the coalescence of gay and immigrant histories.

El corazón nunca me ha mentido: Bodies and Nations at War

AIDS and the specter of death enveloped a great deal of gay and lesbian culture and activism in San Francisco in the 1980s. While the 1970s had been a decade for sexual liberation and celebration, the 1980s was a dif-ferent, less festive one. But many, like Juan Pablo, still came, especially those connected to earlier sexiles. For gay Latinos, the cultural framing of AIDS as white and gay offered a convenient though counterproductive source of denial—a "gay white disease" would not affect them. As soon as gay Latinos began to get ill in visible numbers, however, community-based health agencies could not avoid responding to the growing crisis.

One challenge in this AIDS crisis involved educating Latino men who had sex with men yet identified only as heterosexual. Vesting themselves with gender and sexual capital framed in heteronormativity, these men nevertheless had sex with other men, often while maintaining sexual relations with women partners and, many health workers feared, with-out consistent safer sex practices. That a large portion of these men were undocumented added yet more complexity to the educational response: it required a simultaneous consideration of the men's sexual identity and agency, the necessity of taking an HIV antibody test to ensure they were negative in order to qualify for residency status, and the community's response (or lack thereof) when many found out about their HIV-positive status as undocumented immigrants. Thus, the fight against AIDS among Latinos in San Francisco involved not only those who openly identified as gay or bisexual, but also a large segment of the

Figure 8.1. Flyer for Rodrigo Reyes and Juan Pablo Gutiérrez's *El corazón nunca me ha mentido*. Courtesy of Luis Alberto de la Garza C. and Archivo Rodrigo Reyes.

community of Latino men holding on to a public heterosexual sense of self, and thus engaged in a larger community debate around gender and sexuality, sexual consciousness and secrecy, and immigrant rights and needs.

Juan Pablo's and Rodrigo's theatrical adaptation of *One Day of Life* addressed questions of gender and sexuality directly relevant to this community dialogue. Framing El Salvador's political and armed struggles of the 1970s, the novel narrates the stories of rural poor Salvadorans caught in battle zones: between younger, progressive Catholic priests speaking on behalf of the poor and the military repressive forces targeting any activity deemed subversive; between the need to subsist on an everyday basis and the anger and desire to join the armed struggle against the government. Rodrigo and Juan Pablo's adapted play addressed these personal, political, and emotional battles. Directed by Rodrigo, the play represented the first time in San Francisco Chicanos theatrically addressed the revolutionary period in El Salvador, despite the fact that their presence in the Mission District had been felt strongly long before. Although Chicanos cowrote the play, the production team was an amalgamation of nationalities and (im)migrant histories in the Mission District, with gay and non-gay, Salvadoran, Spanish, Mexican, and Nicaraguan actors. One of Rodrigo's lovers, a Salvadoran ex-soldier, helped develop the dialogue to reflect more closely Salvadoran vernacular Spanish. The then-exiled Salvadoran Argueta in Costa Rica reviewed the adapted script and made no corrections, and the project moved to bring local political attention to an ongoing international crisis.[16]

The play entered several cultural fields of contestation. First, the play represented the first time the long tradition of Chicano *teatro* (theater) in the city concerned itself with Central American immigrants. Second, the explorations of male gender and sexuality brought up immigrant *and* nonimmigrant homosocial visibility. A complex and, for some, controversial text, the play became an intersection for local, national, and transnational representations. Running for five weekends in the Mission District's small Capp Street Playhouse from late June through early August 1985, *El corazón* was a cultural product produced by two openly gay Chicano cultural workers wanting to have the local Latino community engage grassroots political struggle in Central America as well as questions of gender and sexuality there and locally.

Culeros y Cultura

The play followed the general plotline of the novel, but a great deal of the tension in *El corazón* revolved around violence, shame, and stigma on the body. The everyday violence of poverty was present, but so were the gendered ways through which the state and its forces of repression instilled fear in the general population. Both women's and men's bodies were the focus of perceived or real violence in the civil war, but it was the violence on men's masculinity, enacted through the literal and figurative violation of their anus, that became contentious in the play's run in the Mission District. Specifically, it was through the repetitive, excessive invocation of the *culero*, or "faggot"—El Salvador's most popular derogatory term for the man penetrated while having sex with another man—that the play drew attention to the strict policing and punishment of "weak" male gender. The recurrent references by members of the National Guard to *culeros* and any perceived *culero*-like behavior often became comedic. But their use realistically linked patriarchal codes of masculinity to forms of violence in and out of war believed necessary for enforcing a national order. Culturally, the term *culero* suggests that which presumably all honorable, masculine men will not allow to have touched, much less penetrated: their *culo* or anus. *Culero* thus singularly and violently infers a fear of penetration, which is to mark all *culeros* and/ or gay/homosexual men, specifically the "passive" (penetrated) kind.[17]

In one of the scenes exploring this gender matrix of masculinity, propriety, and the need to defend the nation from "weak" ideas, *El corazón* depicted the encounter between two guards and a young priest. In the scene, just as a young couple leaves a store for fear of what the approaching guards might do to them, the guards make not-so-veiled threats against the priest about to enter the store:

GUARD II *(to the store clerk):* Give me two sodas. *(He takes them and moves away without paying for them. He sits next to the other guard at a table.)* Hey look, I think these *culeros* are beginning to respect us. Ah, that's right, you're from here. You must be a *culero*, too.

GUARD I *(as priest enters):* Hey, if you want a real *culero*, one just came in.

PRIEST II: Good afternoon, Don Sebastián. Can you please give me two colones worth of candy.

DON SEBASTIÁN: My pleasure, Padre. Anything else?

PRIEST II: No, that's all this time. Thank you.[18]

Soon after this exchange, in a dramatic turn, repression comes alive as the guards apprehend the priest illegally; following a direct verbal confrontation, they take him out of the store to a nearby river. The store clerk witnesses the kidnapping and decides to inform local residents. The homophobic "playfulness" with which the guards greeted the priest earlier turns to actual violence. While *culero* had been staged only as a derogatory remark in the beginning, the guards turn the stigmatic label into an actual act of violence. After taking him to the secluded area and killing him, they follow with a final symbolic act of sticking a wooden stake in his anus.

Finding the priest's bloodied body proves to be the final blow for Chepe, a local campesino, and his family; they decide to take action despite fears of yet more reprisal. With other neighbors, Justino and Adolfina, they begin to look for the guards. Armed with wooden sticks and an old rifle, they find the guards back at the same small store. The neighbors carefully move in on them, threatening to give the guards a taste of their own medicine:

JUSTINO: Hold it there, fuckers, or I'll send you to the other world right now. (At this moment the others enter.)

CHEPE: Sons of a bitch! Damn you!

JUSTINO: Get out, fuckers, get out. Now we're going to see how courageous you are. (All of them push the guards out and head with them toward the same place where they found the priest. They form a circle around the guards, threatening them with sticks and machetes.)

CHEPE: Take your pants off! Take them off, didn't you hear?!

NEIGHBOR: Now we're gonna do to you what you did to the priest!

GUARD I: No, not that! Anything except that!

ADOLFINA: Ah, you don't like it, right? Shitty monsters! Why do you like to do it to others?

GUARD II: Not that, please, not that! Kill us, but please don't do that to us! (They all form a circle around the guards while they force them to undress.)[19]

Ridiculing the guards who remain naked, the neighbors begin to laugh, their anger subdued through this collective act for justice. They walk away from the scene with the guards' clothes and firearms, leaving them exposed and never carrying out their threats of violence on their bodies.

This comedic effect on stage serves as an entry point for a critique of repressive, military heteronormativity. The fact that the neighbors only threaten but never carry out the act of violating the guards demonstrates the power of this particular threat. In a metaphoric sense, the extreme fear the guards express when presented with the possibility that they too will become victims of this form of gender violence on their masculine bodies is a fear of turning into *culeros*, the penetration of the anus singly responsible for emasculating them.

More broadly, the play's depiction of this encounter between the neighbors and the guards affords the audience an opportunity to consider shame, gender, and sexual violence on multiple levels. The guards fear the actual act, but it is an act socially and culturally experienced and thus vested with more power than the violence alone. Bodily pain but also psychic and social shame would be made real on at least three levels: being penetrated as men in their anus, experiencing this shaming of their gender while in the company of other men, and experiencing this traumatic event while "exposed" before an audience of women and men (the neighbors, but also the audience watching the play).

The play's third act presents the audience once again with Guard I and Guard II. This time the guards are analyzing their situation as U.S.-trained Salvadoran soldiers, comparing the benefits and drawbacks of their new, "improved" diets, the military foodstuffs coming from the United States. Again, masculinity and sexuality around insult and honor play center stage in the dialogue the guards develop while taking a shower together following their day's military training. Appearing completely naked on stage, the guards make sure they reinforce their code of masculinity in the context of the closely erotic homosociality built into the shower scene:

GUARD II: There's nothing like these gringos, man. These people do know what they're doing. Here one becomes a man because the special forces are not for *culeros*.

GUARD I: Fuck, yeah. This is fucking paradise. Although at the beginning I didn't like the food. . . .

. . .

GUARD II: You know what I didn't like? That thing they call mashed potatoes. That damned thing looks like shit and smells like cum. And that other shit, what they call yogurt, if the potatoes smell like cum, that is the actual cum.

GUARD I: And you've tasted it already? If you're still hungry, I have some more here, if you want it.

GUARD II: That one you can keep for your mother, you son of a bitch![20]

This scene concludes with their getting dressed, finishing their political analysis of "traitor" priests and some of their own family members involved in the country's leftist movement. Seemingly unscathed by their mutual playful insults while showering together, they conclude by putting on their Rayban sunglasses. Cleansed and appropriately dressed, they prepare for the day's adventures.

Their washing and simultaneous reassurance of heteronormative positions are diametrically opposed to the two social bodies placed outside
the national membership in times of revolutionary war, the symbolic
culero and the priest. There is a close association between these two
non-manly archetypes in *El corazón:* the *culero* who by definition loses
his manliness through penetration, and the priest for willingly not being
a man actively seeking to conquer women sexually (and thus also suspect for being a *culero*). Standing naked and next to one another, the
guards, as the defenders of the state, could only playfully challenge and
downplay each other's virility to keep their own manliness as intact as
possible and as far away from these "fallen" archetypes of maleness.

The Significance of Bodies

The theatrical acts of resistance Juan Pablo and Rodrigo placed on stage
went beyond the Salvadoran military struggle. The two were conscious
about writing, seeking funding for, and producing a play about a displaced immigrant/refugee Latino community in San Francisco, in Spanish, about a national body at war with itself. In a sense, the play was on
behalf of a national body, but also of the specific bodies in that national
war.

The undressing and dressing of the guards in the scene above held
great significance for the playwrights. In their memories about audience
reactions to the scene, both Rodrigo and Juan Pablo reflected about the
role of the cultural worker in community dialogue and representation.
In one of his last interviews, months before his death from AIDS, Rodrigo
discussed what he felt were the most important challenges in his career,
including his observations of the lasting, unchanging patriarchal roles
Latinos practiced among themselves as men and in relation to Latinas,
and his cultural work and the goals behind his productions in the Mission District. Asked about some of the controversy *El corazón* raised
among community members, Rodrigo explained what he felt were the
links between particular audience members' anxieties and criticism of the
work, and broader issues of sexuality and the body. The scene where the
guards take a shower together and appear naked on stage without their
military uniforms caused a strong recollection in Rodrigo's memory:

> I was aware there were uptight phonies, who anytime they're faced with
> the human body, will become moral arbiters and judges.... And I
> believe that under their own hang-ups, they missed the whole point of

that scene, which was that under the trapping of a uniform, of any form of drag or uniform, we are all human beings. And I was trying to give these guys, who represented the National Guard in El Salvador, who represented monsters, [we] wanted to make them more human beings. Because if you represent them as bad guys, they become two-dimensional, cartoonish. Once they're naked, they become like little boys. . . . they talk about food as something strange and wonderful. In other words, [we] showed them as boys by stripping them of all these power symbols. . . . And gradually, as they finish their showers, and they're putting on their uniforms, they become more and more aggressive, so that at the end when they're fully dressed, and they have their M16s again, they are ready to kill their own families. That was the purpose of that scene. And if all people saw was their dicks hanging out, and they didn't even hear anything, that's where they're at.[21]

In Rodrigo's own words, the challenge was to bring questions of the body in the context of war to the stage. But it was not just the male homoeroticism built into the theatrical scene that audience members most resisted. Some found male gender and sexuality not only not central for addressing militarized violence and national repression, but also largely irrelevant—as I will describe.

The exploration of gender, sexuality, and nationhood in *El corazón*'s treatment of homosocial space and of the *culero* happened onstage as well as off. In a tradition that continues to this day, cultural productions continue after the curtain falls. Following each presentation of *El corazón*, audience members had the opportunity to comment and to question the cast and production team. The last performances were no exception, coinciding with the historic International Theatre Festival in San Francisco. Bringing together Bay Area Chicano and Latino production teams with those of several Latin American countries, the festival was important for facilitating transnational dialogue among cultural workers. The collaborations that occurred through the festival were hardly smooth ones; gender and sexuality became some of the most contentious matters in debate and controversy.[22]

Among the theater groups at the international festival was the Mexico City–based Los Mascarones.[23] According to Juan Pablo, the last evening's performance brought to the surface some of the specific tensions he and Rodrigo wanted to highlight:

And from the back, the director of Teatro Mascarones raises his hand and says, "Well, in terms of a suggestion, I would suggest that you take out of the play the scene where you have the two guards naked." Because the fuckers came out naked. [Showing] dick! They were bathing in the showers. . . . He was suggesting that we remove that because it did not help in any way the development of the play. Now, our purpose in showing that naked scene was to place the guards in a naked situation. To have them in a naked state, completely, from their philosophical theory to their patriarchal theory to everything. And to show them precisely how they were.[24]

Following the director's comments, Juan Pablo recalls, a Salvadoran lady voiced concerns that deemphasized the male nudity on the stage and moved the discussion instead to the more commonplace form of sexual violence in war—that on the bodies of women.

A Salvadoran lady gets up, about seventy years old, raises her hand. And the lady says, "Well, I cannot speak like that gentleman, because I am not educated. And first I want to thank you young men because you're carry-ing out a very important task of showing people here how we the Salva-doran people really feel. And I want that gentleman to please excuse me, but I want to ask him a question. Why did he feel so offended seeing those two men naked, and did not feel offended when one of those naked men raped the young girl?[25]

The exchange exemplified the multiple audiences in El corazón and that Chicano/Latino teatro has had to contend with: the communities it engages through its material and audience participation, and the aes-thetic concerns and interest of its critics. The respective commentaries disclosed some of the structures of feeling produced in the experience of the acts: anxieties about homosociality and concerns for violence against women.

El corazón and the ensuing community dialogue it generated spoke to community memory and history. The refusal to acknowledge the body, gender, and sexuality as fundamental ingredients to the writing and performance of community history point toward what Aída Hurtado has referred to as the politics of sexuality and gender subordination. In Chi-cano theatrical productions, Hurtado notes, the goal originally had been to represent a "collective social vision of Chicanos and to represent all that is valued in these communities," subordinating the varied experi-ences of Chicanas and reducing them to a static virgin/whore dichot-omy.[26] But in El corazón the body and its experiences of violence are present as pivotal landscapes on which history and memory take mean-ing. That both male and female bodies were "exposed" to community reflection in the play afforded those audiences in the Mission District an opportunity to reconsider the violence of Central American revolutionary history and struggle through the lenses of gender and sexuality.

Such exposures of bodies, sexualities, and genders on stage are no simple entertainment. As Susana Peña argues in this volume, the gendered politics of sexuality function through multiple silences and silencing strategies that implicate both community members seeking (in)visibility and those enforcing dominant relations of power. *El corazón* contested such silences by expanding the expected narrative of warfare and human suffering (cast in heteronormative form) to make visible the pivotal role of male homosociality in militarized nationalist culture. The use of soldiers as strong embodiments of manliness and national culture also made male homosociality in war visible. Tactically, this narrative move spoke to some of the tensions that Ramón A. Gutiérrez has found in the interplay of the liberatory politics of nationalism in the Chicano movement of the 1970s. In these conflicted processes of racial ethnic pride, young radical Chicano men responded to their social emasculation and cultural negation as minority men by reasserting, if not exaggerating, their virility, thus reaffirming a rigid heteronormativity.[27]

Del otro lado: Gay Immigrant Crossings

Like *El corazón nunca me ha mentido,* the production of the film *Del otro lado,* depicting the struggles of being a gay Mexican immigrant with AIDS, was a product of cultural and political crossings. Several years before filming it, Gustavo had written a short play version titled *Soy tu madre* (I am your mother) as a window into gay Latino immigrant lives. The city and state's context at this time around immigration mattered significantly, culminating in 1994 when California voters passed Proposition 187, seeking to deny social services to undocumented immigrants in the state, a measure later found unconstitutional. San Francisco was the only city where the measure was defeated, but the anti-immigrant discourse in the state made Latino immigrants (undocumented and not) the scapegoats for the economic downturn. In this period of racialized challenges to immigrant populations, gay immigrants like Gustavo used cultural productions to challenge public discourses of criminalization, of "aliens" invading the land of rightful (white) citizens.[28]

Gustavo's melodrama *Soy tu madre* centered on a heterosexual couple; the husband infects his wife with HIV, and both of them eventually die.

The husband's mother is left to consider how different the consequences could have been had the family been more aware of forms of infection. *Soy tu madre* was his way of bringing AIDS awareness to a heterosexual Latino community in the Mission District, a segment he felt knew even less about HIV and safer sex practices than did gay Latinos.

For Gustavo, his efforts culminating in *Soy tu madre* and *Del otro lado* originated in his public life as a gay Latino immigrant. Striving for such queer Latino cultural citizenship had its particular moments of personal meaning, when culture and politics came alive at once. These individual and collective actions for visibility and space connected the social space of the gay Latino bar, a common destination for many gay Latino immigrants in the city, to HIV and AIDS social service organizations like San Francisco's Shanti, where Latinos also struggled to have visibility as people of color in a mainstream white organization. As Gustavo recalls, public visibility, gay and Latino pride, all came hand in hand:

> One of my most beautiful experiences, speaking of the city of San Francisco as an activist, was during a gay parade in 1991, when we marched for the first time as part of Shanti. And it was the first time we had a huge Mexican flag in a gay parade, with eight people holding on to it. That's when the whole idea of spirit comes out, of doing activism. Imagine the significance of marching, of crossing the entire city, that people see your face and that people say, "That one going there is gay," or, "I know him, I didn't think he was." That's where spirit begins. "Yes, I am, so what!" That was one of the most incredible experiences.[29]

As a gay Latino immigrant, Gustavo highlights the incredible "spirit," in fact, the birth of spirit that comes through the creation of a gay Latino political visibility. It is a visible culture of opposition on multiple levels: a huge national emblem, a Mexican flag, in the middle of an overwhelmingly white and Anglo-centric queer moment; a flag held by *mexicanos/latinos*, somewhat foreshadowing the immigrant and nativist struggles around Proposition 187 that were to come three years later. It is simultaneously a culture of opposition in placing Latino bodies in public space to mark "gay" and for Latinos on the sidelines (and all others) to recognize that gay/queer citizenship can indeed take bodily presence in this racial ethnic group.

Gustavo's own transnational travels were intertwined with these new products of his creativity, using all possible opportunities to carry his vision. *Soy tu madre* premiered at the Mission Cultural Center in 1992 for the annual June Latino/a Gay, Lesbian, Bisexual, and Transgender Performance Art Festival produced by the late Chicano gay activist and cultural worker Hank Tavera (1944–2000). In 1993 the Mission Neighborhood Health Center (MNHC) sponsored a production of it for International AIDS Day in San Francisco. In 1994, also for International AIDS Day, the play was produced in Mexico City, in collaboration with CONASIDA (Consejo Nacional para la Prevención del SIDA), Mexico's National Council for AIDS Prevention. Returning from Mexico City in 1996 after networking with cultural and health workers there, Gustavo approached his close friend Mario Callitzin to write a play about the relationship between gay immigration and AIDS. Following positive response in Mexico to their play *Soy tu madre*, Gustavo returned to the United States reinvigorated, this time approaching Mario to make the film version. To fund it, they established the nonprofit venture of Dos Espíritus (Two Spirits), raising funds in the United States but deciding to produce the film more affordably in Mexico. Three years in the making, with an international crew of queer and non-queer, Mexican and non-Mexican, *Del otro lado* became part of the very process of border crossings both Mario and Gustavo had experienced.

Del otro lado has drawn attention because of its focus on a gay Mexican couple, Alejandro and Beto. Alejandro's HIV-positive status and his dwindling T-cell count present a series of problems for the couple, most critical being Alejandro's inability to obtain adequate treatment in Mexico City. Without informing Beto of his plans, Alejandro applies for a visa to travel to the United States to seek medical help. Once the visa request is denied, however, Alejandro weighs the consequences of staying or seeking help, and decides to cross the border illegally. Alejandro's impending trek to the United States precipitates a series of reactions and possibilities on both sides of the border. In Mexico, his departure signals many losses: his move causes panic in Beto and his own emotional losses around family; it causes fear in his parents, who have been supportive of his relationship with Beto but disagree about his move; and it signals a separation between Alejandro and his extended network of lesbian and gay friends supporting his gay relationship. Seeking medical care in the United States by crossing illegally offers no security either: Alejandro faces the real (and eventual) possibility of getting caught while trying to cross, of facing exploitation along the way, and of encountering racism and discrimination, all alluded to in the film.

Del otro lado presents a transnational gay portrait that cannot be re-duced to repression in the south—Mexico—and freedom in the north—the United States. The film depicts a thriving community of lesbians and gays in Mexico and does not present easy solutions of finding "prog-ress" upon arrival in the United States. Literally having to choose be-tween the potential for health care in the United States versus staying with his family and lover in Mexico, Alejandro embodies the tensions of many queer immigrants in their negotiations of nation and home, blood and queer kinships there, and health and immigrant identity while in the Bay Area and elsewhere in the United States. These ironies addressed in the film speak to the broader social dislocation and marginalization of queer immigrants—as queers *and* as immigrants—but specifically in the "gay Mecca" of San Francisco. That one of the actors herself, male-to-female transgender health worker and artist Carla Clynes, encoun-tered immigration problems before filming *Del otro lado* speaks to the trials queer immigrant productions must face in the making of culture.[30]

According to Mario, legal and financial dynamics in their trans-national production were overwhelming and, once overcome, liberating:

> Carla Clynes was denied a Mexican passport, wanted a passport as a woman, the identity of a woman, and yet her birth certificate is a male name. And she made a scene at the consulate [in San Francisco], from what I hear, demanding that she be given a passport, demanding her rights to be able to travel to Mexico to do this. And eventually she was given a passport, and some letter that said that the Mexican government wasn't responsible for defining the gender of this person [laughter]. . . . "The Mexican government does not do gender."[31]

Taking on a transnational film production, Mario notes, was as much about political border crossing as it was about bridge making—racially, nationally, and sexually. And it involved cultural and political border crossings by queer immigrants who were actually crossing back into the nation they first left for the United States. As Mario describes it, commu-nity was an active process of incorporating multiple identity vectors, a momentary emotional ride focused on this one binational cultural product.

The ability for gay immigrants to travel "back" to their own countries and carry out work linking two homes presents multiple challenges, some legal and financial, such as those transgender Carla Clynes experi-enced, but others that have more to do with the everyday meanings of

Figure 8.2. Image from *Del otro lado*, with Alejandro and Beto together in Mexico before Alejandro's failed and tragic attempt to cross the border. Courtesy of Mario Callitzin and Gustavo Martín Cravioto.

sexuality, race, and gender. As Martin Manalansan explains elsewhere in this volume, the everyday life of transnational queers is shaped by seemingly banal practices that do in fact reveal the constant negotiation of "home" as a matter of "here," "there," and "in between." In the United States this negotiation is neither "a birthright" nor "a romance of dissidence," in Manalansan's words, but, I would argue, the dynamic and not always successful process of seeking cultural citizenship: in this case, visibility and recognition as queer racial (im)migrant subjects in uneven contexts of domination and marginalization.

The challenges transnational queers find in the everyday, including undocumented immigration, gay life, and HIV and AIDS, were present, too, in the making of *Del otro lado*. According to Mario, that the two leading actors and producers were gay Mexican immigrants themselves added to the volatility in their queer moves across borders:

> [That] it was an openly gay production also created certain dynamics, stirred up certain things—not so much the actors, but the crew, because we had to work with them everyday. And I think it went all over the place, from playful teasing to lack of belief in the project. "No es gente seria [These are not serious people]," that kind of thing. To a certain

level of contempt when things went wrong, and we had to put our feet down and say, "No! You're gonna have to do it this way. Period!" Which we had to do many times. Racism towards [African American lesbian film director] Crystal. Racism mixed with homophobia. And eventually in the midst of so many emotions, what ended up happening is that at one point it kind of sank in that this was a very serious project, that we were extremely committed, that it was very personal to us, that we were giving it our best.[32]

Completing *Del otro lado* was not a smooth production process and required struggles for authorial voice and decision making among bodies that were differently positioned by race, gender and sexuality, and nation.

Shown in the Bay Area, Southern California, New York, Mexico, and Ireland, *Del otro lado* explores communities made marginal in the context of migration, queer politics, and AIDS.[33] Depicting the saga of undocumented gay immigration to the United States and the struggles for health care for people with AIDS, the film was neither a romance nor a comedy. As the central character, Alejandro serves as the vehicle for tracking an alternative narrative of migration, identity, and community health, culminating in his tragic death after being attacked on the U.S. side, a most violent "welcome" to the journey he must undertake. In making these writing and filmic choices, Mario argues, their production had a different context for considering merits and criticisms. For him, the effect the film has had on particular audience members who experienced and felt social marginalizations similar to those depicted in the film matters most:

> The film is not this commercial [venture]. It's an unabashedly queer film . . . and it scares people and stirs them up. People sometimes don't know how to react to it. We have seen so many different reactions. . . . I think the more interesting reactions have occurred in Mexico because Mexico is a country where art gets looked at differently. It's not seen in such a utilitarian manner as here. Just outside the United States, I think art gets looked at in a different way; I think that people are more willing to look at the themes, to look at the social context, to look at what is being said, rather than was it technically perfect. . . . This was a very low-budget thing. . . . The way people reacted [in Mexico], people were stirred up—angry, especially in Tijuana. [They said], "The things that we have to do to get people across the border. This is not fair!" And it just like sparked this big debate and set of responses that were very passionate for people. The film is a tragedy![34]

The film's ending dedication speaks to the impetus for its creation: the AIDS crisis, specifically the social networks created and destroyed through the epidemic in Mexico, in the United States, and in between. "We dedicate this film," Mario and Gustavo wrote, "to all our brothers and sisters who have died of AIDS / to those who live with AIDS / and to all those people who work with honesty and respect in the struggle against AIDS."[35]

Conclusion: Transnational Queer Latino Bodies and Cultures

The gay Latino cultural workers conceptualizing and producing *El corazón nunca me ha mentido* in the mid-1980s and *Del otro lado* in the late 1990s in San Francisco had in mind the notions Raymond Williams described as structures of feeling: the making and experience of culture as feeling and as thought. With varying insider/outsider positions to the United States, Gustavo, Mario, Juan Pablo, and Rodrigo engaged public audiences with subjects the nation-state has marginalized or has made outright illegal. The impact of their work as visual (im)migrant acts were certainly felt *and* thought about by audiences interested in the performances and showings. The play and the film spoke to historical conditions very real to their makers and those around them: military repression and economic exploitation linked to Central American refugee histories in the San Francisco Bay Area, gay Mexican immigration, and the crises of AIDS and xenophobia.[36] The histories and politics performed and retold engaged discussions of membership, identity, and community where gender and sexuality did not play second fiddle to race, class, and nation. Enacting historical struggles for cultural citizenship, these gay (im)migrant acts were hardly simple forms for artistic expression; they required community participation and reflection. The queer moves these gay Latinos made through language, geography, and culture represented ongoing contestations for what it means to be simultaneously queer and (im)migrant even in presumably open cities like San Francisco.

Because cultural citizenship takes meaning precisely in nonjuridical realms, we should note one critical intervention in both *El corazón* and *Del otro lado*—the social space of language. Written and produced entirely in Spanish, the productions represented the spatiality of (im)-migrant lives in linguistic movement across geopolitics. For both productions, narrating bodies, desires, and violence took place in what is considered a "minoritarian" discourse in California and the United States, though this is hardly an accurate description for the lives of millions working, living, playing, and surviving in Spanish. As Lionel Cantú argued, the spatial dimensions of queer Latino immigrant lives cannot be reduced to desire, but rather incorporate larger economic and political conditions.[37] In this larger sociopolitical context, language is a tool of resistance to the state's discourses, a form of solidarity for claiming space. Reyes and Gutiérrez's production centered the action through Salvadoran Spanish vernacular, a language that is very present in the Mission District, but largely marginal in Latino cultural productions. Similarly, Callitzin and Cravioto chose the language of the migration process itself, the language that on a daily basis narrates border crossings most intimately. In privileging Spanish as the medium for a political and cultural literacy, they also privileged their audiences: Spanish speakers, those in refuge, exile, and/or migration in the United States, and those still in their own countries but well connected through transnational ties.

Cultural productions can be sites of resistance, alternative ways to engage the ideological state apparatus's forms of exclusion and marginalization. In making themselves visible, queer Latinos in San Francisco have claimed space through poetry readings, writing workshops, films and videos, artistic performances, and pre- and postproduction dialogues to strengthen works in progress. As political interventions, *El corazón* and *Del otro lado* have had multiple effects on their audiences and broader political discourses. Often these effects run parallel to changes in public debate and policy. In 1985, as part of a larger citywide debate on Central American refugees, *El corazón* took a direct stance in their favor. On December 23, 1985, four months after its first performance, the San Francisco Board of Supervisors, with an 8–3 vote, passed a "Resolution to Declare San Francisco a City of Refuge for Guatemalan and Salvadoran Refugees."[38] This San Francisco decision was part of the large transnational movement to support these refugees. Rodrigo and Juan Pablo's production, as a (gay) immigrant act, was part of it. *Del otro lado* is literally a narrative of queer immigrant crossings from the vantage point of queer immigrants themselves. The film ventured into the intersections of sexuality and immigration, offering no easy solutions to ongoing crises built into a globalizing economy. As outsiders in the city's body politic, immigrant gay Latinos occupy a "gay Latino" space filled with cultural and political contestations that involve both the cultural representations of each and their position in the local political economy.

Hardly a static and predictable response to systems of marginalization and exploitation, cultural work travels with its makers. Queers move with their cultures, reinventing in their migrations the forms and meanings with which they invest their products. As cultural productions, they open spaces for dialogue and reflection. As audience members exit theaters, health agencies, and other venues for viewing and experiencing these productions collectively, they engage each other and themselves with the images and the words, considering technical questions along with content, intent, and impact. In this regard, cultural productions construct social space and facilitate further opportunities for creative interplay—feelings, thought, *and* social action thus intersected. In this tradition, *El corazón nunca me ha mentido* and *Del otro lado* were critical interventions into notions of the state, of citizenship broadly defined, and of queer bodies in transit between local and global histories.

Notes

I thank Mario Callitzin, Carla Clynes, Gustavo Cravioto, Luis Alberto de la Garza C., and Juan Pablo Gutiérrez for support in the research for this essay, and for allowing me to interview them about their work in the San Francisco Bay Area. I also thank Luis for technical support, and for giving me access to the Archivo Rodrigo Reyes. I thank Eithne Luibhéid, the late Lionel Cantú Jr., and the anonymous readers for feedback on earlier formulations of the ideas presented here, and the San Francisco Bay Area performance artist emael for pushing me to think more carefully about *Del otro lado.* I am glad to acknowledge that portions of the research presented here were supported by a University of California UC MEXUS dissertation completion grant in 1999–2000, and a University of California, Berkeley, Humanities Diversity Dissertation Fellowship in 2001.

1. *Del otro lado,* 16 mm, 80 min., directed by C. A. Griffith, written by Mario Callitzin and Gustavo Cravioto, produced by C. A. Griffith, Gustavo Cravioto, Mario Callitzin, and Fred Foley, San Francisco, 1999.

2. Two useful analyses of the cultural and political exclusions of Latino immigrants are Leo R. Chávez, *Covering Immigration: Popular Images and the Politics of the Nation* (Berkeley: University of California Press, 2001); and Otto Santa Ana, *Brown Tide Rising: Metaphors of Latinos in Contemporary American Public Discourse* (Austin: University of Texas Press, 2002).

3. Renato Rosaldo, "Cultural Citizenship, Inequality, and Multiculturalism," in *Latino Cultural Citizenship: Claiming Identity, Space, and Rights,* ed. William V. Flores and Rina Benmayor (Boston: Beacon Press, 1997), 37.

4. William V. Flores and Rina Benmayor, eds., "Introduction: Constructing Cultural Citizenship," in *Latino Cultural Citizenship*, 15.

5. Lisa Lowe, *Immigrant Acts: On Asian American Cultural Politics* (Durham, NC: Duke University Press, 1996), 9.

6. Ibid., emphasis in original.

7. Manlio Argueta, *Un día en la vida* (San Salvador: UCA Editores, 1980); and Manlio Argueta, *One Day of Life*, trans. Bill Brow (New York: Vintage Books, 1983).

8. See María Cora, "*Nuestras Auto-Definiciones* /Our Self-Definitions: Management of Stigma and Identity by Puerto Rican Lesbians" (master's field study report, San Francisco State University, 2000); Horacio N. Roque Ramírez, "Communities of Desire: Queer Latina/Latino History and Memory, San Francisco Bay Area, 1960s–1990s" (PhD diss., University of California, Berkeley, 2001); Luis Alberto de la Garza C. and Horacio N. Roque Ramírez, "Queer Community History and the Evidence of Desire: The Archivo Rodrigo Reyes, A Gay and Lesbian Latino Archive," in *The Power of Language/El Poder de la Palabra*, ed. Lilian Castillo-Speed and the REFORMA National Conference Publications Committee (Englewood, CO: Libraries Unlimited, 2001), 181–98; Karla E. Rosales, "Papis, Dykes, Daddies: A Study of Chicana and Latina Self-Identified Butch Lesbians" (master's thesis, San Francisco State University, 2001); Horacio N. Roque Ramírez, "'That's My Place': Negotiating Gender, Racial, and Sexual Politics in San Francisco's Gay Latino Alliance (GALA), 1975–1983," *Journal of the History of Sexuality* 12, no. 3 (April 2003): 224–58; Juana María Rodríguez, *Queer Latinidad: Identity Practices, Discursive Spaces* (New York: New York University Press, 2003); and Horacio N. Roque Ramírez, "The Living Evidence of Desire: Teresita la Campesina and the Embodiment of Queer Latino Community Histories," in *Archive Stories: Evidence, Experience, and History*, ed. Antoinette Burton (Durham, NC: Duke University Press, forthcoming).

9. Manuel Guzmán, "'Pa' la escuelita con mucho cuida'o y por la orillita': A Journey through the Contested Terrains of the Nation and Sexual Orientation," in *Puerto Rican Jam: Rethinking Colonialism and Nationalism*, ed. Frances Negrón-Muntaner and Ramón Grosfoguel (Minneapolis: University of Minnesota Press, 1997), 227n2.

10. A useful, historically revisionist volume on San Francisco is James Brook, Chris Carlsson, and Nancy J. Peters, eds. *Reclaiming San Francisco: History, Politics, Culture* (San Francisco: City Lights Books, 1998). For an overview of (im)migrants in San Francisco, see Horacio N. Roque Ramírez, "San Francisco," in *Encyclopedia of American Immigration*, ed. James Ciment (Armonk, NY: M. E. Sharpe, 2001), 964–73.

11. Raymond Williams, *Marxism and Literature* (New York: Oxford University Press, 1977), 132.

12. Roger Rouse, "Mexican Migration and the Social Space of Postmodernism," in *Between Two Worlds: Mexican Immigrants in the United States*, ed. David G. Gutiérrez (Wilmington, DE: Scholarly Resources, 1996), 254.

13. Cindy Patton describes the "AIDS service industry" as "the private-sector non-profit organizations devoted exclusively to AIDS work... [implying] a set of social relations based on shared norms and styles of organizational behavior institutionalized through patterned power relations, rather than a collusion of the powerful who maintain an 'establishment' by coercion or conscious exclusion, or act purely as a conduit for government monies to communities" (Cindy Patton, *Inventing AIDS* [New York: Routledge, 1990], 13).

14. All quotes from individuals come directly from the oral history interviews I carried out with them, with the exception of Rodrigo Reyes's interview that Richard Marquez conducted and that is now part of the Archivo Rodrigo Reyes in Berkeley, California. Interviews took place in Spanish, English, and/or both, but space limitations prevent me from quoting several passages that took place originally in Spanish and are translated here and presented only in English. It is important to recognize this bi-, translingual exchange in the research process itself, for it speaks directly to the creation and narration of Latino and Chicano cultural production.

15. Two useful discussions of interplay between pan-Latino cultures and politics in San Francisco's Mission District in the 1970s, albeit from male perspectives, are Juan Felipe Herrera, "Riffs on Mission District Raza Writers," in *Reclaiming San Francisco,* ed. Brook et al., 217–30; and Alejandro Murguía, "Tropi(lo)calidad," in his *The Medicine of Memory: A Mexican Clan in California* (Austin: University of Texas Press, 2002), 118–46.

16. Rodrigo's theater company, Yerba Buena Productions, produced the play with financial support from the Vanguard Foundation, the Zellerbach Family Fund, and in-kind support from the Mission Cultural Center. Following the successful production of the play in San Francisco, Teatro Aguacero from Albuquerque, New Mexico, invited and contracted Rodrigo to produce the play there, in October and November of the same year.

17. For a recent, fictionalized exploration of transnational Guatemalan life in Los Angeles, in which the cult of patriarchal, heteronormative masculinity in military life and corresponding derision of *culeros* remain, see Héctor Tobar, *The Tattooed Soldier* (Harrison, NY: Delphinium Books, 1998). Foreigners' anthropological discussions of same-sex male cultures and practices "south of the border" have often reduced these to a monolithic binary of *pasivo/activo,* the passive or penetrated partner seemingly always already marked as the only shamed or stigmatized male (*culero* in El Salvador, *joto* in Mexico, for example), and the active or penetrating man never losing his masculine status. As more and more research and writing, especially from Latin Americans themselves, are showing, same-sex sexual and gender practices among men have historically found greater expressions than those framed in this rigid *pasivo/activo* paradigm. For a critique of this reductive tradition, see Pedro Bustos-Aguilar, "Mister Don't Touch the Banana: Notes on the Popularity of the Ethnosexed Body South of the Border," *Critique of Anthropology* 15, no. 2 (1995): 149–70. For more nuanced discussions on Brazil and Mexico in this realm, respectively, see James N. Green, *Beyond Carnival: Male Homosexuality in Twentieth-Century Brazil* (Chicago: University of Chicago Press, 1999); and Héctor Carrillo, *The Night Is Young: Sexuality in Mexico in the Time of AIDS* (Chicago: University of Chicago Press 2000).

18. Rodrigo Reyes and Juan Pablo Gutiérrez, *El corazón nunca me ha mentido* (unpublished typescript, 1984), 18.

19. Ibid., 21–22.

20. Ibid., 26.

21. Rodrigo Reyes, interview by Richard Marquez, videotape recording, San Francisco, June 16 and July 5, 1991. Archivo Rodrigo Reyes (ARR hereafter), with permission of Luis Alberto de la Garza C.

22. For further elaboration on the gender and sexual controversies in Chicano

teatro in San Francisco, see Yvonne Yarbro-Bejarano, "The Role of Women in Chicano Teatro," *Revista Literaria de El Tecolote* 2, no. 3–4 (December 1981): 10. Important background on the sociohistorical and cultural roots of Chicano *teatro*, including a gender critique of the Teatro Campesino, is in Yolanda Broyles-González, *El Teatro Campesino: Theater in the Chicano Movement* (Austin: University of Texas Press, 1994).

23. According to Jorge Huerta, Los Mascarones had been part of a transnational network of Chicano, Latino, and Latin American theater companies, first coming together at the 1970 Chicano Theater Festival in Fresno, California, sponsored by the Teatro Campesino. See Jorge Huerta, *Chicano Drama: Performance, Society, and Myth* (Cambridge: Cambridge University Press, 2000), 2.

24. Juan Pablo Gutiérrez, interview by author, audiotape recording, Berkeley, California, November 6, 2001.

25. Ibid.

26. Aída Hurtado, "The Politics of Sexuality in the Gender Subordination of Chicanas," in *Living Chicana Theory*, ed. Carla Trujillo (Berkeley: Third Woman Press, 1998), 385.

27. Ramón A. Gutiérrez, "Community, Patriarchy, and Individualism: The Politics of Chicano History and the Dream of Equality," *American Quarterly* 45, no. 1 (March 1993): 45.

28. See Kent A. Ono and John M. Sloop, eds., *Shifting Borders: Rhetoric, Immigration, and California's Proposition 187* (Philadelphia: Temple University Press, 2002).

29. Martín Gustavo Cravioto, interview by author, audiotape recording, San Francisco, April 27 and May 22, 1995.

30. Carla Clynes, interview by author, audiotape recording, San Francisco, January 28, 2000; and Mario Callitzin, interview by author, audiotape recording, San Francisco, October 23 and 30, 1999.

31. Callitzin interview.

32. Ibid.

33. *Del otro lado* had its premiere in San Francisco in 1999 and was part of the closing day of the twelfth annual New York Lesbian and Gay Film Festival, on June 11, 2000. *Mano a mano*, a New York–based transnational e-network of Latino and Latina LGBT organizations and activists coordinated by Colombian Andrés Duque, and the gay Colectivo Mexicano (COMEX) cosponsored the New York premiere. The film also had a premiere in Berkeley in 2000. In Southern California the film has been shown in Los Angeles and San Diego. In Mexico, the film was shown in 2000 in Mexico City, Tijuana, and Guadalajara, and in Europe it premiered that same year in Ireland. In February 2002, the film was shown and used as the point of discussion at the queer Latina/Latino HIV agency Proyecto ContraSIDA Por Vida (PCPV) and at the HIV gay "Latino Encounters" project in Oakland.

34. Callitzin interview.

35. *Del otro lado*.

36. Two analyses of the uses of cultural production in the 1990s to address HIV, AIDS, and health generally in queer Latina and Latino context in San Francisco are Rodríguez, "Activism and Identity in the Ruins of Representation," in *Queer Latinidad*, 37–83, and Horacio N. Roque Ramírez, "Praxes of Desire: Remaking Queer Latino Geographies and Communities through San Francisco's Proyecto ContraSIDA

por Vida," in *Geographies of Latinidad: Latina/o Studies into the Twenty-First Century,* ed. M. García, M. Leger, and A. N. Valdivia (Durham, NC: Duke University Press, forthcoming).

37. Lionel Cantú Jr., "Borderlands: The Socio-Political Dimensions of Gay Latino Community Formation in Greater Los Angeles" (working paper 29, Chicano/Latino Research Center, University of California, Santa Cruz, August 2000, 3).

38. *El Tecolote* 16, no. 4 (January 1986): 1.

Contributors

Lionel Cantú Jr. was assistant professor of sociology with affiliations in Latin American/Latino studies, women's studies, and community studies at the University of California, Santa Cruz. His research interests included international migration, queer theory, feminist studies, Latina/o studies, and the sociology of HIV/AIDS. His work has been published in journals such as *GLQ* and *Sociological Perspectives* and in collections including *Queer Politics, Queer Families: Challenging Culture and the State, Gay Masculinities, The Minority Report,* and *Chicana/o Literary Criticism Anthology.* He died unexpectedly in May 2002, at the age of thirty-six, and is greatly mourned by his family, friends, and colleagues, including the contributors to this volume.

Eithne Luibhéid is associate professor of ethnic studies at Bowling Green State University. She is the author of *Entry Denied: Controlling Sexuality at the Border* (Minnesota, 2002) and coeditor (with Ronit Lentin) of a special issue of *Women's Studies International* on "Migrant Women Transforming Ireland and the E.U." Her articles about the intersections of sexuality, racialization, and migration have been published in journals that include *GLQ, Journal of Commonwealth and Postcolonial Studies, Journal of the History of Sexuality, positions: east asia cultures critique,* and *Radical America.* Her current research focuses on the connections between sexual regimes and asylum seekers in the Irish Republic. She serves as the Latin and North American editor for *Women's Studies International Forum.*

Martin F. Manalansan IV is assistant professor of anthropology at the University of Illinois, Urbana-Champaign. He also teaches in the Unit for Criticism and Interpretive Theory and the Asian American Studies Program. He is the author of *Global Divas: Filipino Gay Men in the Diaspora,* which was awarded the Ruth Benedict Prize for 2003 by the Society of Lesbian and Gay Anthropologists. His other publications include an edited volume, *Cultural Compass: Ethnographic Explorations of Asian America,* and a coedited volume (with Arnaldo Cruz-Malavé), *Queer Globalizations: Citizenship and the Afterlife of Colonialism.*

Susana Peña is assistant professor of ethnic studies at Bowling Green State University. She is currently working on a book, *Oye Loca: The Making of Cuban American Gay Miami.*

Erica Rand teaches at Bates College in the art department and the Program in Women and Gender Studies. Her writings include *Barbie's Queer Accessories,* essays on gender coercion and activist visuals, and collaborative projects on antiracist pedagogy and on sex representation and censorship. Her current book, *The Ellis Island Snow Globe: Sex, Money, Products, Nation,* is forthcoming. She serves on the editorial board of the journal *Radical Teacher.*

Timothy J. Randazzo is pursuing his doctorate in ethnic studies at the University of California, Berkeley. His research and teaching interests include race and ethnicity, immigration, and the law. He has taught a number of courses while at Berkeley, including U.S. Refugee Experience, Race and the Law, and Contemporary U.S. Immigration.

Horacio N. Roque Ramírez has contributed to the *Journal of the History of Sexuality,* the *Oral History Review, Virgins, Guerillas, and Locas* (ed. Jaime Cortez), and the forthcoming *Archive Stories: Evidence, Experience, and History* (ed. Antoinette Burton) and *Geographies of Latinidad: Latina/o Studies in the Twenty-First Century* (ed. M. García et al.). He received the 2003 Center for Lesbian and Gay Studies Fellowship, and completed a commissioned study for the Gay and Lesbian Alliance Against Defamation, "A Language of (In)Visibility: Latina and Latino LGBT Images in Los Angeles Spanish Language Television and Print Media."

He is assistant professor of Chicana and Chicano studies at the University of California, Santa Barbara, and is completing his book, *Communities of Desire: Memory and History from Queer Latino San Francisco, 1960s–1990s.*

Alisa Solomon is professor of English/journalism at Baruch College, City University of New York, and at the CUNY Graduate Center in the PhD programs in English and theater. At CUNY, she served for four years as the executive director of the Center for Lesbian and Gay Studies. Alisa is also a staff writer at the *Village Voice,* where she writes on a range of political and cultural subjects, including a recent investigative series on the INS. Her book *Re-Dressing the Canon: Essays on Theater and Gender* won the 1998 George Jean Nathan Award for Dramatic Criticism. She is the coeditor, with Tony Kushner, of *Wrestling with Zion: Progressive Jewish-American Responses to the Israeli-Palestinian Conflict.*

Siobhan B. Somerville is associate professor of English and gender and women's studies at the University of Illinois, Urbana-Champaign. She is the author of *Queering the Color Line: Race and the Invention of Homosexuality in American Culture,* as well as articles in the *Journal of the History of Sexuality* and *American Literature.* She has also edited special issues, "Queer Fictions of Race" for *Modern Fiction Studies* and (with Judith Roof) "Recent Lesbian Theory" for *Concerns.*

Alexandra Minna Stern is associate director of the Center for the History of Medicine and assistant professor in the Program in American Culture and the Department of Obstetrics and Gynecology at the University of Michigan. She has written numerous articles on the history of race, gender, science, and medicine in the United States and Mexico, including "Buildings, Boundaries, and Blood: Medicalization and Nation-Building on the U.S.–Mexico Border, 1910–1930" for the *Hispanic American Historical Review,* which won the 2000 Berkshire Conference of Women Historians Article Prize. Her monograph *Eugenic Nation: Medicine, Race, and Sexuality in the United States, 1900–1970* is forthcoming.

Index

activism by queer migrants, xxviii, xliiin73, 23, 24, 164, 166, 177. *See also* Cuban American gay male culture; cultural production by queer migrants

adultery, 76–77, 78–79, 80, 83–85, 86, 87, 89n12, 91n41

African-Americans, 40, 81, 88n4, 105, 112–16, 122n58, 143n6, 181

AIDS. *See* HIV/AIDS

Alexander, M. Jacqui, xix, xxi, 104

Anti-Terrorism and Effective Death Penalty Act, 8–9, 26n16

Appadurai, Arjun, xxxiv, 147

Arguelles, Lourdes: and B. Ruby Rich, xxviii–xxix, xlivn76

Argueta, Manlio, 163, 166, 169

assimilation, xxi, xxii, xxiii, xxvii, xxxi, xxxv, xliiin69, xlvn85, 4, 23, 156, 162

asylum: gay Brazilian men and, 34, 38–39, 63; gay Cuban men and, 21, 32–33, 35, 62, 63, 125–42; gay Honduran men and, 41–42, 48–49; gay Indonesian men and, 44, 54; gay Kenyan men and, 46; gay men and, 32–35, 36–47, 48–49, 50, 51; gay Mexican men and, 34, 37, 47, 54; gay Pakistani men and, 20, 35, 52–53; gay Peruvian men and, 48; gay Romanian men and, 72n11; gay Turkish men and, 35; gender and, xvii, 39, 42–45; HIV and, 50, 51; history, x, xvi–xviii, 6, 8, 21, 31–35, 62–65, 70, 71n5; law and, xvi–xviii, 19–20, 21, 30–56; lesbian Honduran and, 44; lesbian Romanian and, 43; lesbian Russian and, 36–37; lesbians and, 32, 35, 36–47, 48–49, 50, 51, 67, 68, 73n28; and proving one's sexual orientation, 40, 41–42, 45–47, 52, 61, 63–68, 70, 72n10; resettlement camps and, 131, 132, 133, 135, 139, 144n30; transgender people and, 18, 21, 22, 30, 37, 38, 54, 55; transsexuals and, 3–24. *See also* detention; Hernandez Montiel, Geovanni; Mariel; Refugee Act of 1980

bakla, 153, 155, 156

Berlant, Lauren, xix, xx, xlin54, 23, 90n39, 104, 148

binational couples, xiii, xxxvin10, xliiin74, 53

biyuti, 149, 152, 153, 155, 157, 159n16. *See also* Filipino queer migrants

Bowers v. Hardwick, 96, 106–8, 109, 116, 117, 119n33

Bureau of Immigration and Customs Enforcement (BICE), 5, 25n4. *See also* INS